GLORIOUS PUZZLE

GLORIOUS PUZZLE

A Personal Experience of the Sovereignty of God

Mary Angelyn Auch

ELM HILL

A Division of
HarperCollins Christian Publishing

www.elmhillbooks.com

Glorious Puzzle

A Personal Experience of the Sovereignty of God

Published in Nashville, Tennessee, by Elm Hill, an imprint of Thomas Nelson. Elm Hill and Thomas Nelson are registered trademarks of HarperCollins Christian Publishing, Inc.

Elm Hill titles may be purchased in bulk for educational, business, fund-raising, or sales promotional use. For information, please e-mail SpecialMarkets@ ThomasNelson.com.

Scripture quotations marked ESV are from the ESV˚ Bible (The Holy Bible, English Standard Version˚). Copyright © 2001 by Crossway, a publishing ministry of Good News Publishers. Used by permission. All rights reserved.

Scripture quotations marked NASB are from New American Standard Bible˚. Copyright © 1960, 1962, 1963, 1968, 1971, 1972, 1973, 1975, 1977, 1995 by The Lockman Foundation. Used by permission. (www.Lockman.org)

Scripture quotations marked NIV are from the Holy Bible, New International Version˚, NIV˚. Copyright © 1973, 1978, 1984, 2011 by Biblica, Inc.˚ Used by permission of Zondervan. All rights reserved worldwide. www.Zondervan.com. The "NIV" and "New International Version" are trademarks registered in the United States Patent and Trademark Office by Biblica, Inc.˚

Library of Congress Cataloging-in-Publication Data

Library of Congress Control Number: 2019910017

ISBN 978-1-400325856 (Paperback)
ISBN 978-1-400325863 (eBook)

DEDICATION

*To my precious daughter-in-law Erica and to any future son- and
daughter-in-law God brings into our lives, it is our prayer
that you will understand and love the family you joined
and glorify God with us.
To my children Jonathan, Matthew, and Julia: may you teach
any children you will have in the future what God has done in
our lives so they will grow to know Jesus as their Savior.*

**"My mouth will tell of Your righteousness,
of Your salvation all day long,
though I know not its measure.
I will come and proclaim Your mighty acts, O Sovereign LORD;
I will proclaim Your righteousness, Yours alone.
Since my youth, O God, You have taught me, and to this day
I proclaim your marvelous deeds.
Even when I am old and gray, do not forsake me, O God,
till I declare Your power to the next generation,
Your might to all who are to come."**

PSALM 71:15–18, NIV

CONTENTS

Appendix

FOREWORD

November 23, 2018 marks the fifth anniversary of our precious son Peter dying from injuries sustained in a car accident. God is bringing healing. One of the ways of moving forward in grief is to find new purpose in life by leaving a legacy for your child. I was listening to a *Focus on the Family* broadcast recently in which parents were telling their story. Their son had died at age twelve due to an infection. To deal with their grief they started a program for children who were rescued from human trafficking in Africa, helping them through art therapy. Their son was developing as an artist when he died. The father advised other grieving parents to do what they had done: leave a legacy for your child the size of your pain. Reflect your child's passions in what you do.

I'm not interested in developing a program overseas. There's too much going on now in our lives to be able to do that. That doesn't fit Peter's story. What would reflect Peter's passion? How can we perpetuate his love for his Savior and zest for life? I want to make sure others know the secret he found, which was his life verse:

"He must increase, but I must decrease."

JOHN 3:30, ESV

I have a fear that Peter's story and legacy will be forgotten. His friends have grown up into young adults and are dispersed around the country.

They hold the memories of what happened, possibly being frustrated that their new friends will never understand the pain they suffered through the experience. The story will remain in their hearts, affecting them for many years to come. People who didn't know him may be able to benefit from the account as well. As his mother, my question is: How can I enable Peter's story and the story of God's glory to be known? The answer came to me that writing a book to share Peter's passion for Jesus and how that transformed my life will preserve it long-term.

The purpose of this book is to share how God created in my heart a trust for Him through all the experiences of my life leading up to Peter's death, and to share how in my grief I learned to grow in love for the wonderful God Peter treasured. God taught me to trust Him in the years preceding the loss of my son through many difficult times. His death launched me into a journey of healing, resulting in joy and loving God more deeply.

To me the most significant aspect of Peter's legacy is to challenge us to allow Jesus to increase in our lives, just as that was his passion. My prayer is that God will be glorified from this story. It would be Peter's desire, as he's in heaven now, to see many people come into the Kingdom of God and let God's Kingdom rule permeate their lives. Peter's number one goal was to "Make Christ the center of my life." He would love it if others would choose the same primary goal for their lives. The changes God can make in people's hearts as a result of hearing his story is the best legacy Peter can possibly leave. My prayer through my story, and Peter's, is that other people, facing very difficult circumstances with their families, would find new insights into God's character that will bring them hope, understanding, and joy.

**"Let this be written for a future generation,
that a people not yet created may praise the Lord."**

PSALM 102:18, NIV

Acknowledgements

Duane Auch, my husband, who was committed to me and protected me as we lived through all these experiences together. And without his support during the many hours of writing, we never would have been able to declare God's glory through this book.

Joy Anna Rosendale, my dear sister, who patiently and lovingly comforted us and helped me to deal with issues in my life. She challenged me to seek God for how to write various sections in the book and wisely guided me on how to tell of God's glory. I can never thank her enough for all the hours she spent helping me to revise what I had written so it would communicate the story.

Matthew Auch, my son, who pointed all of us to see God's glory and purposes in the midst of the most painful time of his life.

Steve Walters, my pastor, and the best shepherd of a congregation that I've ever known. He taught me much about following Jesus, guided me to seek God in the midst of painful times, and challenged and supported me in outreach opportunities.

Martha Rankin, my mentor in missions, who repeatedly challenged me to write this book.

Nancy Mochel, my previous pastor's wife, who taught me by her example to recognize God's hand at work in our lives, to be totally reliant on God in prayer and to give God all the credit and glory for His marvelous deeds.

Carl Gutzman, my Sunday school teacher, who proofread the manuscript and wrestled with me over the nature of God's sovereignty. He enabled me to focus on God's character and goodness as the foundation for seeing comfort in His providence.

Mary Block, my mentor in GriefShare, who allowed God to use her to begin the process of picking up the shattered pieces of our family, and became a dear close friend and role model to me.

Hubert Mitchell, a family friend when I was a little girl, who set the lyrics of "He Giveth More Grace" to music. As I listened to him sing and play his accordion and tell of God's sovereign care for him as a missionary, God instilled in me an understanding of the truth of His grace and limitless love. Every time I sing that song, I am reminded anew of the amazing God we serve, who will never tire of giving grace to us. His example spurs me on.

John Rea, my dear father, who proclaimed God's "hessed" love – His loving-kindness to His beloved people, on a practical level to me at home and to his students as an Old Testament professor. It was my dad who demonstrated to me a solid, bedrock trust in a good, loving, compassionate God in the problems he faced in life. Because of his example, I wanted to seek and know for myself the God he loved.

INTRODUCTION

Glorious Puzzle. What a strange title for a book! I wrestled with the title. I prayed about it, and this title came to mind, as I believe that *Glorious Puzzle* summarizes my approach to understanding God's purpose and role in my life, and in yours as well. It's a worldview that gives hope and joy in the midst of terrible pain and problems.

Many years ago, during a morning worship service, a lady sang a solo that captured my heart. I remember sitting in the choir loft, listening to her and realizing that lots of things could make sense and fall into place if I accepted life the way she did as she sang the song of worship. I cannot find that song to reprint it. I heard it only once. It spoke of the Christian life being like a puzzle God was putting together.

Around the same time I heard that solo, my husband Duane was teaching a fourth- and fifth-grade Sunday school class on the topic of God's providence. God's providence isn't something that's discussed much in evangelical churches. We had to figure out what it meant for Duane to teach the lessons. The "Desiring God" curriculum we used defined providence as:

"God is present and active in all creation. His eye watches and His hand is working to uphold and govern all creation to fulfill His purpose."

A much easier way of understanding providence is to take the word apart:

Pro=before   vid=see   ence=action or process

So pro-vid-ence means to see something before it happens. The word implies having control over what occurs. God is the one who sees what lies ahead. He sees and takes action regarding what will happen in our lives.

Concurrently my kindergarten and first-grade Sunday school classes were studying God's sovereignty. For the little kids we defined sovereignty as: God has the right, the wisdom, and the power to do all He plans.

It seems we as adults just tune out when we hear talk about God's sovereignty. The word makes us think of God being a super power with some overall scheme for what's going on in the world as a whole. He is powerful to do what He wants. We're kind of detached from a sovereign God. He's pretty remote and out of touch with us personally. We may feel that God is too big to care about our mundane everyday lives. We may even believe that God's sovereignty is rather opposed to what we want, and therefore has negative connotations. It can bring fear and resentment toward God. Furthermore if we don't fundamentally believe that God is a good God who loves us, when trouble comes it's very easy to think that He's capricious and has only His interests in mind. A God like that seems cruel. Bad times are signs of His punishment for our wrongdoing. With those beliefs sovereignty is a terrible power that God has over us.

To accept God's sovereignty we have to first of all believe that God is good all the time. He has our best interests in mind as well as those of everyone else's in the universe. All the other aspects of His nature— all-knowing, all-present, faithful, perfect, merciful, gracious, just, loving, holy, and righteous—form a foundation for believing and appreciating His sovereignty. I've seen that when people do not know in their hearts that God is good, gracious, as well as sovereign, they get stuck in grief and don't understand why they are suffering. They may drift away from

God. Why would you want to be close to a God who punishes you and isn't good? But when God is seen as loving and all-powerful, there is an amazing security in life. You can rest in Him, trust Him, and respond to Him in love.

As I have gone through the circumstances and events you'll read in this book, I have learned that God's sovereignty is personal and an expression of His love to me. He is in complete control of my life, down to each millisecond. He plans and orchestrates all things to work out His plans for His Kingdom and at the same time shows me His love and care, and how much He treasures me in that process. My relationship is closer to Jesus whenever I accept His sovereignty as a means of loving me.

My view of God's sovereignty and providence is like a cosmic puzzle that He is putting together piece by piece. He is working out things behind the scenes of our lives that we can see. His invisible hand is making it all fit together. God intentionally arranged events of our lives beforehand as He designed His puzzle for the fulfillment of His purposes. The puzzle pieces of my life fit into those of your life. He puts our puzzles together as we go through experiences. He is putting all of them together to form a picture of something. Just like we find a few pieces here and there that match when we work on a puzzle, that's what God does. It's a gradual process, with Him working on all the areas of the puzzle, a little at a time.

I realize that other people have used the metaphor for sovereignty of God being a weaver who is crafting a beautiful fabric, adding one thread at a time. The underside of the rug or fabric is ugly. But the upper side is beautiful, and the pattern that never made any sense on the backside is clear on the front. However, the weaving process is too methodical and predictable to match my experience. The weaving concept falls short of helping me see how my experiences in life fit in with those of other people's to draw us both closer to God. My life touches yours. Yours touches other people's puzzle pieces, and we affect each other. Furthermore the word "puzzle" brings to mind, partly because of its double meaning, the questions we have with the uncertainty and the unexpected. Puzzle pieces can be laid down at any time, whereas weaving is precise and on schedule.

There is little chance for the design of a weaving to change once it's started. God's overall picture stays the same on His puzzle, but I'm convinced that many times God changes how the pieces fit together. When we disobey and do things our own way and refuse to fit into His plans, He doesn't give up on the overall picture. God may choose someone else to accomplish His purposes. He may fit the pieces together in a different order than was the original design. God is big enough and powerful enough to adjust how His puzzle is put together. He is powerful enough as the sovereign creator to redesign portions of the puzzle and fit different pieces into place with the same end design.

When I was a little girl my dad did some archaeological work in Israel. He came home from surveying on a dig with lots of pots and broken pieces of pottery. What impressed me was a dark-brown pile of ancient clay pieces of something. Each one was no bigger than a 2″ × 2″ jagged fragment. I remember seeing my dad, at his office table, working on putting the pieces together for what seemed like hours. He had no idea what he was trying to assemble. There were no instructions, no picture to give him a clue. We feel like that often in life. We don't know what we are doing or why. Nothing makes sense; we don't know how everything fits together. We only see the ugly cardboard side of the puzzle pieces of our lives. One day my dad's big pot that he had glued together fell off the table. It broke apart on the floor. All the pieces were scattered. It was kind of a crisis because it had taken so much time and work to figure it out. But the second time he put the pot back together, it was much easier. Why? He knew what he was making this time. He had a picture in his mind of what the finished product would be. He knew what the pot looked like. That's like God. God sees the picture side of the puzzle. He has the box top with the overall plan that guides where each piece is to be put. So the question is, what's on the picture side of the puzzle?

On one of the mission trips I took to Haiti, we put on several skits to illustrate Jesus' parable of the Kingdom of God, found in Matthew 13:44. That story tells of the man who found a treasure hidden in a field. In his joy he hid it again, sold all he had, and bought the field. A spark stirred in me as I realized how precious the Kingdom of God is. It's a treasure! If it's worth everything I have to get it, what is it? The definition of the Kingdom of God that I pieced together in my childhood is:

God's rule and reign in our lives and in the world culminate in heaven, when we all go to meet Jesus there and live with Him forever.

This definition sounds dry. It's far off and remote. It even sounds harsh, like a cruel medieval king or slave owner stripping me of all my rights and invading my privacy, taking over. I fight losing control. However, the events of the last few years have taught me to love God's rule and control in my life. It was a choice to accept God's right to govern and control the circumstances of my life, which allowed me to see God as the puzzle maker, putting His Kingdom together. It's become my primary desire to see His Kingdom established in my heart and in the hearts of everyone I know. Seeking the Kingdom of God is what brings joy. Seeing the Kingdom of God being established as He changes my heart and the hearts of other people is exhilarating and exciting! It's worth all that's happened!

It's become clear to me: the Kingdom of God is what is on the box top of God's puzzle. The overall plan for our lives is for God to work out His purposes to bring the Kingdom to every person on earth, so they have the opportunity to join in His Kingdom now and in eternity. God longs for everyone to know of the grace, redemption, and salvation He has offered them. That's why we are here on earth: to accept His gift of eternal life and become part of the Kingdom of God. Once we accept His gift we partner with Him in the Kingdom of God, becoming part of the process as it spreads and is established in the world and in individuals' hearts.

Now as things happen in life I realize that this is another one of God's puzzle pieces. It may not make sense, but it is part of God's plan. As I grow in my understanding of God as the sovereign one who designed and made the puzzle and now is putting His puzzle together, I have grown in my closeness and trust in this loving God. God's sovereignty is best for us because of His perfect love for us. He is working it all out with me for what is good to bring about His purpose, which is how I will feel His love best. Some translations of Romans 8:28 read:

"God works together with those who love Him to bring about what is good, with those who are called according to His purpose."

Romans 8:28, NIV

Often we use the version of this verse that puts the focus on God working hard to make sure that the ultimate result of difficult circumstances is our good fortune being restored. We've heard it said over and over, that all things work together for good for those who are called according to His purpose. The emphasis is on what we feel is good for us. It's as if we are saying we know that God is on our side, and will do good things for us that we prefer if we just hang in there long enough.

But if we as those who are called to play a role in God's big cosmic purpose for establishing the Kingdom take the focus off ourselves, we discover that we are actually working together with God. If we don't fight His purposes, then He can bring good to many people through our painful times. The good He is working out in our circumstances isn't just for us. He challenges us to see the larger context of His plan, and to see what He is doing to demonstrate His love to other people who need to hear the gospel and know God. When we go through hard things in life with God, we are in it together with Him. Things just make more sense when we work together with God as He does whatever He wills. When we work together with God we are living through the experience for His glory.

Around the same time Duane was teaching the Sunday school class about God's providence, I was leading the council time for AWANA for the kids in third to sixth grade. I remember putting together several lessons based on God's purpose for our lives. As I explained and taught the kids for several weeks, I absorbed and accepted that my life purpose is to glorify God. All I do is for His glory. All that happens to me is an opportunity to bring glory to God. That's it. It's pretty simple: a framework of how to act, how to be motivated, and how to have purpose.

If my purpose is to glorify God, what does it mean? My simple definition:

It is to make God famous for His awesome character and deeds.

When we glorify God we talk about His worth in a public or open way. We don't keep God's glory to ourselves. Glorifying God, by definition, involves sharing His glory. We can't keep God's glory as a silent concept in our minds. It must be expressed.

Another simple way of thinking about what it means to glorify God is to cause the truth people know about Him to be magnified. Glorifying God makes Him greater in the eyes of others. It's advertising for our wonderful God.

As Duane and I taught the kids in Sunday school, AWANA, and in Haiti, God started expanding our view of Him, His purposes, and our role in His Kingdom. Little did we realize that through our study, God was preparing us to be able to handle the things that were to take place. God was in control of that time of our lives, putting a puzzle piece in place by teaching us these profound truths that would make the future puzzle pieces easier to fit together.

A few days ago, in my quiet time, I read this verse:

"Blessed are your eyes because they see; and your ears because they hear."

MATTHEW 13:16, NIV

The verse is in the context of Jesus explaining why He spoke in parables about the Kingdom of Heaven. He told His disciples that the secrets of the Kingdom have been given to us. In contrast to those who reject His Kingdom, Jesus wanted His disciples, and us, to understand and see what He was doing. He wants us to see life from the perspective of His Kingdom. He doesn't want us to stay in a state of blindly letting Him take control and "do His thing." It's not fatalism and a sad acceptance of a miserable life of tests and trials to which He calls us. God wants us to see the glorious picture on the other side of the puzzle pieces of our lives. He knows the joy that we will have as we see and understand the picture side of the puzzle. He calls us "blessed" when we see. He displays His glory to us as we understand. This is faith.

It takes faith and trust to see life this way. We have to trust the one who made the puzzle. God is the puzzle maker. We have to trust that He knows what He is doing as He puts His puzzle together, and that ultimately the puzzle will bring about good and His purposes. We may never know the reason for our trials. The answer to our question, "Why?" may never be clear. But we can give Him glory when we have faith in Him during the difficult times, as puzzle pieces are being put in place. We may have to look for evidences of His fingerprints or actions in placing the puzzle pieces of our lives together. Sometimes He isn't clearly evident when He's at work. It's faith that says God is in control of this and this is of His doing.

The problem with this puzzle metaphor is that when events are taking place, especially the painful experiences, it isn't natural to see them as part of God's huge Kingdom puzzle and give Him glory. God started teaching me how to see His glorious Kingdom puzzle long before Peter died. It was His grace and love that gave me practice in less traumatic events so I could be ready for huge problems. As I was growing in my faith in His character and plan, God taught me this truth, found in Proverbs:

**"In all your ways acknowledge Him, and He will make
your paths straight."**

Proverbs 3:6, NIV

What He taught me is that in everything that happens ("in all your ways"), look for God's actions and how He is showing me His love. Look for ANYTHING that is good at the time it's happening. Then give God the credit ("acknowledge Him") for doing it in order to demonstrate His love and care. Don't just think of things as coincidences. You'll rob God of glory if you do. You'll rob yourself of feeling near to Jesus in the midst of your pain.

When I started looking for God in hard times, I've always found evidence of His loving-kindness. It might be just a smile from someone or the perfect timing of an event, or it might be a more obvious gift. Once I recognized something positive, I could give God praise and dwell on His goodness and love. I found that praise magnifies God's role in the situation. A thankful heart brings peace. Gratefulness brings joy. I learned to rest and let the anxiety go as I trusted in His faithfulness. As I learned to focus on Him, the pain and awfulness were minimized to a more tolerable level.

When I look back on some very sad things that happened when I was a young adult, I wasn't able to get to a place of joy until I could see some evidence of God's love as He put the painful puzzle piece into place. I will tell you that story in a later chapter. Acknowledging His role in situations has been key to healing. So one of the primary goals of this book is to demonstrate to you how to look for evidence of God in the puzzle pieces and hard times in your lives so you can work together with Him to bring about good for the Kingdom. It is in that context that He can make your path straight. The barriers and rocky places of fighting what's happening and struggling with it all are removed. We avoid going down side paths that lead to trouble. We can move forward with God on a straight path when we acknowledge Him.

This next principle regarding how to view painful times may seem too radical. But how else can we make sense of verses like James 1:2–4?

"Consider it pure joy whenever you face trials of many kinds, because you know that the testing of your faith develops perseverance. Perseverance must finish its work so that you may be mature and complete, not lacking anything."

JAMES 1:2–4, NIV

There is joy in the trials we face when we know the picture on God's puzzle box. When we understand and grow to love God's purpose and plan to form the Kingdom, maturing us in the process and making us more like Christ, then it's exciting to see it happening! The current puzzle piece that's getting put into place may be painful to us. It may take a long time for God to put it into place. It takes waiting on God to allow Him to teach us what's necessary with the current piece. It may be hard, heartbreaking, draining, and frustrating at a human level. But it's also another chance to see God's glory being displayed for us to see. There's joy in that. We may have to wait a long time to see anything positive, which develops perseverance and strong faith in God's character regardless of the circumstances. Ultimately Jesus' Kingdom advancing, gaining members and becoming more like Jesus, is the most glorious thing ever. Keep persevering in joy. Jesus is worth it!

A summary of all of this is that the sovereign puzzle maker, God, is establishing His Kingdom here on earth so that as many people as possible will have their relationship restored with Him to enjoy Him in heaven eternally. This is the puzzle to which I will refer. We are all part of the puzzle He has designed and is putting together. Our purpose in His puzzle is to glorify Him and make Him famous to others. We may have to look hard for evidence of His presence when difficult puzzle pieces are being put in place. But when we do, we see evidence of His love and care for us. And as we recognize that God is placing pieces of His puzzle through the events of our lives, we grow in faith. It is then that we can work together with Him to establish the Kingdom of God on earth. God's priorities take precedence over our own comfort. We love His puzzle and purposes more than our own lives. God's puzzle is a glorious one. We can even find joy in our difficulties.

This is the story of my part in God's huge, cosmic puzzle. It starts with how I learned to understand what God was doing and how to look for Him in circumstances. Through those early times in my life God was laying the outline or border puzzle pieces in my life. I was learning to understand His sovereignty. My faith was tested in many types of problems. I learned to trust the puzzle maker. When really tough situations arose, faith that the puzzle was being put together by God held me together. But it was in the journey of recovery from the death of my son that I grew in my love for the puzzle maker. It was then that I found joy. I trust that God is glorified in this story of His glorious puzzle. My prayer is that as you read this you consider this awesome God and how He is putting your life together for His purposes, find God's presence in all the circumstances you face, yield to Him, love His purpose, find joy, and thereby glorify Him.

**"But as for me, it is good to be near God.
I have made the Sovereign Lord my refuge;
I will tell of all Your deeds."**

PSALM 73:28, NIV

PART 1

FAMILY: A CONTEXT FOR LEARNING TO TRUST

Border to the Puzzle

My Childhood

I really hate to put puzzles together. That may seem rather odd, considering I'm writing a book about God's divine puzzle. Puzzles seem like such a waste of time; usually I have way too much on my "to do" list to stop and put one together. But when I go to spend time with my oldest son Jonathan, doing a puzzle is a nonthreatening way of being together and talking about things at the same time. Recently I visited him and spied a twenty-five-piece puzzle on a shelf. That's about my level of skill. Actually I wanted to take out the puzzle to trace the pieces to get some graphics for chapter headings for this book. I copied the shapes quickly and then Jonathan and I started by sorting out the pieces with straight edges to form the structure or border of the puzzle. That's what these first pieces that God put into my life are: the border that surrounds everything else and forms the structure of what God has done in me.

I suppose the puzzle box with my pieces was opened when my husband Duane and I were born. I was born into a family with three older sisters. My father was an Old Testament professor at Moody Bible Institute. He loved and doted on the four of us. He made our childhood fun with all his stories he'd create to entertain us on long road trips and when he woke us up from naps. My mother was the household organizer, a disciplinarian with a mission to teach us to work and to know as much about the Bible as possible. She was sickly due to chronic renal failure, so we had ample opportunity to learn to manage the household for her. She knew her days were numbered so she taught us to memorize as many Bible verses as possible. We listened to Bible stories over and over again on our little record player in the basement. We were paid for each chore we did and each verse we memorized. Work and God's Word were the priorities she instilled in me.

I prayed with my mother to accept Jesus as my Savior when only two and a half years old. I was a happy little person then, singing all the time. My nickname was "Mary Sunshine." I was reinforced for being cheerful. I don't remember ever feeling free to express feelings of sadness, anger, or anxiety. If I was feeling "down," I was reminded of my nickname. My mother didn't want the four of us girls to express any "negative" emotions; we were made to feel those feelings weren't "Christian." I was her good little girl. I learned to be a plastic shell with a smiley face, while inside rage and frustration built up.

I recall going to kindergarten, and hearing on the first day of school the story of the three bears. I had never heard a single children's story or nursery rhyme before then. I had only learned Bible stories. I had no idea there was fun entertainment in the world! I can see now that God was protecting me from a lot of ungodly stuff, but it sure wasn't a fun childhood at home.

My mom was usually sick, staying in her room in a remote part of the house. I took advantage of that and used the two-block walk on the way home from school to play with my friends. I knew I had to be home by 4:00 p.m., and used every minute after school to have a normal life, free of work and chores. My best friend Ruth had a very healthy home life. I am convinced that God placed her mother Irene in my path as a puzzle piece in my life. That kind lady modeled what a good, loving mother does to care for her children. I had no idea moms were supposed to make

4

cookies, find out how their kids' days went at school, and listen to them share their dreams and troubles. To this day visual memories of being in her beautiful, homey kitchen where she was blessing me, make me feel secure. I had some idea how I should treat my children because she was a wonderful role model. I was so glad I could meet with her several years ago and let her know how important she was to me.

The whole time I was growing up I obeyed and tried to please my parents out of a sense of duty. I couldn't really see much that I did that was sinful. I didn't try to break any of their rules. The only time I got in trouble was if I was caught reading a book when my mom thought I should be working. The punishment usually involved a severe verbal chastisement and occasional spankings doled out by my subservient father. I tuned it all out and just thought they were being ridiculous in their expectations. A person should be able to take a break once in a while! My resentment grew with each time I was punished. Once my mother locked us all in separate rooms for two to three days with some water and a can to pee in because we hadn't done something to her level of satisfaction. At that time all respect for her drained away. She became an obligation in my life. My sense of self-righteousness increased. I couldn't see that my heart was full of pride. I knew God loved my parents, but I didn't have any sense that He loved me at all. He had done some amazing miracles in their lives, but God wasn't personal to me.

When I started high school I went to a huge place in Oak Park, Illinois, which was a suburb west of Chicago. I walked into the cavernous lobby of the school the first day, and decided I hated it and was going to get out as quickly as possible. I figured out how to get all the required courses and credits by working very hard to get out in three years instead of the usual four. My sisters had all left for college when I started my freshmen year. I was put in full control of the household for three years until I graduated from high school, doing all the cleaning, meal planning, shopping, cooking, gardening, yard work, and laundry. Life was so filled with taking care of a large house and two parents that I recall only going to one event during high school—a gymnastics meet at which my best friend's brother was competing. But I learned to be in charge. One of the good things my mother did was to shower us with praise and admiration for things we did that met her standards. She worked to perfect the abilities she liked in us. As a result I felt I could handle it all. I could do anything.

At the end of the summer, at just seventeen years of age, I went to Messiah College in Grantham, Pennsylvania. I was ready for this challenge. After all, I was able to handle everything with success. I went there to major in home economics education in a Christian environment. It wasn't my choice of a major. I really didn't want to learn in depth about all the domestic things I did from day to day at home for my mom, but she wouldn't hear of me considering any other major. To her, girls could only prepare to be nurses, teachers, secretaries, home economists, or missionaries. I couldn't stand body fluids so nursing wasn't a real choice. Typing nearly cost me a decent GPA, so becoming a secretary was not an option at all. Teaching didn't seem too bad of an option, but I didn't really relate to children. I wanted to do something interesting, such as archaeology or architecture, but had no support to do so. So with my desire of pursuing a degree in some type of science or design squelched, I took off, going far away from home. Looking back, God was moving a puzzle piece into place around which much of my life would be shaped. Praise God, I had a way to get out of the abusive environment of home sooner than most kids! It was His faithful protection of my life that got me out of school a year early.

God, in His providence, placed me in a safe Christian college in a suite for four girls. All of them were very mature Christians. They saw through my happy façade, recognizing a hurting, angry person. They lovingly challenged me to express my feelings. They taught me that being able to give a voice to anger and disappointment and inadequacy and fear was human. They encouraged me to not let my parents control me anymore. They saw through my shallow faith in God that was based on my parents' experience. Those friends pushed me to seek God for myself.

I started to acknowledge my deep-seated anger at God. It was based on reading the story in Luke 7:36–50. In that passage I read of a woman who had lived a sinful life who came to Jesus and washed his feet with her hair and tears. The Pharisees were critical. Jesus then told them a story of two men who owed a money lender various sums of money. The debts were forgiven. Jesus noted that the one who had been forgiven much was more grateful and loved the money lender more than the one who had been forgiven just a few coins. He compared it to the sinful woman who was washing His feet and stated, "Her many sins have been forgiven – for she loved much. He who has been forgiven little loves little." I was so angry when I read that story. I was a still the "good little girl" my parents expected me to be. I had never done anything very bad. God didn't have to forgive me much. I felt I wouldn't be able to love God much, feel His love, and have a close emotional relationship with Him because I didn't see that there was much to forgive. It seemed I was doomed to a mediocre spiritual life, feeling distant from God.

In my immaturity I decided that to be able to be forgiven much, I needed to sin much, just like the woman who washed Jesus' feet. I was scared of the long-range consequences I could face, and really couldn't think of anything horrible to do. It gnawed at my heart. I was desperate to know Jesus and be close to Him. The only testimonies I had ever heard were of people who had done horrendous things or who had experienced terrible abuse and were miraculously saved. My parents valued the dramatic stories of salvation or conversion other Christians shared. A common Christian life of following Jesus day to day wasn't valued by them.

I needed to do something dramatic to demonstrate my conversion to Christ so they'd value me. So at the end of my freshmen year of college I went home to practice my newfound liberation in Jesus amidst the oppression I felt when around my parents. I was determined not to be fake, but to be authentic with my feelings. It didn't go over well. They couldn't understand why I was acting sad, moody, and angry at times. They interpreted it as being rebellious. I wasn't "Mary Sunshine" anymore, and I felt rejected. Those conversations were awkward. It was clear to them I wasn't acting like a Christian when I wasn't happy. I couldn't effectively voice what I was feeling. In my frustration I wanted to get back at them and get God's attention. I pondered what I could do that would be terribly sinful to them, but not harmful to me in any way. Therefore the worst thing I could think of doing was to buy a bikini! I wore it down by the lake and my dad saw it. That was a sign to my parents that I was really falling away from my faith. I was overjoyed inside. I had done something terrible enough in their eyes for God to forgive. There was hope I could have a close relationship to God like the sinful woman had. It's kind of pathetic now that I look back on it. What I did was safe and protected me from long-lasting miserable consequences and yet caused me to find forgiveness in Jesus' love.

A family who worked for my parents saw my need and could identify with why I was so frustrated. They spent a day with me before I returned to college for my second year. That day they prayed with me, assuring me that God loved me. I felt close to God and liberated to follow Him. I was filled with joy for the first time in my life. From that time on I had an intense desire to follow Jesus and serve Him. My feelings of being distant from God persisted to some extent. But God had laid down a significant piece of His Kingdom puzzle.

Duane's Story

A few states to the west of me, Duane grew up on a family farm in rural southeastern South Dakota. He is the middle of three sons. They went to a country grade school a little over a mile from home. The family worked hard together raising a variety of animals and crops. Duane has always been thankful for the opportunity to grow up in such a stable family and wholesome community. On the farm Duane's parents instilled skills, character, and faith needed for the ups and downs of his life.

Duane's dad was a wise and intelligent man who probably could have gone to college to pursue a more lucrative career. That was the hope for his sons, so he encouraged them to get good grades. As it turned out none of them would turn their backs completely on farm life. Duane's dad allowed them to learn responsibility through caring for their own crops and livestock. Duane experienced the joy of seeing his own sows with big litters of baby pigs and sorrow of his own calves dying during birth. More than in most vocations, a farmer learns that God is in control.

Duane's mom was a "stay at home mom" but not in today's sense. She cared for her three sons who were born within a five-year period, but she also milked cows, tended a large garden, preserved the produce, cared for the yard, drove tractor when needed, ran errands, and more. However, her children were never neglected. Throughout his life Duane always felt loved and accepted by his parents. Their commitment to him and each other were examples to be followed.

Duane's family was part of a local Reformed church and attended services every week without fail. Christian education was very important, so Duane was well taught in the Bible and church doctrine and was confirmed. He knew that salvation comes by God's grace but he didn't know whether he really believed. In life he strived for acceptance and affirmation by working hard. However, his efforts to please God were not enough to allow him to feel secure. He feared death, because he had no assurance that God would accept him.

One night in high school he attended a revival meeting. He went up to talk to the speaker at the end of the evening. The speaker, Vernon Dirkson, asked him whether he was going to heaven or not. Duane answered, "I hope so." He then heard about the assurance of salvation, based on grace, not works. Vernon explained the truth of 1 John 5:13: "I write these things to you who believe in the name of the Son of God so that you may know that you have eternal life." Duane then realized he had assurance of salvation and acceptance before God, based solely on Jesus' sacrifice for his sin. There was no more he could do to earn God's approval. Jesus had done it all for him and suffered in his place. Duane's life was changed. He went to college and got involved in the Navigator's campus ministry right away. He became a disciple, learned the scripture, and he grew in his faith by leaps and bounds.

Vernon was killed in a car accident on the way to a mission event, when he was taking lots of Bibles for high school kids to distribute. This was soon after Duane came to a trusting faith in Jesus by his ministry. Fast forward to many years later, when Vernon's wife heard of Peter's accident, she realized that her husband died on Highway 46, just two miles from the place of Peter's accident. She and Duane both found comfort in that coincidence. Vernon must be in heaven, visiting with Peter, and realizing the ripple effect of his ministry.

Even though the boys made good money on their farm projects, their dad insisted on paying their four years of college. Duane studied in Brookings, South Dakota, at SDSU. He majored in agricultural education as an undergraduate and went on for a master's degree in agronomy, with a focus on weed science. He is a born researcher by nature, quiet, detailed, committed, serious, and faithful to any task he has to do. He is the most diligent, responsible person I know. He models doing a quality job for the glory of God in everything he does. One of his top priorities is to maintain high ethical standards in the research process, even when the results are disappointing and he could be tempted to hide the truth.

The difficulties, including the death of our child, that could have split our marriage and our family apart have actually drawn us closer together. This is because of Duane's integrity, persevering faith in God, and faithful spiritual leadership of our family. These qualities have carried over into how he handled the challenges of all the puzzle pieces God had planned for us in His providence. He has been committed to doing the right thing and following God no matter how hard it is. He learned these skills in his profession and has applied them to his relationship to God, his marriage, and the family. His model of quietly following God has been what gave our kids stability in the midst of trouble. He has been diligent to teach them the truth and has lived it out daily in front of them.

Bangladesh

I continued at Messiah College, being too timid to change my major for fear of family repercussions. I got through all the courses easily and was bored with everything related to home economics. It was just glorified "work-a-holism" to me. It symbolized being bound to my parents, with no freedom to be myself. The thought of teaching home ec day in and day out was deadening and depressing. If I had tried to change my major, I was afraid my parents would have a fit and possibly disown me; I didn't have the courage. I found that I loved other classes that I took: anthropology, archaeology, world religions, and a course on translating the Word of God. God was making a move to get me interested in missions.

During the interim January term of my sophomore year, I went to Israel for a biblical archaeology course. We traveled each day to sites in Israel where significant biblical events took place. However, it wasn't being where Jesus walked that rocked my spiritual life. One day I was taking a break after a hot day at some archaeological site. My favorite way to spend free time was walking through old Jerusalem, shopping in the little stores in the bazaar. That afternoon I looked into a shop that seemed to be tucked into a cave under an ancient building. There was enough light to see piles of oranges, apples, dates, spices, and green produce. It was beautifully arranged, but my "home ec" brain saw germs and contaminated foods and potential illness. At that moment I distinctly remember hearing God say to me, in an almost audible voice, "Mary, are you willing to serve Me in places like this?" He was asking me if I could handle working with poor people in wretched, dirty circumstances. I felt challenged to get out of my comfort zone to follow Jesus on the adventure of the Great Commission.

My world was rocked. God seemed to be calling me to serve Him in what I would perceive to be a tough place. Perhaps I wasn't doomed to teach home economics to American children after all! Perhaps there was an exciting life ahead in missions! I went back to Messiah College that semester and took anthropology to get prepared. The next January

I took another trip to study practical anthropology. The month spent in South Africa, Zimbabwe, Botswana, and Zambia was filled with learning how to interview people in order to learn about their culture, and with seeing missions in action. We learned how to be careful not to destroy positive aspects of culture when evangelizing and planting churches. We were challenged not to evangelize with the purpose of turning churches in foreign places into copies of American worship centers. The purpose was to determine what was cultural in a foreign place and what practices needed redemption and transformation by God's Spirit. God was at work in my heart, getting me ready for the next very significant puzzle piece of my life.

Messiah College is an Anabaptist school, holding some of the same beliefs as Mennonites. They support the efforts of Mennonite Central Committee or MCC. MCC is the relief and development agency that works alongside the Mennonite missionaries. Recruiters often came to Messiah College to find potential volunteers. I was fresh on the heels of my trip to Africa and readily took the challenge to become a volunteer for three years after graduation.

The first assignment was to go to Nepal. I was delighted. To work in the Himalayan Mountains with an experienced nutritionist seemed too good to be true! I don't know why, but I was reassigned to go to Bangladesh instead. The reason given was that MCCers could do no overt evangelism in Nepal, as it was outlawed. Perhaps I said in my application how important evangelism was to me. How ironic that I couldn't go to Nepal! The situation was the same in Bangladesh. In that Muslim-majority country we could legally answer any questions about our faith, but never initiate a conversation about spiritual things. God was clearly deciding where I should be. In His providence this puzzle piece of my life involved Him placing me in a rural area along the coast of the country to work as a nutritionist with a family planning organization.

I traveled to Bangladesh with a nurse who was to be my coworker. Erica and I were going to live in Maijdi with a group of guys who worked in the agriculture program. We landed in Dacca (now called Dhaka). It was

July, which is the hottest, rainiest, most sticky, miserable time of the year. The temperature was around ninety most days with 90 percent humidity in the rainy season. I had no idea the climate would be so oppressive. I was taken to the MCC Guest House and crashed in bed after the long trip. I must have left my Bible on the coffee table in the living room. Duane recalls being at the guest house the day I came. He had come from Maijdi, where he was living and stayed in Dacca overnight as he was on his way to a study tour in India. He saw my Bible. It was a big, thick well-marked NASB with a heavy leather cover. The words to Isaiah 40:7 were engraved in a floral design on the cover: "The grass withereth, the flower fadeth, but the word of our God shall stand forever." He knew two girls were to join the large group of male agriculture workers. He was intrigued to meet the owner of the big Bible when he returned after a week. God was doing something that would have lifelong implications for both of us by using my carelessness when I left my Bible out in the main living area.

I absolutely loved working in Bangladesh: crowds, curry, heat, humidity and all. It was a joy despite the rule that we couldn't openly share Jesus with anyone there. I loved working with the Muslim ladies in the small cooperatives we formed. My role was to teach them home-management skills and nutrition so their children would survive and be healthy. At that time they usually gave birth to ten or more children, hoping that at least half their kids would survive to support them and help with farming. The infant mortality rate was high, which drove the high fertility rate. The population was 75 million in a country the size of Wisconsin. Since I was there in the late 1970s the population has increased by another 100 million people. Bangladesh was the most densely populated country on earth. God was putting down another puzzle piece: a love for Muslim people.

Concurrently Duane was working on establishing soybeans as a crop that farmers could grow and sell locally. There were five guys and two girls living in the MCC house. I took over the management of the household, organizing the Bangladeshi staff every day in cooking, cleaning, and washing our clothes. I was known to be pretty bossy and controlling, to say the least. We all ate together three times a day and played games at night to keep occupied in our compound. Our weaknesses and strengths were evident to each other. God was so good to me then. I had never been around any guys on a day-to-day basis; I never had had a date in my life. Guys were aliens to me, but I wanted a husband. I prayed every night in my bed on the upper floor under the mosquito net for God to find me the right man. Little did I know that my future husband was in bed in his room on the floor beneath me of the very house where I was living! For those years God got me used to being around men day in and day out. I could see what I liked and didn't like in guys without having to play the dating game. By the end of the first year I decided that Duane had the least objectionable characteristics of all the men in the household. He was a good possibility.

After a year of working I was ready for a vacation. I went with Duane and another guy, Greg, to Thailand. We spent the first week in the northern part of the country, sightseeing and riding motorcycles. I remember very little except that Greg got very ill. The second week we traveled south to a lovely little tourist island of Ko Samui. Greg was still sick. Duane and I had lots of time together in a tropical paradise. We swam at night in the moonlight, with each stroke creating phosphorescent greenish blue lights in the water. We snorkeled and saw beautiful coral and fish. It was a paradise.

It was while I was cleaning up Duane's scratched and torn-up feet after that day snorkeling when I decided I loved him. The feelings were mutual. We returned to Bangladesh, in love, to get back to work. God gave us two years to get to know each other by talking together for hours in the compound. We never had a formal date outside the building, because to appear in public together as single people in a very conservative Muslim area would have been a scandal.

When our term of service was completed we returned to Duane's home state of South Dakota. I decided that I needed to get another degree besides home economics so I could get employment I'd enjoy. I enrolled at South Dakota State University (SDSU) to study dietetics and get a master's degree in nutrition. I also had to decide whether our relationship would last the cultural change of being in the USA. I realized I would have to learn to accept the local farming culture, one I had never known before, if I were to marry Duane.

Repentance

Duane and I were married on March 7, 1982. I continued studying at SDSU until 1985, when I graduated with a master's degree in nutrition and a concentration in dietetics. While at SDSU, I had to take an undergraduate economics course as part of my requirements. The class met in one of the largest lecture halls on campus. It wasn't a tough course for me. I had studied enough for one of the unit tests to have been able to do well on the exam. But halfway through it I must have been stumped. The guy sitting next to me was pretty close so it was very easy to see his answer to the question. I copied his answer and finished the test. The problem is that immediately I was flooded with so much guilt I could hardly stand it.

Up until that day I loved God and wanted to serve Him with everything in me, but I really hadn't ever come face-to-face with my own sin problem. I hadn't ever felt that I was cut off from God due to my sin and in total need of forgiveness. I had never repented of anything. I was pretty self-righteous. God put an end to that pious faith that day. I realized for the first time that even just that one sin of stealing was enough to separate me from God forever. I was doomed without grace. I needed Jesus' punishment and death for that one sin just as much as someone needs forgiveness who lives a very sordid life, scorning God and the Bible. One sin is enough to break communion with God. His holiness is so pure that just one sin, let into heaven, would mar its perfection.

I prayed and repented, but realized that I had to confess what I had done to the professor. God states in 1 John 1:9, "If we confess our sins, He is faithful and just to forgive our sins and cleanse us from all unrighteousness." Only in that way could I restore my relationship with God. I planned to talk with the professor quietly after class the next period. The class met Mondays, Wednesdays, and Fridays, so I had to wait two days. It was a terribly miserable time, feeling the guilt of what I had done and anticipating the possibility of being expelled from the graduate program for cheating. I was terribly anxious.

The tests were returned and I had a good score. I could have just walked out of the classroom that day and no one would have known. But I couldn't deal with my guilt any longer. So after class I hung around, hoping the line of students who were complaining about their test scores would diminish so I could talk to the professor alone. I waited long enough. I joined the line when I thought no one else would come after me. But at least ten others lined up behind me for their turn. Ugh. How embarrassing! Everyone would be able to hear what I was to say. They would think I was so stupid to tell him. But I just couldn't leave the room until it was done.

Finally it was my turn. I blurted out to the professor that I had cheated on the one question on the test, and I didn't deserve the grade he had given. He looked kind of shocked. Maybe no one had ever said that to him before. He just said it was "OK" and quickly sent me on my way.

I nearly danced out of the room. My guilt turned to joyous liberation from the debilitating shame. I was forgiven, not only by the professor but also by God. I was totally amazed at the fact that Jesus had been punished for that sin when He didn't deserve it at all, just because He loved me. John 3:16 was suddenly not just a verse I had memorized as a child, but reality: "For God so loved the world that He gave His only Son, that whoever believes in Him will not perish, but have eternal life." For the first time in my life I knew the joy of forgiveness. I knew I had repented. I was certain that God the Father saw Jesus' righteousness instead of my sin. I accepted the gift of forgiveness and the promise of life in heaven forever with Jesus. Now I felt like I really was part of the Kingdom of God. I had allowed Jesus to take over my heart. He exposed sin and other areas of my life I kept hidden from Him. I was assured I was forgiven and had a clear relationship with Him.

Establishing Our Family

Infertility and Miscarriage

Recently I was listening to a message given by David Jeremiah. His topic was "The Faithfulness of God." He reminded me that many people, including myself, go through times in their lives when they cannot see anything positive in their circumstances. This puzzle piece is one of those. It has only been in retrospect that I have been able to see God's loving-kindness and faithfulness. At the time things were grim and very painful. I could not see God's love in action, tenderly taking care of me. But now, looking back on it, I clearly see God's love and protection.

After I graduated we moved close to the farm where Duane grew up. He started farming with his dad, and I began work at the Human Services Center in Yankton. Although I only stayed there one year, God was preparing me to understand and navigate the world of treatment for mental illness to enable us to handle one of our kids. It's amazing how God, in His providence, plans and prepares us for what lies ahead. But that's for a future chapter.

While working at my first job after graduation, we decided we had waited long enough to have kids. It had been four years since our wedding and about time to get our family started. I was twenty-nine years old by then, and the biological clock was ticking. I expected to get pregnant right away, but nothing happened. Finally, after about a year of frustration, I went and had the first procedures done to evaluate the condition. The gynecologist realized that the problem was more than he could handle and sent us on to a specialist in Sioux Falls. I was immediately scheduled for laparoscopic exploratory surgery.

It turned out that I had endometriosis—my tubes were blocked, the whole uterus was covered in scar tissue, and I wasn't ovulating due to cysts on the ovaries. Getting a diagnosis of infertility is equal to learning you have cancer. I was devastated. My plans and dreams were shattered. I wasn't in control at all anymore. Then Dr. Lee did another surgery to clean it all up, and I started taking Clomid to increase the chance I would ovulate. He gave us hope that we'd have a baby within a few months.

Meanwhile Duane got the opportunity to work as a consultant and specialist in Burma (Myanmar) for Ohio State University. He was to help the seed farms there to improve their operations. We prayed about it to seek God's will. Duane had to give an answer regarding our decision within a very short time. His family wasn't too supportive. We didn't know what to do. Duane and I will never forget the Sunday we sat in church and heard a sermon from a visiting speaker. He challenged everyone to go where God was telling them to go to serve Him. It was intended for the younger people in the church, primarily, but he spoke directly to us. God's answer could not have been clearer! I was so excited to go overseas again! It had been so awesome the first time. God was getting ready to put into place another puzzle piece of our lives. I was happy; this would be the perfect time to have a baby. We planned to be there four years, and I wouldn't have to work.

However, as we prepared to go, the months wore on and there was no sign of a baby. I remember getting more and more depressed and anxious. I remember the day I was alone and had a knife poised at my wrist, ready to end it all. I caught myself in time. We stopped the medication for a few months while we were packing up our household to leave, since a side effect of the drug can be suicidal thoughts. Just prior to leaving the USA, I restarted the medication to be able to ovulate and conceive.

When we got to Burma we were sent to live in Meiktila, which is a city about 330 miles away from Rangoon (Yangon). There were no other American expatriates living outside the capital city. We were isolated. But God put us in a compound next door to an elderly couple. She was an English nurse, and he was a retired Burmese physician. Their daughters wanted to learn to speak English, so they came to visit every afternoon to chat.

Burma has a socialistic government. At that time it was illegal for anyone to talk to me beyond a normal conversation at the market without permission from the government. I walked to the open-air market to get groceries each day with the cook, and we went to the local Baptist Burmese church (established by converts of Adonirom Judson). The cook and drivers and housekeeper gossiped around me as I cooked over the fire in my wood-fueled stove every evening after English class. The neighbor girls must have had permission to talk with me. They may have been given that privilege so they could act as spies and report back to local authorities, but they were also my link to the outside world. There was a missionary couple in Rangoon, but I only saw them infrequently. These were all the social contacts I had.

It was through those girls that we learned of the student uprising that began in the spring of 1988 in Rangoon, which quickly spread to remote areas of the country. I recall hearing demonstrations out on the street as people, led by the Buddhist priests, shouted and clamored for freedom and democracy. One day I snuck to a building close to the bazaar to get an upstairs view of the demonstration. That was quite dangerous. The American embassy told us to stay clear of all the turmoil. But it did something in me to see people so desperate for freedom of expression. To this day I realize that the USA is a wonderful country, giving us privileges most of us take for granted.

Meanwhile I got pregnant. I was delighted and ecstatic. Despite the embassy doctor's fear of me having twins or triplets, due to the infertility drugs I was taking, I was on cloud nine. God was good; my plans were working out. We weren't infertile anymore! All was sunshine and happiness. At that time I was traveling around the country with Duane, to the seed farms where he worked. I felt happy when we stopped to fill the car with gas; the smell of gasoline made me nauseated. We were going to have a baby!

However, one day while at the market, terrible abdominal pain started. It wouldn't go away. It was just a solid contraction that didn't come and go as it does in labor. I couldn't figure out what the pain could be. It was nothing like I had ever experienced before. I went to bed for about a week. The doctor next door came over to check me. He had no diagnosis, or if he did I couldn't understand what he said in his broken English. About a week later, when in the bathroom, I passed two strange-looking pieces of flesh-colored flat tissue. I flushed them down the toilet. That was the end of the pain. Nothing else after that.

The morning I got ready to go to my prenatal checkup with the embassy doctor in Rangoon, I recall looking in the mirror and thinking, *You don't really look pregnant anymore.* God softened the blow by putting that thought in my mind. When the doctor looked at me he broke the news, saying, "You're not pregnant. You lost the baby." Devastation and shock aren't strong enough words to express what I was feeling at that moment. I was alone; Duane was at work. I have no idea how I ever got back to the guesthouse to collapse with my broken heart.

Somehow we got back to our place in Meiktila, isolated, away from anyone who spoke English. It was an eight hour trip to anyone who could offer any support and help. My world was shattered. Now, as I tell people in the GriefShare groups I lead, that my miscarriage was the worst loss I've faced, they look at me dumfounded. (How could it be worse than losing your teenage son?) It was, though. I became depressed. The sunshine outside couldn't permeate my frozen heart. The ice inside me was broken in pieces. God was far away and hadn't answered my prayers for a baby. In fact He had let me ignorantly flush its remains down the toilet in a terrible burial. How could God do this to me? I became terribly angry inside. The rage I felt consumed me. Then as the months passed on it subsided into apathy. From then on all I recall of my relationship with God was that it was like a frozen desert wasteland in the winter. There was total dryness. The distance between me and God grew.

As I look back on the experience I realize this was a puzzle piece in my life. God was shattering my façade so He could enter all the places of my heart. I had given Him some control of my life, but He wasn't king over everything. The Kingdom of God involves God ruling and reigning in every area of our lives. There were lots of remaining areas to give over to Him to control. I was so self-sufficient and arrogant then that it took a loving crowbar to start to open my heart to Him. God was at work, but I was totally unable to see anything good in the situation.

What made matters worse is that the embassy doctor refused to make arrangements and refer me to get further treatment. I never had a D&C or any evaluation after his dreadful news. I would have had to go to Thailand to see a specialist. Why did he refuse? I have no idea; he just didn't think it was necessary when I asked him repeatedly to get a referral for the procedure. And month after month I didn't get pregnant again, either. Anger, disappointment, and depression became the backdrop of my life.

The political situation worsened. The demonstrations for democracy grew more dangerous. The day shots were fired in the American embassy compound in Rangoon, the decision was made by the ambassador to evacuate all the US citizens. We left Burma, and spent a month in Thailand on the way home. When we got back to South Dakota, Duane nearly forced me to go back to the infertility specialist to get help. I was done with any treatments. I was grieving too badly to be able to make a rational decision about my health. I had had enough. I just wanted to adopt and forget about it all.

The infertility specialist was furious when he did an exploratory surgery. What he found was that all the remains of the pregnancy tissues had gone through the fallopian tubes and into my abdomen, where they encased everything in what became a ball of scar tissue. If the embassy doctor had referred me for help when I suspected I needed it, I may have been able to get treatment in time without extensive surgery. I gave in and let the specialist go through with the procedure. He took care of an even bigger mess in my abdomen than he had cleaned up when he first treated me for endometriosis before leaving for Burma. The specialist gave us six months, in which time we had a 30 percent chance of getting pregnant while I took more fertility drugs. After that he didn't think there was any hope. My heart grew more bitter and angry. This time my feelings were projected toward the embassy doctor. I just couldn't understand why God would allow him to do something so stupid as to prevent me getting help in a timely basis.

Little did I know that God was in the middle of the whole sad, ugly thing. I just couldn't see it at the time. When we settled back into our church after returning home, I looked around and realized that EVERY one of my friends had a baby the year we were gone. If I had miscarried living in the USA while all of them were giving birth to their second or third child, I don't think I could have handled my jealousy and rage. God protected me from that horrendous possibility. He really was there, loving me and keeping me secluded away from the horrific emotional pain I would have had. His loving-kindness and faithfulness are apparent to me now. How I praise Him for protecting my heart in that way!

Several years later I overheard a lady describing the symptoms she had when she had a miscarriage. I was horrified to learn how life-threatening it was, as she nearly bled to death before getting help. I had always wondered why I had such a weird way of losing my baby. There were none of the usual signs at all. I think that's why the embassy doctor refused to really take it very seriously. When I heard her story my heart melted in repentance. I realized that God was protecting me by the way He arranged the circumstances. When I was living in Burma, where I lost the baby, it took a day to drive on bad roads to get meager health care in Rangoon. There were absolutely no emergency services available anywhere. I could have bled to death for sure, if things had gone wrong.

God was faithful and good by causing things to happen as they did. Once I understood that He was working behind the scenes in this very ugly, sad puzzle piece of my life, I was able to move forward from my grief, forgive the doctor, and praise Him. The joy was freeing and exhilarating. I wasn't stuck in a very ugly place with a bitter heart any longer. Why? I could trust a God who, in His providence, orchestrated the circumstances of this painful event to protect me. I felt so loved by God then. His sovereignty was trustworthy, and not only a means of working out His purposes for His glory but also a means to shower us with His love.

God doesn't promise that His kids will be immune to the problems people face in life, but He does promise to be there with us. Once my eyes were opened to how God demonstrated His love in the situation of the loss of my baby and how He was there with me, I tried to look for signs of His goodness the minute ugly things surfaced. I changed from viewing circumstances as just coincidences to seeing them as God's hand at work. Those little things that just seem to fall together sensibly and nicely, with an outcome that ultimately brings good, are actually God-ordained and planned events. They are part of the way He foresees events and works them out for His good and purposes. Although I had a glimmer of this understanding after the time in Burma, that skill had to be honed further through more tough times.

Adoption

The six months passed during which time there was hope I could get pregnant. There was no baby on the horizon. I gave up and we turned all our attention and financial reserves to adoption. It was a hard time. If infertility is hard, working on adoption with a raw, grieving heart is just as hard. We approached the whole issue with no emotional reserves, having been totally drained of hope during all the medical procedures we endured.

A social worker tried to link us up with mothers who were putting up their babies for adoption. One day she gave us the news about an African American young woman who was having twins. They were a boy and a girl and were due in a month, but expected to be born at any time. We agreed to the arrangements. Two at once! How wonderful! I named them Rocky and Julie in my mind. We were delighted, but didn't let many people know just in case things didn't work out. The social worker cautioned us to resist the urge to buy everything we'd need to take care of twins. There would be a chance to do that when they arrived. I silently disagreed with her; I couldn't see how I could go shopping with two tiny babies for everything we'd need the minute we'd get custody of them. Furthermore I didn't think anything would really happen to change the plans. But we complied and resisted the urge to get prepared.

Duane and I got the call that the babies had been born. Everyone was so excited for us! We needed to drive from South Dakota to Ohio to get them. I cancelled everything at work for the next week. The plan was for Duane to be the stay-at-home parent with the babies. We packed that night to take off in the morning, full of anticipation and excitement. We were to become parents at long last!

Just as we were getting into the car we heard the phone ring in the house. It was the social worker. She told us that the mother of the babies had been forced to change her mind. The grandmother was insisting that the mother keep them. The adoption was not going to happen. There was no way to get the grandmother to reconsider.

Once again we were devastated. Duane called the pastor of our church. He must have sped the forty miles to our place, because he was there in less than half an hour. Pastor Glanzer picked up the shattered pieces of our lives and our faith and lovingly pointed us back to the Healer. He loved us through that horrible experience. He was Jesus with modern clothes on, loving and helping us to face life once again without children. What an amazing pastor! I was able to tell him just lately of how much his ministry meant to us. Because of this pastor's care I didn't turn back into a bitter, angry mess. He directed me to seek comfort in Jesus. It was easier to allow God to fit that piece into His overall puzzle, because I could see God's love in action through other people.

We gave up on that social worker making any feasible arrangements for adoption. We found a good adoption agency to work with instead of trying to adopt privately. Holt International Children's Services nearly guaranteed that you would have a child in your home within a year of beginning the application process. We needed a guarantee we could get a child. We just couldn't face another disappointment. We were exhausted emotionally from so many losses. We plunged into the application process with Holt.

Most of the kids Holt placed were from Korea at that time. Soon a referral was sent to us for a little boy who was twelve months old. A "referral" means we got a picture of him and a few details about his birth and health. From that information we could agree to the adoption or ask instead for other possible kids to consider. Most people accept the first referral unless there is a health problem the adoptive parents don't think they can handle. All we knew about this little boy was his Korean name, and that he lived with fifty to sixty other children in an orphanage in Seoul. He was a year old and healthy. He was considered to be a "special needs child" due to being biracial (African American and Korean) and therefore was considered to be hard to place. We didn't see any problems with adopting him if it was just his mixed ethnic heritage that made him stand out. He was smiley, cute, and energetic-looking in the picture. That's all that mattered to me. We agreed to the referral and the process was started for Jonathan to come home!

I don't recall feeling or thinking much at that time regarding God's role in the process. I think we were just too relieved that the long, painful road of infertility and childlessness was over. I was still thinking that we were in control; we had wasted a few years by getting the advice and services of a social worker for the adoption that led down a fruitless path. By just being logical about it and working with an agency that was efficient, we were to have a child in a predictable amount of time. My thoughts were that finally things were going to work out for us. Maybe there were distant thoughts of Jonathan being planned by God, but it wasn't my predominant belief at the time. I realized Jonathan was God's gift to some extent, and that was reflected in selecting his name, which means "gift of

God." However, I think any person who has experienced infertility sees their children as gifts.

Parents at Last

In the process of adoption from Holt, there is a time when you have to pay the full bill. It was more than a year after the doctor gave up hope of us conceiving. I sent in the check; Jonathan would be on his way as soon as the adoption agency could get all the legal arrangements made. Duane and I were rejoicing that we would finally have a family. I recall going to a concert the night I paid the bill, on a date with Duane. When we returned home we learned that Duane's brother's baby boy had just been born. Jon would have a little cousin his age. All was good.

A few weeks later I started feeling funny. It couldn't be! I bought an at-home pregnancy test and did it by myself without telling Duane. It was positive. It couldn't be right! There was no chance left of having a baby according to the infertility specialist. I did another test and it came out positive, too. Then I told Duane. We got at third test kit and watched the little blue line form on the tester. All I remember is dissolving in tears of laughter, just as I'm doing now as I write this. We were going to have our very own baby!

The ironic thing is that I had just been to the doctor for a checkup a week before we did the pregnancy tests. I have a deformed cervix with a high risk of cancer developing resulting from a drug my mother took when pregnant with me. The doctor had done a very painful procedure to kill abnormal cells, and told me he needed to repeat the procedure. That day on the way home from the appointment I decided that it wasn't worth it to have any more medical procedures. I just wanted to have a hysterectomy since I was infertile anyway. Since Jonathan was coming soon from Korea, we didn't need to hassle about my fertility anymore. That issue was settled as far as I was concerned. Why not just end the whole mess? So I decided that day to change the purpose of the next appointment with the doctor, from having another painful procedure into a discussion of having a hysterectomy.

But just in time, I got pregnant. The purpose of the appointment changed one more time, from a painful procedure, to a discussion about a hysterectomy, to telling him I needed him to confirm that I was pregnant. My doctor was so happy when the test in the office came back positive! I was pregnant for sure! God was definitely in control! He sent me off to my infertility specialist to check to make sure it wasn't an ectopic pregnancy, for which I was at very high risk due to all the scar tissue. As the ultrasound was being done, the speck on the screen began pulsating. The technician sucked in her breath and said, "The heart just started beating!" I got to see my baby's heartbeat begin. I was bonded to that child. He was mine. God was blessing us so much. That little heartbeat became a precious little puzzle piece, my baby, fashioned for His glory.

When I consider now how close I came to the changing course of my life and Duane's, it makes me stop to glorify God. God was sovereign over the timing of the conception of my baby. It was no coincidence at all. He planned that child and had to organize the timing perfectly so that I wouldn't destroy every possibility of becoming pregnant. His timing at putting puzzle pieces in place is precise. Sometimes the timing is so perfect that you can't miss His hand at work. This was one of those times. I wasn't yet thinking of this as being evidence of God's sovereignty. The term wasn't part of my thinking. But I recognized God's hand at work in the whole situation. All we could do was praise Him for the little ones He had planned for us to parent.

Meanwhile we had to notify Holt Adoption Agency of the pregnancy. They had a policy that an adoption would not be possible if the parents got pregnant during the time the adoption was being processed. But due to Jonathan's special needs, they would consider the situation further. I remember calling my sister Joy, to discuss it. She wisely said, "God is sovereign to determine what kids you get by birth, and He's sovereign to decide what child you get by adoption. It's just as much His choice by adoption as by birth. If He wants you to have Jonathan, He'll make it possible."

I think that may have been the first time I was aware of the personal nature of the sovereignty of God. He wasn't just a remote God with some vague interest in me since I had trusted Jesus as my Savior. My sister put a term (God's sovereignty) to what I was starting to understand and feel. She gave me this verse:

"I prayed for this child, and the LORD has granted me what I asked of Him. So now I give him to the LORD. For his whole life he will be given over to the LORD."

1 SAMUEL 1:27–28, NIV

This was a prophetic word of faith for Jonathan with all the problems we faced with him later in his childhood and life. We had an inkling that the sovereignty of God would work for our good and His glory.

It was rather mind-boggling to realize that God is so involved in my life that He picked my kids. I had a lot to learn about the nature of God! But I was growing in my trust of this amazing God who was obviously planning things so precisely.

The pregnancy was rough. I had contractions from twenty-four weeks on. The months stretched on and on, with holdups in getting Jonathan home. We moved many miles away during that time of waiting, to our house and farmstead where we still live. God blessed us with providing a small farm closer to the place where I worked. It was just the type of place I always wanted as a child: a creek that runs beside the driveway, a weeping willow tree, woods and a hill that surround the farmstead with space for hobby animals (ducks, chickens, sheep, goats, and a donkey), and a big yard for our many farm cats and two dogs. We left our church and all our friends behind to start this new phase of our lives.

Finally the arrangements were made for Duane to go to get Jonathan, flying to Seoul and back. The day Duane was to arrive back with our little son, the doctor told me I needed to stay home on bedrest from then on. I couldn't work anymore. What timing! I had to be at home with my new little adopted boy to begin the bonding process. It wouldn't have been possible without God intervening with a health issue. Jonathan (Jon) was nineteen months old then. I realized God was in control of this whole thing, down to the day I started my maternity leave. I would be able to have several weeks at home with Jon, getting to know him. After the baby would be born, my attention would be torn between the two of them. I was so grateful for God's action on my behalf to organize this time without the pressure of work and a new baby. I felt God's care and love for me personally. He knew what Jon and I needed most, and even though it caused lots of discomfort physically for me, God worked it all out for His glory and plans. Once again the timing was proof of God's love for me.

Duane and Jonathan arrived in Sioux Falls the evening I took off for my maternity leave from work. I made it to the airport to meet them. To our surprise, despite the fact we had moved seventy to eighty miles away and were part of a new church, Pastor Glanzer was there. He was the one who had picked up the pieces of the failed adoption of the twin babies. He came to rejoice with us and glorify God for His action in our lives to resolve this terribly painful experience. What an amazing pastor!

Ten weeks later, on June 30, 1991, Matthew Isaac Auch was born late one Sunday afternoon. We gave him the middle name Isaac, meaning "laughter." God filled us with laughter and joy when we learned we'd have him. We had been married for nine years when Matt was born. Our infertility was over! He has been a joy ever since. He's made me laugh over and over in the last twenty-seven years, when things got grim. What a huge blessing he's been!

Special Needs Child

Jonathan became a huge puzzle piece in our lives. Maybe he's several pieces fitted together with many other pieces of our lives and our kids' lives. God put those pieces there to bring Him glory. What we went through with Jon never would have been anyone's choice. Nevertheless because of Jonathan, and the way he's influenced our lives, he has been the impetus of much of our spiritual growth.

A few weeks before Jonathan came home I heard about a seminar in Sioux Falls concerning attachment disorder. Somehow I felt compelled to go. I never did things like this on my only precious day off from work. There was too much to do on the farm to catch up. But God sent me to that seminar to prepare my heart. I learned there of the terrible problems some parents have when they adopt, due to the difficulty of forming a good bond. I learned that the kids don't learn to trust anyone when they don't have a consistent person taking care of them before they are adopted or live in a stable foster home. When no one is there in the orphanage to calm them and reassure them, they think that no one will meet their needs. They learn to control things to get what they want. These kids can resort to dangerous and inappropriate ways to meet their needs. And as hard as adoptive parents try, the child just won't trust them. They take it out on the mom most of all. The attachment disorder cannot really be reversed unless God does a miracle of healing in the personality; it can only be managed to minimize harm to everyone involved. It sounded terrible. I kind of tucked it away in the back of my mind. But looking back, I see that God was preparing me for what we were to face.

Providence is "seeing before." God was certainly acting in His providence, as He could see what was to happen when Jon came to live with us. He compelled me to go and learn about what was going to happen so I could be aware and not totally blindsided. Neither Duane nor I had much previous experience taking care of children. We been married for nine years by this time and were pretty settled into a comfortable life. The only problems we had were work stresses. We didn't realize how challenging it would be to suddenly have two children at two different ages coming at nearly the same time. And although I had some child development background as a home economics major, I certainly wasn't equipped to be a parent of a child with a major personality disorder. There's not much that can prepare you to handle a special needs child day in and day out.

When Duane saw Jonathan in the orphanage in Korea, he noted some bruises on his forehead. One day he observed Jon banging his head on the floor. Jon was in constant motion with the other little kids, running around the room and jumping from crib to crib. By this time he was nineteen months old. He didn't have any toys in his room. Duane learned that he had been moved from one room to the next about six times since he was born. The orphanage had the practice of moving all the kids of a common age together to the next room as they grew older. There weren't any consistent caregivers who went with them as the children moved to a different room. Duane had the feeling that Jon was the butt of some discrimination from the Korean workers due to looking different than all the other full-blooded Korean kids. He stood out due to being biracial with predominant African facial features. Due to behaviors he has had, we suspect he was neglected.

When Jonathan came home he did not understand anything we said and couldn't really communicate much verbally. He had never heard any English until he was on the plane on the way home with Duane. He seemed to be a happy little person who was very active. He had minimal skills with manipulating toys and small objects. He had to crawl on my lap to be held, as I couldn't lift anything before Matt was born due to my physical condition. He learned to crawl up on me quickly. When he wasn't snuggling on someone, he seemed to bounce around the house.

One night after Matt was born we took the kids to a Right to Life event on campus at the University of South Dakota. Protests were planned by advocates of Pro-Choice, so there were security guards in the building. At the meeting there were several speakers who got pretty long-winded for two children. Matt and Jonathan couldn't tolerate being quiet for the whole meeting. When the graphic videos depicting abortion started I took them out to the lobby. Jon ran around and kept trying to get attention from the guards. He was overly friendly. I had noted this behavior before. He would try to entice any stranger to give him attention wherever I took him. I just thought he was a friendly little guy. But the security guard gave me a dose of reality. He said that most kids at that age stay by their parents and are naturally afraid of strangers. It planted the thought in my mind that something must be wrong with Jonathan. It sounded like a symptom of attachment disorder that I had learned about at the seminar.

After about six months Jon was able to speak a little English. We read and read to him and got him to play with toys. I didn't really think there was anything unusual about his development at that time. When I took him to get his immunizations, the community health nurse suspected problems when she did a Denver Developmental Screen. He wasn't doing things kids should be able to do developmentally by his age. She suspected he was rather delayed developmentally due to not being able to handle small objects, an inability to copy simple shapes with a crayon, and unclear speech. She made arrangements for me to take Jonathan to a specialist in Sioux Falls.

By this time Jonathan was three years old, and Matt was about eighteen months. One day I looked down the steps to the basement and nearly freaked out. The two of them were at the bottom of the staircase. Jonathan had Duane's shotgun between them. There were shells lying around. I got the kids out of the basement and got Duane to figure out what had happened. We didn't have a gun-safe cabinet because gun safety wasn't stressed as much then as it is now. Instead Duane crammed his shotgun and rifle in the rafters of the unfinished basement. They were wedged in between the supports in the ceiling. The shells were stored in another place in the ceiling rafters. Jonathan had stacked two folding chairs on top of one another and had gotten the shotgun down. He had loaded it. Fortunately he put the shell in upside down so it couldn't be shot. God's protection was clearly evident, but I was terrified at what this child could do.

The next week we took him to the specialist for the appointment that had been arranged. By the end of the morning we had a long list of diagnoses for our little boy. He had reactive attachment disorder, oppositional defiant disorder, ADHD, and was developmentally delayed. (To this day he functions at a fourth-grade level intellectually.) The psychologist couldn't prove fetal alcohol syndrome, but suspected it. That morning he said quietly to Duane, "This type of child usually ends up being institutionalized." Although seemingly unkind, it prepared Duane's heart so that when things got worse he wasn't shocked and didn't blame himself as much as he otherwise would have done.

Those years are full of many painful memories of Jonathan. I feel exhausted just recalling them. It's only by God's grace, loving-kindness, and faithfulness that we made it through that time. I often felt I was going to end up at the mental health institution about forty miles from our home due to the difficulty in parenting our son. It got to the place that I prayed constantly for strength to make it through the next minute. Verses such as these became real to me:

"Praise be to the LORD, for He showed His wonderful love to me when I was in a besieged city."

PSALM 31:21, NIV

"Praise be to the LORD for He has heard my cry for mercy.
"The LORD is my strength and my shield; my heart
trusts in Him and I am helped.
My heart leaps for joy and I will give thanks to Him in song."

PSALM 28:6–7, NIV

I had very little time to spend alone with God at the time. Jon could be up at any time so I couldn't really settle into a good habit of having a quiet time and being alone with Him, and as most mothers know little kids are a danger to themselves 24/7; they need to be watched constantly. In Jon's case he was a danger to the rest of the family as well. I had to draw on what I could glean from snatches of sermons and time driving to work listening to Christian radio. My prayers were more pleas from desperation than time spent with God, allowing Him to calm my heart. But those prayers were real. God knew all I could manage was asking for emergency help.

We had a terrible scare when Matt was eight months old. In those days there were walkers you put your babies in so they could get around without crawling. It helped them be up off the floor and strengthened their leg muscles to be ready to walk. Jon liked pushing Matt around the house in it. One day they were playing beside me in the kitchen. I was looking in the refrigerator with my back turned for a minute. The door to the basement was open. Jon pushed little Matt down the stairs in the walker. Matt went flying out and landed at the bottom. By God's providence there was a piece of carpet at the bottom. Matt hit the carpet, which must have prevented a skull fracture. God's faithfulness was in action. God even plans and gets carpets for soft landings in place to accomplish His purposes! We rushed him to the ER. He didn't have any long-term effects from that accident. It scared us and we were more careful with Jon and Matt playing together from then on. I praised God for saving my precious baby's life.

Jonathan started taking medication for his ADHD when he was three and a half years old. It slowed him down a little, and medication blunted his impulsivity to some extent. But the pills could do nothing to change the fact that he trusted no one to meet his needs. Pills could not improve his lack of appropriate reserve around strangers. He found ways to control situations because the only one he trusted was himself. As he got older Jon developed a fascination for knives and fires. At nine years of age, he lit a match in his room the night after new carpeting was put in, making a burn mark. One night he took the TV off the stand in the living room, brought his red wagon into the house, and took the TV out to Duane's office, which was attached to the garage. Jon had amazing strength for a skinny little kid. On another occasion he ransacked Duane's office, spreading papers and documents all over. He threatened me and the other kids with knives. One day when Duane was at work he locked the kids and me out of the house, holding us hostage with a knife. Another day he got in Duane's little pickup with Matt, and got the vehicle in neutral gear. The pickup started rolling backward toward the bank of the stream on the edge of the driveway. I raced across the yard, jumped in, pushed the kids aside, and put the break on before he caused an accident. Another day he jerked the steering wheel while a babysitter was driving the kids home from swimming, causing her car to go through the ditch and into an electric fence by a field. When he was about eight Jonathan got on the roof one day to taunt me to get him down. I learned to act nonchalantly to avoid reinforcing his antics. Amazingly he never got hurt or broke any bones.

Jon usually refused to do whatever I told or asked him to do. It was either a sassy type of refusal or a refusal that conveyed total defiance. "Yes" wasn't part of his vocabulary. He was so active that my usual feelings toward him were total annoyance and frustration. Counselors varied in what they suggested. My recollection of the books written by Christian childhood specialists was that any defiance in a child warranted correction and punishment until they learned who was boss and obeyed. With Jonathan that didn't seem possible. But I did my best to stand my ground, spanking him for outright defiance, and putting him in "time out" when he needed to calm down. The only place I could put him in "time out" was on the staircase to the basement. Anywhere else he would thrash around so much he'd be totally disruptive to everyone else. On the stairs he'd hurt only himself if he didn't sit reasonably still. Why he just didn't run down the stairs to get away from it all doesn't make any sense to me. But he did quiet down there to some extent. He smashed a hole in the wall beside the staircase that kept him busy, as he made it bigger and bigger with each punishment.

At times the "time out" was not possible. I couldn't get him to go to the staircase. He needed to stop his behavior immediately. We were advised to use "holding time" to try to create a bond for times when he was really out-of-control. The theory was that the child never learned to be calmed by a parent as a baby, so when he'd get upset as an older child he should be held down until calm, and therefore learn to trust the parent and relinquish control. That's fine if it's a twenty-pound child. But a six- to eight-year-old seventy- to eighty-pound skinny little kid with boundless energy is really hard to hold on to when he's angry and out of control. He never really calmed down that way to look lovingly up into my eyes as the theorists said should happen. The approach degenerated into restraining him until he was tolerable. I spent hours holding him down on all fours, as he writhed and spat in my face. It took all my energy to get him to give up. I was usually totally exhausted from those encounters. I was too tired to be angry. I just grew indifferent and distant from him. He just got worse.

To be honest I grew to detest him. I really resented God for allowing such a little monster to invade our lives. How in the world did I deserve to get such a horrible kid when all we wanted was to be able to be parents? Was this some sort of mean trick? What kind of God would make us endure this torture on a daily basis? I remember telling people I saw my job at work as "respite" from all I endured at home. Who goes to work for peace and safety from home? Where was God when I needed protection? Would this ever end?

Others in the family didn't see Jon in such a bad light. He tended to express his problems most around me, which is characteristic of attachment disorder. Duane and Jon were much closer and had fun times together. He was a fun-loving little boy much of the time when around other people, and entertained his aunts and uncles. Jon was particularly close to his grandfather, who seemed to love him unconditionally and didn't make any demands on him to cooperate and behave. He loved fishing with Jon and overlooked his hyperactivity and difficulties.

Jon loved to play tricks in a sneaky way. The funniest thing I recall is a day I drove him to his special ed preschool. He took a backpack with him every day with extra clothes and snacks, so I didn't notice anything unusual that morning when he headed into school with his backpack over his shoulder. I had parked the car by the library, which is quite a distance from the front door to the school. For some reason I didn't pull away from the curb to head home right away. But soon the principal, a fifty- to sixty-year-old woman, came tearing out of the school, brandishing the backpack with Jonathan following her. It was pretty hilarious to see a normally reserved lady desperate to get my attention, running so fast. I asked, "What is the matter?" as I braced for the bad news. Jon had smuggled our kitten into his backpack to use for show and tell. The kitten had been quiet during the five-mile trip to school, but once inside it made its presence known with some loud meows. Apparently pets weren't allowed as show-and-tell items!

At that time Jon needed speech therapy, and we were able to get free services from students at the University of South Dakota. He was so terribly active that teachers and professionals were at a loss to get him to sit still for evaluations and therapy. I took the other kids with me to these appointments. I realized how much of a problem he was the day I watched him through the one-way observation window. The student was trying to do her basic tasks to evaluate his speech. The room was rimmed with low cabinets with a table in the center where they were supposed to be working together. Jonathan taunted her and ran around and around on top of the cabinets, refusing to cooperate with her. He looked like an animal in a zoo that is trapped and just runs in circles. It was a horrible sight. No wonder I had so much trouble at home.

Jonathan thought nothing of seat belts and restraints. He could get out of them easily. One terrible day, on the way home from speech therapy, he was angry and out of control. It was a twenty-three-mile trip on a two-lane highway. Fortunately there wasn't much traffic. Jonathan was trying to get at the steering wheel. He was hitting the other kids. By this time Jon was nine years old. Matt was seven, Julie was five, and Peter was a baby. (I'll tell you about them in future chapters.) All three cowered under the dashboard as I drove and tried to restrain him behind my back with my right arm. Keeping them in their car seats would have caused them to be harmed by him. The kids were terrified of him and what he'd do. In desperation we cried out to God for help. Jonathan was too much to handle. I was broken and at the end of my rope. My self-sufficiency was gone, stripped from my soul and drained out of my life as I tried to manage Jonathan.

The danger to the kids increased. We had just completed putting an addition on the house with bedrooms for all the kids. The contractor had forgotten his big hammer with a big claw end and left it behind. I heard a terrible sound out in the garage. Matthew and Jonathan had gotten into a fight about a bike. Duane was far away from home, working out in a field. There were no cell phones then to contact him. Jon picked up the hammer and smashed Matt in the head with it. By God's plan and providence Matt was wearing a cap. He rarely wore anything on his head. But that day, for some reason, he did. Jonathan hit him with the claw end of the hammer and his scalp split open. I got the blood stopped and called the ER. With Jonathan so out of control, there was no way to drive twenty-three miles to get Matt there for stitches with all the other kids with me. We went there hours later once Duane came home. Matt has a scar on the crown of his head as a testimony to God's grace. He didn't have a concussion or any permanent brain damage. He even graduated at the top of his class years later as proof that God protected his life and health that day! That experience marks another time I started to realize God's amazing intervention in very minute details of our lives. I started to acknowledge God's sovereignty was being displayed before my very eyes. He loved us all enough to preserve Matt's life, and worked out a way to make sure he was protected from permanent harm.

Our little boy Jonathan began stealing money from anyone. We were totally clueless that this behavior could happen. He stole any cash he could find from his siblings. Their piggy banks weren't safe from him; it was nearly impossible to teach the other kids how to give, save, and spend wisely when their brother could ransack their banks and take it all. I resorted to a system of marking all the dollar bills with color codes on the margin to indicate to whom the money belonged. That didn't faze him. He took it anyway; at least I could identify from which sibling he had stolen the bills. We became a cashless family, relying on checks and debit cards. The envelope system advocated for money management would have been a disaster!

We really couldn't get anyone to give us respite. Jon bit me whenever he wanted something. He bit me when he was angry. He tormented babysitters and didn't act any better for them. They were at risk of real danger. We couldn't trust anyone to take care of him; how could you pay a babysitter enough to endure the problems? Duane and I felt isolated and alone. People cast their pitying looks on us in public when he'd act up. Their glances seemed to border on disdain at what terrible parents we were that we couldn't control him in pubic.

When we were at church he was in constant motion. He caused a commotion in the back row each week during the service. He took money from the offering plate if we didn't pay attention. I couldn't send Jonathan to children's church for others to take care of him; everyone would be at risk and in danger. Recently I went to a funeral in that church and sat in the spot where Duane and I struggled each week with Jon. I could barely hold back the tears, as the memories surged over me. Sitting there gave me a chance to reflect and pause to glorify God for what He did to rescue and sustain me.

One weekend when Jon was about eight years old, I took all four kids to an Asian multicultural event in Sioux Falls downtown. After the event we were all tired and headed home in our van. After a few blocks I heard a loud *Whap! Whap! Whap!* sound that just got louder. I looked up at the sky through the windshield thinking perhaps it was a helicopter; there was no sign of one. Then I realized it must be our car. At the next possible place I pulled into the gas station and convenience store on the corner of West Avenue and 12th street. It's a sacred place to me now because of what happened. I drove past the places to fill the car with gas to a far parking lot near the back of the lot. It was a little secluded. I got out and spied a flat tire on the rear passenger side. This was before the days of cell phones. I had four kids with me, and Jon could easily get out of control in an unstructured situation. He was already tired and on edge. How could I take all of them into the store to call for help? I needed Duane with me to take care of it. Panic started to take over.

Suddenly, out of my peripheral vision, I saw a vehicle zoom past the cars getting gas. Without any hesitation it parked right beside me. Out came a twenty-five- to thirty-year-old big guy. He wore a white tee-shirt and jeans. He had silver earrings and a silver chain necklace. He didn't say anything at all, but confidently found the spare tire up under the car, found the tool kit, and began changing the tire. His helpfulness disarmed me, but I was still scared. I kept Jon with me, knowing he could shoplift if he were in the store by himself. Matt and Julia remember watching what took place. Peter stayed in his car seat, unable to see what was happening. I feared that the guy could hurt me, but tried to be calm in front of the kids. As he worked I asked him where he learned to change tires so well. He replied, "In my father's place." That's the only thing he said. When he emerged from lying under the car, all I recall is that his tee-shirt was still snow white. It looked almost as if it were dazzling. As fast as he zoomed into the parking place, he jumped into his vehicle and took off. I was stunned. The only way I could make sense of it was that God had sent an angel to me to take care of the problem. It could only be a divine messenger sent to come to help. I felt so loved and cherished by God for days. God saw my pain and all our problems. He hadn't forsaken me at all. He was right there, protecting and helping me through all the difficulty. He knew exactly how difficult life with Jonathan could be and didn't fail to fulfil His promise to "never leave or forsake us." He could be trusted.

When Jonathan was in second grade at age nine, the school board president at the Centerville school expressed some empathy for what we were experiencing. Her encouragement was welcomed and rare. Most people communicated that we were terrible parents and had no idea how to discipline our kids. We felt shunned or pitied by many in the community. The president had a daughter with Down's syndrome. She was sympathetic to the problems we were having. She told me to just patiently wait; when the school was no longer able to handle him, the school system would enable us to place Jonathan in an institution for kids, providing schooling and residential care. The school would fund whatever was needed. By the end of the school year her predictions came true. Jonathan was running off the school campus, hitting staff, and they couldn't handle his problems or tolerate him any longer. They made arrangements for Jonathan to be placed at Children's Home Society in Sioux Falls.

Having brought Jonathan home when he was nineteen months old, we had endured over seven years of total stress with him. I barely knew my other kids. It was blessed relief to have Jonathan out of the house. The healing started to begin in my heart without constant chaos and fear to live with each day. I don't recall anything but desperation in my relationship with God after Jonathan came to live in our home. It was fear and tension from the minute I woke up each morning until Jonathan finally went to bed. God got me through it all, and I could see His protection and strength daily. I grew to rely on Him as I poured out my heart to God. He changed me during those long years. He taught me that my self-sufficiency didn't work. I needed Him and He was a God who could be trusted to be there when we were in danger and when there was no strength left. He was there giving ideas how to handle things wisely. I couldn't make it without Him. He wanted to show me His care and favor, but had to get me in a position in which I needed Him. Parenting Jonathan was the means by which He broke through to my heart.

During those bad years people would ask me about adoption, and I'd give a very negative response and try to guide them to get a newborn baby rather than accept an older child. I tried to steer them clear of any child who had been raised in an orphanage who possibly could have some degree of attachment disorder. But one day, many years later after Jon was placed outside our home, someone asked me for advice about adoption. She asked me point blank if I'd do it again. To my surprise I heard myself answering with a resounding, "Yes!" It was at that moment I realized how much God had changed my heart. How did that transformation happen? He had uprooted the bitterness and anger in my heart and had replaced them with joy and a positive attitude toward Jonathan and the whole experience we had had. He had healed my heart to the extent that I realized that I needed Jonathan to enable me to develop a real relationship with God. Because of Jon, my arrogant, self-sufficient exterior was cracked. It had broken due to all I faced on a daily basis with him. I am so glad that I came to the end of myself and learned to depend on Him. That closeness and trust and humility I had gained with Jesus were worth all the trouble in those bad years. It was a rough lesson, but I'd never trade it for an easy time. Letting God take charge of this part of my heart so His Kingdom could be established in my life was the end result. Jesus was and is worth it! That puzzle piece was a tough one to experience, but God has been glorified in it and I'm glad.

Jonathan continued to live in several different residential school settings as a child. He came home to attend eighth grade in Centerville, having achieved some degree of control in his behavior. Things were initially okay, but his tendency to steal started surfacing at school. Toward the end of the year he stole something from the boys' locker room. Jonathan was a master at manipulation. He was confronted by the principal, superintendent, PE teacher, local police, and his parents in a conference room one afternoon. He talked his way out of it all, convincing all of us that he hadn't stolen anything. How a kid who is developmentally delayed with a borderline IQ level could fool everyone is amazing. But they still suspected him and had cameras put in the office and some classrooms during the summer.

That summer after eighth grade Jon worked with Duane. Things got very stressful again. Jonathan does well with structure and in an enclosed place. That's not possible on a farm. There are different things to do each day, and there is no set schedule. There is minimal predictability. A lack of routine creates feelings of insecurity in Jon, and he begins acting out to find some clear boundaries. The stealing intensified at home. He got more and more violent. This time he was much bigger and stronger than when he was out of control as a little kid. We lived in fear again. He got ahold of cigarette butts from an employee who left them lying around on the farm, and got a taste for nicotine that led to an addiction. Things deteriorated. He ransacked Duane's office one day, setting fire to papers on the desk and overturning cabinets with delicate equipment. I was at work. Duane had to call the police, and Jonathan was taken away to the juvenile detention center for a while. When he came home he started back to school to begin ninth grade. Within days he was caught stealing money off the secretary's desk in the office. It was very clear from the video footage that Jon was guilty. He couldn't fool anyone this time. The police came to take him away. He never lived at home after that. He was sent to Redfield, to the South Dakota Developmental Center (SDDC), which is the institution for developmentally delayed people with severe behavioral problems.

When Jon was taken away to SDDC, we realized that it was only by God's grace that he was able to go there. His IQ was just low enough to enable him to qualify for services, which means that the state of South Dakota has funded all the educational and residential care he's needed. (Many, many thanks to all the hardworking taxpayers of South Dakota!) What an awesome display of God's provision and sovereignty in planning even the scores your kid gets on the IQ tests he has to take! How many people praise God for their child being developmentally delayed? I certainly did. It was the way God made a way of escape for us. It was the way God planned in His providence to meet Jon's educational needs. SDDC was the place where he was finally able to feel some success and gain some control over his behavior. Jon was able to develop lots of friends there and feel accepted for the first time in his life. God was clearly at work putting all the pieces in order to give us peace and rest. Because we could acknowledge His actions on our behalf, I'm convinced He made the "path straight" for him to live there for his high school years.

Jonathan did well at SDDC and was able to complete his high school credits. He completed the program when he was twenty-one. Soon after that he was transferred to another program in Brookings, South Dakota. He was to share an apartment with another guy with periodic supervision from staff at the main office. That arrangement lasted about a week. Jon started stealing from his roommate. He was transferred to live at a group home. Unfortunately the only home that had space was a place for people who were pretty severely impaired. Jon's needs were very different from the others there. The program wasn't set up to handle a strong young man with all his problems. He didn't like living with the others in his house. He began running away from his group home. One day he was angry at being accused of stealing. He ran to the center where his case manager worked to talk to her. She had left work for the day. He was so angry that he put his fist through a security glass window. He severed arteries, broke bones, and tore ligaments and tendons in his dominant hand. He bled profusely. At the ER he was still so worked up that he didn't want to allow the doctor to treat him even though they threatened that he would bleed to death if he didn't cooperate. His hand required extensive surgery. After that he was considered to be quite dangerous and was transferred to a locked unit with Volunteers of America in Sioux Falls.

God wasn't finished with Jonathan yet, though. He was working in his life all along to cause him to realize his need for Jesus. Jon was part of God's cosmic puzzle. The Lord was establishing the Kingdom of God in his heart, piece by piece. There were lots more pieces that needed to be fitted together, but that story will be told later.

Our Firstborn Son

Matt, our firstborn son, was a happy little boy. He was Jon's little pal. The two of them got into numerous scrapes together. One day I found both of them hiding by the back door, covered in chocolate syrup. They were too cute to get too mad at. But when Jon became defiant, Matt quickly learned that it didn't pay to disobey Mom! Either he was naturally a compliant child or he learned the lesson of obeying his parents at an early age. Or perhaps I was oblivious to naughty things he was doing because he managed to fly under my radar screen. Maybe Matt used the chaos Jonathan created to hide his true attitudes and behavior. But whatever the truth is, I really don't remember having to put him in "time out" more than a few times, and I probably only spanked him once.

One of my clearest memories of Matt as a very little boy is of him sitting in his sandbox with his back to the kitchen window. He spent hours in there digging trenches, and making waterways and dams. He also thoroughly enjoyed playing in mud puddles. His nickname when very little was "Mudball Matthew." Kids often show their "bents" or interests when very young. Matt displayed his love of water, mud, sand, and dirt, which led to his interest in civil engineering when a young man.

Until younger siblings displaced him, he was always at my side when cooking and baking. He liked to help with everything, just being his little cheery, smiley, easygoing self. He picked up lots of survival skills that way, and developed a heightened level of common sense. He was very detailed and precise in what he created. His artwork showed an amazing sense of observation. Matt loved to get little kits of models to put together. My favorite was the replica of King Tut. He carefully put the little skeleton together, wrapped it in the grave clothes, put it inside the inner coffin, and painstakingly painted the ornate outer cover of the sarcophagus.

I asked God one day why He gave us Matt. He didn't have to; we were able to adopt Jonathan to start to fill our home with children. We anticipated adopting two times, once for Jonathan and a second time for another child. But Matt was a total surprise gift from God. God told me that He gave us Matt as reassurance when we were having difficulties with Jonathan. Our problems with Jonathan weren't the result of bad parenting. God wanted to bless our home with some normalcy and peace. Matt became a stabilizing force in the family. He brought fun and laughter when things could be grim. He was understanding and considerate to everyone.

My little boy had such a tender heart. He was the reason I got involved with kids' ministries at church. When he was two years old he just couldn't separate from me to stay in Sunday school with the other kids and the teacher. (He was probably just too young to be there!) But being a "green mom," and not knowing any other way of handling the problem, from then on I sat in his class and soon became the teacher of the littlest children. He developed confidence pretty quickly, and I was able to move on to teach other classes than his. I kept teaching some grade in Sunday school for the next twenty-two years.

The day he turned nine years old, I looked at him and blurted out, "You're half-done!" What I realized is that our eighteen years with him at home had reached the halfway mark. I was a bit freaked out that he was growing up so quickly. I thought he'd take it as a compliment, as if he was very mature for his age and learning to be very independent. But poor little Matt dissolved in tears, feeling like I was going to kick him out of the house much more quickly than he ever expected. We were both glad we had a remaining good nine years left to be together as he grew up.

Matt had a dreadful flaw as a little kid. When he threw up he made a huge mess. That's a little gross to talk about. He was known to cover most of the bathroom when he'd get sick. But I'll never forget the night when he was about ten years old. On the way to AWANA he told me he wasn't feeling well. I was a leader and couldn't stay home. And it was Valentine's night so there would be more activities than usual to help manage with the other leaders. I had had a fender bender in a snowstorm on the way to work, so the day didn't have a good start. I was pretty stressed out. Matt got to feeling worse as the evening progressed. So he went into the men's room to throw up. Someone was using the toilet, so in desperation he filled up the urinal with his stomach contents. One of our friends told me what Matt had done. I refused to let that sweet man clean up after my boy. But that was the worst, most awful mess I had ever faced! To make the day worse, Duane was on the way to church for a deacon board meeting after AWANA, and the car ran out of gas about a mile from church. I just tucked that problem in the back of my mind and went home with the kids. I had bigger problems to face—alone. When I got home I put the kids to bed, which involved lying down with them to get the youngest ones to sleep. Within a few minutes the radiator/heater beside the bed started to hiss and sputter. A greenish-blue vapor filled the room! We were pretty terrified and decided to vacate the house so we wouldn't breathe the fumes, not knowing what they were. Duane wasn't home yet. I packed up all the kids into the car, including poor, sick Matt, and headed back to church to get Duane's help. He left the meeting when he saw the look on my face. We all spent the night camping on the floor in the living room, with the door shut to close off the wing of the house where the kids' rooms were located. What a memorable Valentines' Day!

Matt grew in his love for Jesus. To this day I really don't know how he developed such a keen understanding of His need for salvation. But very early it was clear he wanted to serve Jesus with his life. He was very disciplined and let God's Word penetrate and change his heart. God preserved him from lots of problems. He never got in trouble at school or with his friends. He did very well in everything he tried to do and wasn't afraid to get involved in any sport or activity. He faced a difficult time at the public school, being ridiculed for playing violin and piano, and for being the smartest kid in his class. But because of that harassment Matt developed a toughness to stand up for what he believed. And he developed a tender heart for guys who didn't know Jesus. He wanted his peers to know Jesus, too.

When Matt graduated from high school I wrote him this letter. He was ready to go into the world to get prepared for the mission to which God was calling him.

Dear Matt,

You have lived up to be the meaning of your first name and middle name: Matthew = "gift of God," and Isaac = "laughter." As a baby you were the gift God gave to us when we thought we'd never have a baby of our own. How Dad and I laughed and laughed when the doctor was proved wrong and we found out that we were going to have you. You were the gift I needed when parenting became very difficult at times. You were usually obedient, compliant, and always helpful and sweet. You made us laugh so many times with your wit, your sense of humor and jokes. And now as you graduate, you are becoming the gift God intends to give to others as you devote your life to serving Him with the talents He's given you. We are so proud of your devotion to God and your love for Him. We are so glad that you've allowed Him to control your life. So go now, Matthew Isaac, and keep filling other people's lives with laughter and joy. Keep spreading the news of the greatest gift God has given, that of His Son, Jesus our Savior. You are free now to continue to be the gift God made you, wherever you go.

Love,
Mom and Dad

A Daughter

When God put these next puzzle pieces in place I started to understand how sovereign He is in the timing of events in our lives. When Matt was about one-year-old we decided we really wanted a girl. Duane had grown up in a family of all boys, and I had only sisters. We wanted our boys to have a sister. So the poor boys were plagued with a mother who asked them repeatedly whether they wanted a sister or not. I wanted to make sure they were involved in the decision. They were too little to possibly understand the implications of having a girl in the house, but they agreed to get a baby sister (whatever that would mean). Our biological clock was ticking. We had to get the application completed before Duane turned forty, because Holt Adoption Agency wouldn't place a child if there were more than forty years between the age of the oldest parent and the kid. So we proceeded without incident to get Julia.

When I was growing up I listened to a record of a Korean Orphan Choir singing for World Vision. I loved looking at the cute little girls and boys in their traditional *hanbok* costumes on the cover of the album. They were adorable. I really wanted one of them to be my child. Years later, when traveling with Duane in Bangladesh, long before we were engaged, we had a discussion about adoption. I found that he also wanted a cute little Korean girl! So God had planted the desire for a Korean child in both of our hearts. I envisioned a sweet, quiet, shy little girl like the ones we had seen at the Holt picnics. But the words of my sister, stated many years previously, rang in my ears: "God is the one who selects our kids, not the adoption agency." God knew what child we needed, and He knows exactly which parents the child needs for the purpose of His Kingdom. He matches us up with our children, using our unique relationships with them to mold and shape all of us to be like Jesus.

Julia had an atrial septal defect in her heart. She was born C-section, so the flap in the septum between the upper chambers of her heart didn't close during birth as it usually does. She was finally medically stable and available to come to us when she was seven months old. She had been living with foster parents since the day she was born. Her first months were vastly different from what Jonathan experienced. She had developed a very close bond to her foster parents. It was considered more likely that she could transfer that good bond to permanent adoptive parents. I flew to Korea to get her and spent a week traveling and learning as much as I could about the country where two of my kids were born. I met Julia and her foster mother at the beginning of the week. It's totally amazing to meet for the first time the child you have dreamed of having ever since childhood! She was a sweet, precious baby, and was thoroughly bonded to her foster parents. I was so encouraged to see her relationship to that wonderful mother, knowing our relationship with Julia could be very close as a result of her good parenting in the early months of her life.

While in Korea I visited the orphanage where Jonathan had lived for nineteen months. Seeing the conditions there helped me see why he had so many problems with attachment. The staff there remembered him. He looked different than all the other kids due to his African heritage, so he still stood out in their minds two years after he left. I also got the feeling that there was a grave possibility that he had less attention than the others and was possibly deprived of food because of his heritage. I had brought many toys for the children as gifts, but the director took them all and gave them to his own little boy. My heart hurt for all the little kids in there who were longing for a relationship with parents, and who needed mental stimulation.

Finally the day came for the long twenty-four-hour plane ride home to the USA. I gathered up baby Julia and all her clothes and took her with me. She wouldn't settle down to sleep at all during the entire flight. The only way to calm her, most likely because the air pressure was bothering her ears, was to feed her. She drank eight eight-ounce bottles of formula during the sixteen-hour flight! I sat by a Korean lady on my left side. She was silent, but watched what I was doing. After many hours she mustered the courage to state the sentence in English that she had been working on the whole time: "Your baby must look like her father." How funny! I blandly stated, "Yes, I'm sure she does." The lady didn't seem to have a clue that this was an adopted child and not mine by birth. I was secretly glad that she didn't seem to sense my ineptness at getting Julia to calm down and think I was a terrible parent.

While the kids were little, Duane stayed at home with them most days, farmed the land he inherited from his family, and began working for Herb, a man who did research on new agricultural chemicals that were being developed. Duane had always wanted to own his own business, doing that kind of work. Being Herb's employee gave him experience and a foot in the door for that profession. I was working as a dietitian in Vermillion, at the hospital and care center, at that time. I was the director of the department, which was a salaried position. I managed the kitchen and took care of the clinical needs of all the patients. I had an assistant, but most weeks I put in at least sixty hours. I was really stressed with work. I recall taking walks outside alone and pleading with God to some-how change our work and parenting roles. I just couldn't bear being the major bread winner. It was too much pressure.

When Julia was a baby I experienced how God is sovereign in His perfect timing. I was working full time and was never sick. I never took any time off. There was too much to do on the job. One Saturday I decided to make the whole family go to the mall in Sioux Falls to get a family picture taken at Penney's. Posed pictures are hard for most families. They are a hundred times more difficult with a child who has severe ADHD and oppositional defiant disorder and rarely cooperates with anyone. Getting everyone to cooperate for the picture was a challenge, but not so stressful that I would feel totally drained and ill when walking to the car. We went out to eat afterward. By the time the meal was done I was feeling really sick. I just didn't have any strength left. When we got home Duane took care of the kids, and I went to bed with a fever. My temperature stayed high no matter what I did. I stayed in bed on Sunday, feeling like a wet, floppy noodle.

Monday morning I called in sick, which was the first time in five years I missed work. I went back to bed. Later that morning Duane burst into the room, holding Julia. She was stiff, foaming at the mouth with her eyes rolled back. I struggled out of bed as he thrust her at me, asking what was wrong. It was a seizure. She had never had one before. She hadn't been sick at all. There had been no fever to cause a seizure. The only thing we knew was that she had been rocking on a chair. Matt saw her flopping around and then she fell onto the floor. He couldn't describe more than that at just three and a half years old. Duane called 911 and an ambulance came. He had to go to the hospital with Julia. The boys needed someone to take care of them. Duane's mother lived an hour away. There would have been no one to help Duane if I hadn't been at home. The boys certainly could not have gone with Duane by ambulance. Because God had sent me home sick for the day, I was at home just when needed. His timing was perfect. It turned out that I had pneumonia, and Julia was diagnosed with epilepsy. I'm convinced God planned for me to get pneumonia out of the clear blue to enable me to be at home to help during the emergency. Her problem was well controlled by medication after a few days, and she's never had any more problems as a teenager or adult. But I learned in the whole process that God is sovereign in orchestrating even our illnesses to work out for the good of everyone in the family.

As Julia grew into a little girl, she had had multiple ear infections and was rather sickly. Just as she'd recover from one problem, she'd develop another one and be in more pain. She was a miserable little child. To make matters harder for her, we realized something was quite wrong with her speech. We just couldn't understand much of what she said. Finally we went to a specialist. She had a deformity in the structure of her throat, causing all the air to come out of her mouth when she spoke. Some breath should resonate in the sinus cavities to have a good vocal quality. After surgery to correct it, she was somewhat improved. But the procedure had to be revised somewhat because all her air was directed into her nasal passages instead, and she sounded like she had a very stuffed-up nose. In the process her uvula at the back of her throat was removed.

Suddenly after the second surgery Julia could make herself understood. Her speech was clear. She wasn't frustrated with us as much anymore, due to her inability to express herself clearly. Her crazy, funny personality could shine through. What a fun person she became then! She started to blossom and we grew to be totally amazed by the little girl God had given us. I had always told people when explaining why we adopted her that "we wanted a girl for fun." She became that fun person! A wonderful thing about adoption is that you bring totally unexpected genetic traits, bents, and abilities into your family. You cannot predict what you'll get. You are surprised by how God blesses you with unique, amazing skills and personality traits in your child. Anyone who knows Duane and me realizes that Julia's traits of being outgoing, vivacious and dramatic are not something in the genetic pool coming from us or our ancestors! What a dull place our home would have been without the wonderful blessing she became to us.

Julia used her voice and speaking ability to stand out as a witness at her school. Her kindergarten teacher recalls hearing her share the gospel with other kids in her class. She was known to be very outspoken in science classes, pointing out the problems with the evolution theory that was presented. She did not shy away from proclaiming the truth from the Bible with her classmates!

God blessed Julia with a trait for being very musical. She took violin lessons as a small child and got quite proficient in playing. She also liked to sing. When young, her voice was very breathy and soft. I feared that it was the surgery to her throat that had caused significant impairment, and that she'd never be able to sing well. I recall the day when she was preparing to sing a solo part for a Christmas cantata, that she worked with our friend Julie, who was a music teacher. She was in the sanctuary of our church, which had a huge cathedral-type ceiling. Her voice was barely audible to me. Julie the music teacher taught her how to project her voice that day, and Julia's voice suddenly filled that large space. I realize that it was largely a technique she needed to learn, but to me it was as if God had healed my daughter's voice problem for good.

Julia went on to major in vocal performance. She has an amazing high soprano operatic voice that is beautiful to hear. She has used the story of God working to heal her throat as a major evidence of His love and providence in her life. I had the joy of meeting up with the surgeon many years after he did the operations. He still remembered her, and rejoiced with me at God's healing power, transforming her into a musician who is using her talents for His glory.

Julia has a strong personality. Our relationship had lots of ups and downs, as many mothers and daughters experience. I had learned to shy away from conflict and give in when challenged due to experiences I had as a child. The conflicts Julia and I had were the typical spats that occur between two females in a household, but were rather dramatic at times. They were not the type of control issues I experienced with Jonathan. But I realized that I couldn't give in and let Julia grow to be disobedient and self-focused. I am forever grateful to God for giving me my daughter, who taught me to stand up for myself, be the parent in the relationship, and be loving but firm when needed. The males in the house shuddered when Julia and I would clash, but we always ended up closer after an argument or conflict. She was always able to see through my façades to expose the motives I had. She has challenged me over and over to examine my life and face my pride and sinful attitudes. God knew I needed this girl, and chose her specifically for me, and has enabled us to become best friends as adults. He doesn't make mistakes.

.

FAMILY BUSINESS

Career Change

God's providential timing really became apparent in our work and career situation. Because I was working in a salaried position, I was away from home many hours a day. Duane was the stay-at-home parent and working part time. I just didn't feel right about the situation. The stress was enormous on me. I wanted to be able to be with my children more. I struggled with respect for my husband. Our roles were just not right for the two of us. I didn't feel secure financially, realizing everyone was really dependent on me. I recall crying out to God to change the situation. Nothing happened. God didn't seem to be hearing my prayers. Things just got worse, as there was more and more to do at work. The situation with Jon was nearly unbearable at home. Why wasn't God doing anything? Would this go on and on forever?

At that time the medical center where I worked needed a major upgrade to the facility that was to involve gutting the kitchen down to the dirt under the floor. The whole kitchen was to be replaced, which involved starting over with a new configuration of the floor plan and buying some new equipment. Usually the architect hires a kitchen design consultant to do all the planning, but to save funds the decision had been made to do without one. That meant, in my opinion, that I was responsible for all the planning. I wasn't going to let such an important project be done solely by the architect who had minimal knowledge of institutional food preparation and service. It was pretty scary to me to think of planning the kitchen design by myself. Of all the dietetics classes offered at SDSU there was only one course that was optional: equipment layout and design. I didn't take the class, but it was exactly what I needed to know to plan a new kitchen and reorganize everything. I would have learned to understand issues in the plumbing, electricity, building codes, and the workflow that influence the design of an institutional kitchen if I had taken the course. But I had to learn it on my own instead. So I bought the textbook and started to plough through it by myself. This was long before the days of Internet classes. The problem was so large, there would be no way I could do the other aspects of my job, study the subject, and work with the architect. This experience took place about a year before Jon was placed in Sioux Falls at Children's Home Society. I was broken and exhausted from my home life, being totally dependent on God by this time. But I was still pretty confident at work that I could handle on my own just about anything that I was called to do, given enough time to do so. Therefore I decided to ask the CEO to hire another dietitian for a year to free me up for this kitchen design work.

The CEO knew vaguely that I had trouble with Jonathan at home. He could see that I was tense and stressed with a thin cheerful veneer pasted over my anger toward my son. I was close to blowing up at both little things and big things that went wrong in the department. Therefore when I brought up the subject of getting help to manage the department, he thought of other options on the spot. By the time that conversation with the CEO was done, instead of becoming a novice kitchen design consultant with oversight over another temporary dietitian, he changed my position to half time involving only the clinical care of the patients and residents. He promoted the assistant manager to be the director of the department, and made arrangements with the architect to get a professional kitchen designer. I was no longer the manager.

I left the meeting that Friday afternoon in terror! My benefits had just been slashed. My income was half what it had been that morning. By Monday, three days later, I would be a part-time employee. How in the world were Duane, Jonathan, Matthew, Julia, and I going to survive and keep paying the mortgage on our house? How would we have enough to eat? I really wondered what God had in mind and how this could possibly be anything but terrible.

Duane had been working at his part-time job with Herb that Friday. When I got home Duane mentioned that Herb had said he wasn't feeling well on the trip they had taken to a research site in the middle of the state. My mind was filled with anxiety over our new financial condition, so I didn't really notice what he said. Sunday afternoon, I took a nap. The phone must have rung while I was sound asleep. I will never forget Duane flinging open the bedroom door, lunging for the bed, sobbing and saying, "Herb died!"

Herb was only fifty-five years old but had had severe heart problems. It turns out that he went to the ER that Friday night and had emergency heart surgery. He died in recovery after the procedure. Unfortunately Herb's wife was at end-of-life, dying of cancer. Everyone expected her to pass within a short time, but not Herb! The family was left with a big problem. Contracts had been signed for research projects, and some of them had been planted. Only a person with a masters in agronomy (plant science) was qualified to do the research and take over the business. The season for intense field work during the day and long into every evening had begun. They really needed someone to take over and get the rest of the research plots planted, or it would be too late. Consequently Duane helped Herb's wife, who knew a little about the business, and started working full time the Monday after Herb died. I was free to stay at home with the kids half days starting that Monday because my job had just dramatically changed as well.

Herb's wife died about a month later. Duane's bid to buy the business was initially rejected by the family. However, by God's grace, after an evening of negotiation with the brother-in-law, he was able to buy the business at a reasonable price. It couldn't have been better timing! Duane makes decisions methodically and doesn't take risks financially. He probably never would have started a research business on his own. His new job enabled him to continue working from home, available for his kids and helping to supervise Jonathan. God put down a major puzzle piece that weekend. God answered my prayer for help dramatically. He reversed our roles overnight when we were unable to get out of the situations we were in vocationally. He took care of our needs by giving Duane the control of the business.

The experience of God starting South Dakota Ag Research was a time I really sensed that God's sovereignty involves working in the lives of other people as well as in my own circumstances to accomplish His will. He fits our pieces together with other people's pieces of life to accomplish His overall purposes. Now I know that the waiting time as I prayed and prayed for a change in our careers was needed so God could work in the life of Duane, for him to get a good understanding of the research business, and in the timing of the death of Herb and his wife. God had heard me and was quietly answering my prayers. He had to prepare Duane for a new role so he could support our family. At just the right time He put it all together. God is making a huge puzzle that involves not only my life but the life of others. It involves the really big changes as well as the small details. It's fascinating to think of what God is doing to orchestrate everything when I have to wait for my prayers to be answered.

Farm Accident

Some of God's actions to work out His purposes are so complicated, involving so many details, that it makes your head spin. There's no coincidence to this one. It's purely a story of God's sovereignty. Here's one of those stories that shows His glory demonstrated in loving-kindness on our behalf. Duane often had to work away from our farmyard on his own.

Each year he put some research plots about thirty-five miles away on land by his brother's house. At harvest time he pulled his little miniature combine over there on a trailer with his pickup. He was working alone one afternoon, combining samples of wheat bunch by bunch. It was a very old piece of equipment, without any modern safety features. When feeding a sample into the combine, his thumb got caught in the blades and was nearly severed at the base of his fingernail. He managed to stop the combine. He got pressure on his thumb to stop the bleeding and somehow got the trailer unhooked from the pickup hitch. He drove out of the field. A tiny rural hospital with an ER was about five or six miles away. About two miles down the road he ran out of gas. The rest of the way to the ER would have to be on foot. By this time the adrenaline coursing through him was wearing off. There wasn't any super flood of energy left to walk so far, but he started trudging toward the town. God intervened. Just then Duane's brother came driving down the highway.

That doesn't seem so remarkable, considering that Dennis lived about a mile from where the accident took place. But Dennis had a job that involved working four consecutive days followed by four days off, with changes in day and night shifts as well. The likelihood of him ever being around was minimal. It just happened to be his day off, and Dennis, by God's plan, picked Duane up on the highway and drove him the remaining four miles to the ER, where he was stabilized before going on to Sioux Falls for surgery on his thumb that night.

Meanwhile the ER personnel called me at work. I needed to get to Sioux Falls quickly to be with Duane when he got there. The problem was that it would take at least two hours to get home, pick up the kids from day care, and drive up there to the hospital. I drove home, wondering how to handle Jonathan with his behavior issues and the other three kids to spend an evening in a hospital waiting room. When I got home there was my sister Beth and her husband! They had arrived unexpectedly on a trip across the USA, raising support for their work as missionaries in Pakistan. They had never dropped in like that before, and haven't since.

The chances of them being there when I needed them most was about zero. But God was secretly planning it all!

My brother-in-law Jim was my kids' favorite adult relative. He could, and still does, enchant children with the stories he tells. He can keep them entranced for hours with tales he concocts of "Alf the Elf" and the "Abominable Snowman." He keeps adults in stitches telling about all his travel adventures around the world. I was afraid of managing four restless children for what could be hours as Duane got his thumb reattached. Who else but Jim could have entertained the kids for hours as we waited for the surgery? Who else could God have used to bless me so much but Jim and my sister Beth?

Meanwhile Duane was learning different lessons from this providential action on God's part. As the shock wore off and the pain increased as he lay in the ER at the little hospital, he caved in emotionally from the stress of what had happened. He recalls that God planted a song in his mind and heart that kept him calm. The words to the song "Now Is the Time to Worship" rang in his ears and heart. He was encouraged by praising God through a very tough, painful time. What a lesson! Who would ever think of singing a worship song when your thumb on your dominant hand is nearly severed? But God encouraged Duane through singing praise. He showed Duane that He was a God big enough to handle all the problems with the upcoming surgery and the pressure that would mount from the interruption in his research work.

Fire

God taught the whole family how sovereign He is in protecting us from harm. One day I picked up my three younger kids and two neighbor kids from grade school and drove them to their piano teacher's house, which was a drive of about twenty miles from our home. I did this every week. It was just another uneventful time of hauling kids around and waiting during their lessons, and then driving everyone home again. However, as I drove them home that day I was a few miles from the gravel road where I turn off the highway to go south toward our house when I saw a dark, huge column of smoke reaching high up into the sky. The closer I got to 463rd Avenue where we live, the more fear and anxiety gripped my heart. The terrain in that area is pretty flat, so it's hard to get a good feeling for distances. But it certainly looked like the smoke was coming from our farmyard. It's common for farmers to burn trash in their yards or weeds in a field or ditch, so seeing some smoke around a farmyard isn't unusual. But this fire looked big. I picked up speed as I drove south toward our driveway. It was clearly apparent that flames were coming up out of our yard. I feared the worst as I drove in the driveway, praying and pleading with God that the house would be spared.

We finally entered the yard and were relieved that the house wasn't burning and seemed okay. I could see the fire trucks in the back yard, hosing down the area where we burn our garbage. The fire was burning and flames were still leaping high. Gary, our neighbor, rushed over and said he had noticed some smoke a half hour before, drove into the yard, and realized that the fire was spreading. He didn't see Duane anywhere, so he called 911 and then rushed home. He got his truck that had a large tank used to transport water to his cattle. He fought the fire alone until the fire department joined him and took over. The kids all saw the flames and billows of black smoke rising up over the yard. They stood by the house with me and watched it in fascination while I prayed.

The fire had started in the middle of an open area where there was a huge hole for burning refuse. (Duane has a lot of stems, stalks, and grain that has to be destroyed after it's been harvested and analyzed for his research studies. Because he is in product development, the crop that's been tested with a new fertilizer or pesticide or other chemical has to be destroyed before the Environmental Protection Agency has approved its use. If the product has not passed all the safety standards, none of the grain or soybeans can get into the food supply. It has to be burned, even though it seems wasteful.) So Duane had burned a load of dry material a few days before the big fire started. Apparently remaining embers ignited when more refuse was put into the pit.

Around the perimeter of the yard is a parking lot for many pieces of equipment that we use during the year to plough, plant, and harvest. We also have two large tanks full of gasoline and diesel fuel, and three small buildings with chemicals he uses in his research studies. There were three old vehicles that no longer worked: a pickup and two cars. A large trailer was parked just beside the burning area. Surrounding the whole area is what's called a "shelter belt," which is a forest of trees and bushes that are intentionally planted to protect the farmyard from wind and storms. I knew that if the trees around the edge of the yard would catch on fire, it could be disastrous. The firemen concentrated on keeping the fire from the trees, and at the same time made sure it didn't spread to the fuel tanks to cause an explosion. I told the firemen of the danger of the fire spreading to any of the little buildings that stored the vials of chemicals. The toxic effects of one of those buildings catching on fire would be horrendous. Furthermore Duane's business would be ruined if he didn't protect the chemicals properly. The ramifications we'd experience from the EPA would be disastrous.

Somehow we were able to contact Duane to come home. He had been working far away at a place where he rented space for an experiment. Gary, Duane, and the firemen worked feverously to put out the fire. As I watched during those awful minutes, something in my heart changed as God was putting a puzzle piece in place. I couldn't control anything. I was completely dependent on God to take care of the problem. The kids were too little to have any sense of the possible consequences if Duane's business was burned up. We were totally at the mercy of God's grace. Only He, using the firemen, could protect us. Only God could keep the wind from taking a spark away to ignite something hazardous. All I could do was stand there and trust the God who had been with me before in trouble, allowing Him to rule and reign in my heart.

It was so smoky that it was hard to tell what damage was occurring as the fire burned. But the fire stayed contained. They were able to stop it just yards away from the fuel storage tanks that contained many gallons of gasoline. The fire stopped about 100 feet from the house and chemical sheds. When everything cooled down and the smoke drifted away, we were amazed at God's protection. Not even the tires on the trailer were burned! None of Duane's equipment was damaged. But the three old vehicles were shelled out and completely burned up. God has a sense of humor in His sovereignty. Duane had contacted the insurance company to stop the coverage on the three vehicles earlier that week, but it hadn't been processed yet. We were able to get insurance to pay for the damage to the pickup and two old cars!

God is so good. He taught us all a huge lesson that He protects us. We as Christians aren't immune to the problems that everyone else has in life. In fact at times it seemed our family got a larger share of trouble than most families. But God proved to be faithful. He enabled the neighbor to drive by the yard at just the right time to call 911 to get help. If he hadn't done that, it would have been too late by the time I got home. I think it made a huge impression on the kids to see God stopping the fire before disaster occurred. Not only did my trust in God's loving-kindness surge that day but also God proved Himself to be real to my kids.

4

SURPRISE

Childhood

"Duane, I think I'm pregnant."

"What?!" he responded.

I had purchased a test kit. To get the results without curious little eyes and ears, we settled our three kids into watching a movie. Then while waiting for the results, the phone rang. The caller was a friend with whom I went to college several years earlier. I told her what we were doing and pledged her to secrecy. I didn't want anyone to know yet; the chance of losing a baby was too great and I didn't want to face that emotional pain again with everyone knowing what I was experiencing.

Because we had such a hard time getting pregnant with Matt, we kind of assumed we were infertile again, and never imagined we could possibly have another baby. Who gets two miracle kids? We no longer considered ourselves to be fertile. We were just too busy with the three kids to even think about another baby, or even want one.

The dipstick was blue—a positive test. I called back my friend to relay the news, and then sat down to absorb it all. I was shocked. What a change in our plans!

God was showing us another puzzle piece of our lives. This puzzle piece was to be a new baby. How did this one fit in? Why in the world would God think we should have another baby at this stage of life? I did the math quickly. I would be forty and a half years old when the baby would be born. Duane would be sixty-three by the time high school graduation took place. That's a little old to be chasing a kid around to attend all the events in which they would get involved! Besides, the last pregnancy was rather challenging. Could I handle this again, being six years older? How could I possibly handle all the challenges with our oldest son Jon, the middle two children and their needs, plus a new baby?

But God had a plan in giving us this precious puzzle piece. I didn't know why He thought we needed a fourth child, but it had been planned since before time. The psalmist wrote:

"All the days ordained for me were written in your book before one of them came to be."

PSALM 139:16, NIV

By that time in my life I realized that God was in control and had something planned for good in creating this new child. Despite the fears, I just decided to wait and see how this puzzle piece would fit into God's overall puzzle of His Kingdom.

Peter Benjamin Auch was born on September 19, 1997. He was a very healthy eight pounds and thirteen ounces baby. The older kids just loved and adored him. I was so busy then that I rarely thought about God's plans for Peter. But the issue laid dormant at the back of my mind, in a similar fashion to Mary, Jesus' mother, who "pondered all these things in her heart."

In the last days before Peter was born, Duane and I struggled with his name. Should he be Benjamin Peter or Peter Benjamin? We liked the concept of "Peter," meaning rock of salvation, and also felt "Benjamin" was appropriate as the last son of Jacob, the biblical patriarch, who was the treasured little one of the family. That's how we thought of our son. But eventually "Peter" won out as a first name. His name literally means "rock of salvation who comes with divine power to save His people." Built into his name, Peter had a mission to proclaim Jesus' salvation and strength.

On the night Peter was born Duane took all the older kids to a Franklin Graham crusade in Sioux Falls. I was pretty tired out and really didn't want their company at the hospital, so I willingly sent them on their way. That night all three kids, Jonathan, Matthew, and Julia, responded to the invitation to accept Jesus as their Savior. It was pretty amazing that they were all three born into God's family the night their little brother was born physically.

When Peter was born Jon was still living at home with us, and Duane was at the height of being busy getting his business established. I worked part time, about five hours a day at the medical center in Vermillion. It was a busy time with the kids, loaded with tense moments with Jon. I had more time to spend with Peter when he was a baby, though, than I had with any of the other kids.

He was a good little baby, liking to cuddle and be with me. I was so busy with the housework, yard work, and watching the other kids and my job, that Peter had a permanent spot perched on my left hip for the first two years. He loved to listen to me read to him. We would sit in the large, blue recliner chair with Peter taking the prime spot on my lap while Julia and Matt were squished on either side. Before he was four years old he was looking at books by himself and learning to read.

Peter liked toys, lots of them. Around age four, his love of Rescue Hero figures far outstretched our budget for his toys. He jumped at the chance to work to earn money to buy them. He soon was frequently seen sitting on top of the clothes washer, digging down head first to get the clean clothes and emerging to hurl damp items into the dryer located on the other side of the room. He swept, put away clean dishes, and did anything possible to earn a dime or quarter. As soon as he had $3.00 saved he'd be ready for the weekend trip to Walmart to pick out the next Rescue Hero to join his throng. I marveled at his determination.

Peter played and imagined and read most of the time. He really wasn't an outdoors kid when he was little. But he would spend time with me in the garden. If he was outside I usually could find him in my rock garden. I have no idea what he was thinking about, but he expertly jumped from rock to rock, avoiding a fall into the geraniums growing between his targets. He seemed fascinated with rocks. His name, Peter—the rock— seemed pretty fitting for him.

Gradually my responsibilities at the medical center increased, and I had to work full time again. Peter and Julia were cared for by a sweet lady who had an in-home day care at her house. The little kids loved Peter. He had a way with winning everyone's hearts. I recall the screams of delight as we opened the day care door in the morning: "Peter's here! Peter's here!" Peter learned to play well with other kids at her house during those long hours with her.

Because his birthday was in mid-September, Peter missed the cut-off date to go to kindergarten by about two and a half weeks. He would be nearly six years old by the time he'd go to school. The other kids at day care went to preschool each afternoon. But we just couldn't afford that additional expense. So I got a homeschool preschool program for his day-care provider to do with him. He polished off all the worksheets in no time at all. Then I got the kindergarten book. Again, he got that one finished before he turned five. With another year to go before he'd go to school, and with increasing evidence that he could get quite bored, I had him work on the first-grade book. That wasn't much more of a challenge to him than the first two books.

At church, Duane and I were involved as AWANA listeners, and we were teachers of Sunday school. Due to his age Peter started the Cubbies program in AWANA just before he turned three. He liked it initially, but considering he wasn't supposed to move up to the Sparks level until he was in kindergarten, this posed a problem. The two-year curriculum started over, and Peter had to do it all again. He began acting out. By then Duane and I were leaders in the AWANA program. We'd have prayer and planning meetings with the staff. The staff were encouraged to discuss particular kids and issues they had with them so we could problem-solve together and pray for the situation. In that setting, at the March meeting, his leader brought up how troubled she was with Peter Auch. "He has such a behavior problem, I need prayer to know how to handle him." It was terribly embarrassing! Immediately we suspected that the poor child was bored out of his mind and didn't have anything to do but create trouble. He was five years old then. We moved him up to the Sparks program designed for kids in kindergarten through second grade. Sure enough, he completed the entire first Sparks book in about five weeks. He was cooperative again, as he was challenged to learn. And he was memorizing God's Word quickly, like a little sponge.

When Peter was four years old, Child Evangelism Fellowship (CEF) made arrangements to have the *Jesus Film for Kids* shown in a theater in Sioux Falls. I took him there with me one Sunday afternoon. Peter was entranced by the story of the children woven into the gospel message he already knew. But God touched his heart that afternoon. When the CEF leader asked children if they wanted to confess their sin and ask Jesus to forgive them, Peter went up and prayed to accept Jesus as his Savior. I remember sharing it with the choir at practice later that evening. We all rejoiced at the newest member of God's Kingdom!

Peter was a determined little boy. If he set his mind to do something, he got it done. When young, he really didn't come off as stubborn. He was obedient. But he'd work very hard to get something he wanted. For some reason, after his bottom two teeth came out around age five, he decided it was time to work on his upper teeth. He must have realized that was the natural progression. However, his observation wasn't keen enough to notice that it's the middle two upper teeth that come out next and that most kids wait until the teeth become wiggly on their own to fixate on getting them out of their mouths. He began wiggling the next one over from the middle left tooth. Sure enough, after a few months of constant wiggling trauma the poor tooth came out (way too early). The middle two teeth came out a little later. All three teeth were gone at once. He had a huge gaping expanse across his face for a very long time as a testimony to his perseverance to reach a goal.

Keeping my kids challenged with learning God's Word and fascinated by Sunday school became a huge task. I'm convinced now that because of the passion God gave Duane and me for the children's ministry at church, it proved to our kids that spending your life in service to God and devoting huge amounts of time to open up kids' hearts to God are worth all the effort. They realized God was first place in our lives. We didn't intentionally try to model it. They just saw that we weren't wasting time on other hobbies that wouldn't last. I think they realized that it wasn't an outward expression of religion or an attempt to earn God's favor. We were totally captured by the Truth and wanted to convey it to kids, no matter the cost. They had to consider what that meant to their own relationship with God. All those hours of having a child sit on my lap as I typed and devised kids' ministry plans and activities sank into their hearts. It paid off. Years later I read a book about why kids fall away from the faith. The thesis of the book was that unless parents, by their actions, prove that God is worth everything and deserves the best of their lives, kids won't think God is any real big deal at all. They may fall away from their faith if other things capture their interests, hearts, and minds. God has protected my kids from that outcome.

Duane was in charge of the whole Sunday school program by this time. He gave me a wide-open task of developing special summer Sunday school programs. Our favorites were the summers studying creation, the flood, how the ark could have been able to hold all the animals, and the study of the tabernacle. None of the kids who came to church at that time will forget taking the two paper-mache goats, which Matt made for us, to the back yard of the church. One kid took a goat out to the shelter belt of trees surrounding the property to set it free as the "scape goat." The other was "slaughtered" as the atoning sacrifice. We slashed its neck, and out poured the red tempera paint that Matt had hidden in a balloon inside of it. We burned up the sculptured animal, as they did in the Old Testament, as part of the Day of Atonement.

Several years later, for a period of time, I spent hours writing Christmas plays. It was my job to come up with a program, as I had been elected to be in charge of the children's ministries. There were no commercially available plays that had enough parts for the forty or more kids in Sunday school. The only thing to do to accommodate everyone was to write it myself, making sure each sheep, shepherd, wise man, star, and so on had their own line to say. The plays had to get more and more creative as the years went on. I wonder if Peter will ever forgive me for the year we told the Christmas story from the perspective of ornaments on a Christmas tree. Julia played the part of a foreign exchange student who knew nothing of the nativity story. In the play she went to the living room on the set, and the ornaments (kids playing the parts of them) told her about Jesus' birth. When writing the play, I noticed the tendency at that time for Christmas ornaments to become secular. Many had no resemblance to anything traditional or religious. It was as if Jesus was being crowded out of Christmas, as evidenced by the pathetic, secular ornaments on sale. So Peter's ornament represented that concept, telling of the people who had crowded Jesus out of their lives. He was a golf ball. I'll never forget the disdain in his voice as he had to announce to the audience, "I'm a golf ball," and explain his role. He thought it was totally stupid.

Peter went to grade school in Centerville. He had six other boys in his class. We lived five miles away from the town, so he really didn't play with them too much after school as he had to come home on the bus. Making friends was tough there. The kids seemed a little awed by his academic ability. He felt lonely. He did join the little league baseball teams and played as a catcher most of the time. He understood the rules of the game thoroughly, and could instinctively tell what to do in that position to get the kid on the opposing team out. There were no boys his age at church, only a large class of girls and himself. His brothers were six and eight years older than he. He played with Julia a little bit, who was four years older, but basically he learned to occupy himself alone. Reading became his world. He didn't read any fantasy books, as I recall. It was all prose. Christian missionary biographies, stories of sports heroes, presidents, and other influential people occupied much of his time. In second grade he knew just about every useful fact regarding each president of the United States. He studied geography, pouring over maps and globes. His favorite Christmas gift each year was the latest *World Almanac* and *Book of Facts.* I'm looking at a copy now. It's well worn, the cover is torn, and the binding is broken. He absorbed much of it each year until a new copy came out and appeared under the Christmas tree for him.

What an amazing planner he was as a little boy. I wanted to take the kids to Yellowstone for a vacation. Peter, with his love of maps, swung into action. He planned the trip. He mapped out where we would drive to each day, the routes, at what towns we would stay for the night, what we would stop to do along the way. This was long before our family began using *Map Quest.* He did it all on paper, laboriously calculating with a ruler the distance from spot to spot and the time it would take to get there, traveling about sixty-five miles per hour. Unfortunately he didn't account for the slower speed limit in Yellowstone, and the fact that we might actually want to get out of the car to look at anything. His itinerary couldn't be followed once we were in the park, but we pushed ourselves to follow his plans as much as possible to keep him from feeling bad. What long rides we had some days! He was about nine then.

Around that time, a friend gave me two nanny goats. Peter loved them. We bought a billy goat for them, and the herd increased. Peter loved playing with the babies. The herd became even more entertaining when another friend gave me a pair of fainting goats and a donkey. We eventually expanded to ducks and turkeys as well. Peter was known for his love of his goats, and as you'll read later God used that trait to bless people.

Peter started being more concerned about health in fourth or fifth grade. He signed me up to be a judge of a recipe contest for healthy foods the school kids created. He decided that he would develop a muffin recipe with flax, bran, and strawberries. After all, if you can put blueberries in a muffin, why not chopped strawberries instead? I have to admit I was a little biased as a judge, but his muffin recipe was the best thing in the competition. It was the main snack served after the races held in his honor many years later. (See the appendix for the recipe.)

When Peter was between nine and ten years old, God laid down a significant puzzle piece around which many other things in the Kingdom fit. When our twenty-fifth wedding anniversary was approaching, I expressed a wish to Duane to be able to go to the Caribbean on a cruise. I wanted to snorkel again with him and repeat our amazing experience of falling in love while hunting for coral and seeing tropical fish. Duane heard me, but he also thought of other ideas. One day he surprised me by asking, "How would you like to go on a mission trip for our anniversary?"

I felt my hopes of romantic coral hunts draining away. I responded, "Uh, maybe. Where?"

He replied, "Haiti."

Good grief! I thought. Of all the places to go, Haiti was hardly a romantic getaway! What was he thinking? But I could tell he was pretty excited about the possibility.

A few days later he asked, "How about taking the kids with us to Haiti?"

Again I thought, *Good grief! This is supposed to be our anniversary, a time to be AWAY from the kids for once in the fifteen years since they started accumulating in our house.* But the look on his face, and the fact that he was leading the family in our spiritual growth, captured my brain and heart. I agreed.

So in the spring of 2007, we joined others from Iowa to go to Pignon, Haiti, to work with a ministry called UCI (United Christians International) under the direction of Jean Jean Mompremier and the board of the mission. We took Matthew (age sixteen), Julia (age fourteen), and Peter (age ten). By then Jon was living at the Developmental Center in Redfield, SD, needing constant supervision. He therefore couldn't go with us. As it turned out Julia and I slept in a large room with all the women, and Duane and the boys slept in a large room with all the guys. I hardly saw Duane the entire trip; we were pretty busy with a variety of projects. It wasn't exactly a romantic time for a twenty-fifth anniversary! But the trip set the stage for our purpose and passion for the next ten years.

Peter was pretty little and didn't quite know how to cope with the language barrier he faced in Haiti. He basically observed what was happening. We all saw God at work there, utterly transforming the life of a voodoo witch doctor when he repented and accepted the gift of salvation. They heard incredible stories of Jesus transforming the lives of people who were held by Satan's bondage. I think the kids were blown away by the power of Jesus. They had never seen anything so dramatic. Peter never went back to Haiti until he was fifteen in 2012, when we took the church youth group and many of Matt's friends from college. But those experiences went deep into his heart, giving him a passion for Jesus. He also saw from his parents that serving Jesus was rewarding and fun and worth everything.

Each Christmas Duane organized a local Angel Tree project for Prison Fellowship. For the first few years we delivered all the gifts for kids living in Vermillion and Elk Point, South Dakota. Those were rather uneventful times. By the third year Duane expanded the geographical area to which we were going to distribute gifts. This time he sought families living in the Pine Ridge Indian Reservation on the western side of the state. The five of us gathered up all the gifts and our luggage and set off for a Christmas vacation on the reservation. We had about ten gifts to bring. What an eye-opening experience it was for all of us. The kids had never seen such poor living conditions in the States. They could see the needs and heartbreaking living situations of kids whose fathers were incarcerated. They got a chance to be Jesus' hands and feet. Peter mentioned to me, years later, that this trip was one thing that God used to capture his heart to serve Him.

Fun Times

The years after Jon was placed in Sioux Falls to live in a group home hold memories of happy, fun times together with the five of us. They are rather a blur now, with few distinct events to recall. The stress and tension we had was lifted. We could enjoy being a happy family. God was at work, though, putting another puzzle piece in place. He was teaching me to know Him, to understand His Word, to serve Him, and to enjoy being part of the body of Christ at church. He was healing me and strengthening my heart that had gotten rather smashed up in the difficult lessons I had learned.

Up until the time Jon left there was no way I could ever attend any Bible study outside of the time at church on Sunday mornings and evenings. I recall going to a Beth Moore Bible Study by myself after Jonathan was out of the house. It was mind-boggling to be able to have the freedom to learn with other women while Duane took care of the three little kids. I could step up to the challenge of spending forty-five minutes every morning doing the required personal Bible study.

The pastor we had at our church, Pastor John, was a good expository preacher. He dug through vast, long books of the Bible, Sunday after Sunday, showing the congregation how to interpret what God said. I grew to have a clear understanding of God's character and how He works in the world. I also grew to have a much clearer understanding of the contents of the Bible. You might think this is strange, when you consider that it was my mother's priority to teach her four girls the Bible before she died. However, I was the youngest. She and my father did a good job teaching my three older sisters, but I think they didn't know how to keep up with the older girls' interest in the Bible and repeat what they had taught them to me at a younger child's level of understanding. So I really had had a pretty foggy understanding of the Bible.

It was my very own kids, though, who challenged me to put what I was learning in Bible studies into lessons for their age. I had so much fun in those years, developing Sunday school curriculum for our summer sessions and writing plays for Christmas and Easter. Peter, Matt, and Julia were my inspiration. They inspired me to dig into God's Word, find the truth, and figure out how to make it clear to children. The simplicity that was required to explain principles to children forced me to find the essence of what God was saying in the lesson. They were such good sports, acting in plays and helping to create things that were needed for lessons. I'll never forget Julia being willing to be the star in several plays, putting her acting ability to work. Matt, with his detailed, artistic, creative side, helped create props. In one of the last Christmas plays he helped with as a high school senior he willingly dressed up as a high priest and made sure two little boys, dressed just like him as priests, were able to light incense without causing any harm.

Duane was very busy with his business in those years. It was based from home, so the kids could work with him. In the summer he worked around the home and farmyard while I was away at my job, and he taught them to work with him. They learned to do very tedious tasks required in research. They didn't complain much. Because Duane focused his efforts during the summer months on his experiments on the farm, we struggled to take long vacations away from home. But we did have some very fun times on a weeklong fishing trip at a cabin, driving to California to visit my parents, and going to Yellowstone. We took opportunities to go camping, celebrate holidays, visit the kids' grandparents, and travel over the Christmas holidays. The family traditions we established built stability into their lives. We were able to live on the same farm, in the same house, for all the years they were in grade school and high school. I'm sure God kept them grounded in that stable home so they were better able to handle the emotional struggles that their brother caused.

The best times I recall together with my kids were on mission trips to Haiti. Julia went with me eight times. She was a great companion. She just blossomed there, developing amazing skills at acquiring the ability to pick up languages by listening and practicing all she understood. Julia plunged into learning Kreyol and making many friends. Her ability to learn and speak languages surfaced then. Matt went with us three times and had great times with the young Haitian people, learning about the water resources and infrastructure there. Matthew's interest was captured by the spiritual needs he saw, and the need for water, roads, and basic services. Perhaps it was then that his interest in civil engineering was confirmed.

Peter didn't accompany me on the second trip, but Matt and Julia did. He stayed home with Duane. While we were in Haiti that time, several tarantula spiders visited the room where the guys on the trip were staying. We found out that it was legal to bring a tarantula across the border into the USA. The kids knew their little brother was feeling a little left out at home, and they decided to bring a pet home to him. They found an empty little plastic container that had been used for frosting, punched holes in the top for ventilation, and captured the next eight-legged visitor to their room. We taped the lid on securely and I carried the spider in my carry-on luggage. What fun we had at the airport customs in Florida! I declared on the form that I had "agricultural products" in my possession, and had a thorough search of my stuff. I produced the frosting container with the spider. The official didn't think it was legal to bring it in, but he didn't really want to handle the critter if he confiscated it. He called over a supervisor, who verified that it was legal to bring them in. So Peter's new pet joined the family. We got home very late that night. I will never forget the surprise on his face when we gave him the little container the next morning with his new furry friend.

He took pretty good care of it, but the tarantula stopped eating and died. Pastor John brought one back from a mission trip for his kids a year or so later. We gave them our cage to use. But their tarantula was a little freakier than ours. It liked to hang on the mesh cover of the cage. Their youngest daughter couldn't handle the spider doing that and one day broke down and demanded that her parents get rid of the tarantula instantly. The pastor's wife Nancy called me and kind of begged me to take their spider as soon as possible, cage and all. So Peter had responsibility of another furry-legged critter. This one was hardier and ate all the bugs it was given to nourish it. One day I went in his room and noticed a small crack in the lid of the cage. The spider wasn't anywhere to be found in there! It had squeezed through the crack and was loose! Knowing Julia was terrified of it, I pledged all three boys to secrecy while we casually searched the whole house when we thought she wasn't looking. However, she eventually found out that the spider had escaped and was pretty freaked out for a while. A few weeks later our cat got rather sick with diarrhea. This was uncommon for her. It took a long time for it to stop and remained a mystery why she got sick. After Christmas, a few months later I did a pretty thorough cleaning behind all the furniture and found a dried up tarantula carcass that was missing a few legs. We put two and two together, and pieced together a feasible story: the cat had attacked the spider and ate a few legs before it got away to die in peace. Tarantulas digest their prey by liquefying them with powerful digestive enzymes. We supposed that the legs might contain some of these digestive chemicals, and the poor cat had a pretty nasty time with its intestines getting harmed by the caustic effects of the spider's legs. I must say things were more peaceful around the home once the mystery was solved.

New School

Julia endured racism and some bullying from some of her classmates for many years at the school in Centerville. It was very difficult for her to be in that environment and learn. She did get tough, though. As soon as she got her driver's license at age fifteen, so she could get herself to school, she transferred to the Beresford High School, which is ten miles away from our house. Thank God for open enrollment laws in South Dakota that enable parents to choose what school their kids should attend! She thrived in the new environment. One day a boy at the new school made some racial slur that she heard. She shoved him against a wall, using all the fierce power that a 5′4″ teenage girl can muster. The boy looked at the teacher, pleading with his eyes to help. The teacher just said, "I think she's going to beat you up!" No one ever messed with her again in Beresford!

Peter watched to see whether he should follow in her footsteps and transfer to Beresford. He wanted to make sure he'd get a good education there and be challenged to keep learning up to his potential. When he learned that Beresford offered more math classes than Centerville he decided to change schools at the start of seventh grade. Once classes started, he quickly established himself to be at the top of his class academically. He could have alienated himself by acting arrogant, but instead he somehow made it "cool to be smart" as his friends described it. He got his peers to want to excel in their classes instead of being content with medi-ocrity. Peter created a healthy competition to reach the top of the class. His teachers really appreciated those leadership abilities!

When he started to attend Beresford Middle School, Peter traded in the long boring rides in the school bus for trips to school with Julia speeding in the ugly, beat-up green van. He usually had to wait more than his patience could bear for her to be ready to go. One day on the way to school they had to drop off Duane in one of his fields to do some work on an experiment. That set them behind schedule and they were going to be late for school. Julia tried to compensate, and recalls going so fast over a bump that they were airborne for a while and then bottomed out when they hit the ground. Those stressful minutes of waiting and waiting for Julia to get ready for school, followed by hair-raising frantic trips in the old van, must have been really worth it. Peter loved school in Beresford!

There was a large class of at least forty kids at Beresford. Half were boys. There were many potential friends. He went to the huge outdoor LifeLight Christian music festival a few days after seventh grade started. I was pretty surprised to meet his new friends Mike and Caleb. Duane and I had never seen him having such fun with other guys! They were quite the group: two redheads, and tall, lanky Peter. We were more astounded a few days later when he said he wanted to run for middle school student council. All the other candidates were girls, so he figured that if all the boys would vote for him, he'd have a chance at winning. I don't think he realized that the girls were starting to sit up and take notice of this new kid and might cast some votes for him as well. This little guy (in my mind) was starting to display some ability at strategizing and some latent leader-ship abilities. He won the election.

School became a whirlwind of opportunities and fun and mind expan-sion. Peter joined the cross-country team that fall, following the athletic path of his older brother Matt. Always feeling rather inadequate on baseball and basketball teams as a younger child, he found his niche in running. And to our surprise he did quite well. That story will be told later.

Peter wanted to join Boy Scouts. The local troop was small. Parents had to help lead. I was qualified to help the boys with some of the essential badges: cooking, personal management, and personal fitness. Peter was older than most of the boys. His leadership skills became apparent. He didn't think it was beneath him to teach the younger boys. He excelled in his personal management project, developing goals he wanted to attain and plans to achieve them.

In eighth grade Peter asked his dad to help him start a junior high Fellowship of Christian Athletes (FCA) group with his new friends. He was gaining respect with the boys as a good runner. He was getting tall, and had some basketball skills. Through his deepening friendships with the people on his cross-country and basketball team, he saw the spiritual needs of his friends that year. Those kids who joined FCA learned of God's desire to save them and establish a relationship with them, which would help them through the tough times they were to face.

In the spring of his eighth grade Peter had to write a research paper on a person. He chose William Wilberforce. This was before the movie about Wilberforce was released. He was interested in this man who devoted his life to helping to abolish slavery. It seems that in retrospect, working on this paper did something significant in his life. He won two awards for his paper: the South Dakota National History Day Best Project in British Oral History, and first place for the Junior Research Paper Project. He was more serious after writing it. His search for a purpose for his life and cause to promote seemed to awaken. He took Wilberforce's perseverance so seriously that it seemed to us that Peter began searching for some way to serve God by having a big impact on the world. Here are some excerpts from the paper he wrote. It's given me some insight into the effect William Wilberforce had on his thinking:

> *"William Wilberforce's great faith and hard work allowed him to change Great Britain and the world by ending the slave trade, helping to rescue an oppressed people and a nation's character and changing the way people see others.... Wilberforce had amazing perseverance, as he never gave up on his mission. His goal in life was to*

honor God first and then his country. He truly did set about reform as he led the long campaign to abolish the slave trade and eventually slavery. He has inspired many abolitionists all over the world and truly was the citizen of the world that he wanted to be. He changed the way people see each other today because his work ended slavery in Great Britain and served as a model for abolitionists in America and all over the world. Wilberforce's reforms brought an end to an age old idea: the ownership of one person over another."

Matt recalls the day when Peter visited him at his apartment at South Dakota State University. Peter scanned Matt's bookshelf. He spied the book *Don't Waste Your Life* by John Piper. Peter asked Matt if he could borrow the book. Matt recalls replying, "Only if you read it." Peter read it and it shaped his determination further to do something significant with his life. The book played such an important part of his thoughts that he once again asked his dad to lead a study of the book with his friends. Duane gladly supported Peter's newfound passion and met with a small group of guys on a weekly basis. They were challenged to give everything to serve Jesus and not waste all the talents, skills, and opportunities on selfish ambitions. They were challenged to make their lives ones that exemplified service to Christ.

Peter was not an angel. He earned enough money working with Duane in his business to get a smart phone. The phone captured his interest and time. His almanacs and books laid untouched in his room. Instead of engaging in conversation on shopping trips with me, he played games on his phone. We didn't have any other video-gaming devices. I vacillated between feeling really frustrated and wondering if his brain was going down the tubes, versus realizing that he needed to develop some fine motor skills. He wanted to be a surgeon at this point, and understanding that much of what he might do would involve robotics, I decided not to say much to him or curtail his cellphone use. He needed to develop some of those abilities. However, he became so engrossed in it that he wasn't very compliant with coming when I called him to do something. He wasn't obedient by my standards. But when he did emerge from his phone he was usually totally engaged in what the family was doing. Even though it could be an hour after I had requested his help when he finally decided to obey, he worked fast, efficiently finishing the task about the time I had planned it should be done. I was frustrated by my ineptness at not getting him to comply on my schedule. But when he did such a good job in his own time frame, finishing the task within my schedule, how could I say much?

His procrastination came to a head the day we were butchering turkeys in the fall of 2013. He was sixteen by then. The birds had gotten way too big. They were monster tom turkeys (over forty pounds each, dressed!). We had three to butcher. I called to Peter to come help. There was no answer and no sign of him, despite the fact that he liked butchering. Duane tried to tackle the first turkey to slit its neck. The technique is to straddle the turkey from the back, put a knee on each wing, stretch the neck back, and do it in. However, the turkeys were powerful and strong. Duane is strong, too, but a huge flapping bird requires two guys to subdue. The tom was literally beating up Duane. I ran back to the house and screamed at Peter to come instantly. He had never seen me so angry at him. He jumped up and ran with me to the barn. The two of them finished off all three birds. Peter learned a lesson that day.

The boy lacked common sense and mechanical ability. His Boy Scout skills didn't extend to building very good fires. Matt relayed to me an incident in which Peter was frustrated when setting a bonfire in our backyard; the fire just wouldn't get going. Knowing lighter fluid is used on grills, but that we didn't have any, Peter instead got an ice cream bucket of fuel from one of the tanks on the farm. He was just ready to douse the pathetic little pile of coals when Matt, age twenty-one, went over and watched what he was doing. Matt, who has a unique amount of common sense and a calm demeanor, asked just in time, "What color was the liquid you poured into that container?" Matt knew that if it was pink, it was diesel fuel for farm use and wouldn't cause much harm. But if it was tan or yellow, it was highly volatile gasoline and there would be a huge danger.

Peter responded, "It's the color of beer."

Matt says he took his life into his hands by not stopping Peter immediately. He recalls vacillating between letting this be a life lesson for Peter to bear the logical consequences of a bad decision or preventing an accident. Sure enough Peter had chosen the fuel from the gasoline tank. As Peter started to pour the gasoline from the bucket and onto the fire, the heat from the puny little fire ignited the whole bucket of gas! He tossed the bucket with its remaining gasoline into the flames, which suddenly became an inferno. Being fast on his feet, he got away. Matt feels a little chagrined that he allowed Peter's ignorance to nearly burn his little brother. They both learned something from that experience. Maybe what they learned best is, "Don't tell Mom." I didn't hear the story until much later!

Our friend Mike Sveeggen never seems to tire of telling a story about Peter. It's pretty funny now in retrospect. We were preparing to take the high school youth group and some of Matt and Julia's friends from SDSU on a mission trip to Haiti. To raise funds the kids were selected as servants to do any jobs people in the church needed to have done. Donations for their support were given in exchange. Peter and I were selected to help Mike paint the trim on his house. The color he selected was a pretty dark forest green to accent his cream-colored siding. I settled into working on trim at ground level. Mike and Peter were going to handle the gable of the house and high parts on the second story. Mike had a tractor there with a loader. For people who aren't familiar with farm equipment, a loader is an attachment on the front of a tractor that's shaped like a trough. It scoops up things and can hold heavy big loads. Mike decided to sit in the tractor loader with his can of paint and asked Peter to drive it up close to the house. He just assumed Peter could drive a tractor and understood how the controls would raise and lower the loader. He was a farm boy, right? All farm boys know how to drive tractors by the time they're sixteen for sure. But Peter never took much interest in doing real farm work, and Duane's research tractors and equipment were miniature in comparison to the large tractor Mike had borrowed. Peter said nothing and confidently got in the cab, and after a little orientation started driving Mike close to the house. Mike was up high enough by then that Peter could see where he was going. But remember that his eye-hand coordination was not the best? Mike saw himself getting closer and closer to the side of his house. He yelled, and I rounded the corner to see Peter in the cab, and the loader with Mike about an inch away from the house. Mike and I screamed. Peter jumped, put on the brakes hard, and got some control of the tractor, but not before he hit the top of the trim work. Mike's gallon of green paint splashed all over the bottom of the loader bucket and Mike's pants. I think the two of them switched jobs so Mike's house wouldn't have any more gashes. We'll never forget that incident!

One summer we raised about twenty chickens to butcher for meat. My mother-in-law had taught me how to do this on the first day I spent in South Dakota. It is a rather involved process, better suited to a group of four to five people. But I planned to do the job with Peter one Saturday afternoon. There was no one else to help. It was at least 3:00 or 4:00 p.m. when we got started. I knew that we just didn't have time to kill and process all twenty birds before dark. But Peter had so much fun watching them run around without their heads and flopping until they collapsed that I relented and let him finish off all of them. The wheelbarrow was full of birds to de-feather, gut and clean, and cool down and package before we could have supper. He diligently learned the process, worked fast and hard, and we got them all stashed away in the freezer located in the garage before nightfall. It was one of those fun bonding times I enjoyed with him. He made everything fun. We looked forward to yummy meals of home-grown fried chicken.

About four weeks later a bad smell developed in the garage. Every day it got worse. Finally late one Sunday afternoon my nose was drawn to the aroma coming from the upright freezer in the garage. I opened the door and gagged in horror at the sight. Everything inside the freezer had thawed. There were stinky pools of reddish liquid dripping all over the shelves and pooling on the bottom. The meat in the packages was discolored and rotten. Somehow the freezer had gotten unplugged and everything in it spoiled. I shut the freezer door, called Peter, and told him the horrible news.

We plotted how to cover up the problem. We felt horrible our chickens had spoiled, but we couldn't quite tell everyone about the stinky situation yet. My thought was that the shame would be lessened if we cleaned up the mess before anyone knew. I wouldn't feel as badly if I just had to tell Duane and the other kids a sanitized version of the story. If they saw and smelled the situation for themselves, we'd never live it down! There wasn't time to clean up the mess before church; if we got any residues of the chicken remains on our skin, we could smell too terrible to be around anyone! Peter and I planned to get the family to take two cars to church that night, so we could leave together as soon as possible after the service to get home while everyone else stayed to chat. We left a wheelbarrow in the garage, positioned to carry the putrid bags away as quickly as possible when we got home. Peter and I attacked those bags of chicken with amazing speed, hurling them into the wheelbarrow. I disinfected the freezer while Peter's long legs took the wheelbarrow rapidly over to the burning pit to dump out the foul mess. We were just finishing up the cleaning when everyone else returned from church. Peter was my partner in crime.

Although Peter was a big, strong athlete, he still was my little boy at heart. He was at home alone with us during his freshmen and sophomore year, because Matt and Julia had graduated from high school and were studying at SDSU in Brookings. At the end of his freshman year he was on a prom-planning committee. That enabled him to go to the prom if he went with an upper-class person. He invited an upperclassman from our church, and she accepted the invitation. Somehow prom night fell on the night the older kids, Matthew and Julia, had parents' night for the Navigator ministry at their campus in Brookings, South Dakota. Duane had the job of attending the event at SDSU. I got to prepare my son for his first prom. We washed the pickup truck inside and out, polishing it so he had a macho vehicle to take his date to the high school. He looked adorable and handsome. I sent him off in the late afternoon to get pictures taken before the grand march. A few minutes later the phone rang, and a terrified Peter was on the phone. The vehicle wouldn't go any faster than forty miles an hour on the highway in a sixty-five-mile-an-hour zone. He was petrified. He turned down a dirt road when he couldn't figure out what to do. In his panic he attempted to turn around in a driveway and sideswiped a set of mail boxes. After all this I called Duane and found out that I inadvertently switched the transmission to low range when I was wiping off all the farm dust from the dashboard. Now he was delayed for picking up his date. He was a totally distraught, emotional mess. His usual composure was shattered. Poor guy, he was humiliated that he had wrecked the truck. It looked horrible on the driver's side. He was usually very prompt and now he was going to be terribly late. He would miss out on all the pictures with his friends and their dates. And even worse, after getting some of the mess sorted out with the highway patrol, he had to take a very dirty old car of ours to pick up the young lady. All his pride was drained away.

I'll never forget the day the last summer we were together when he was fifteen. I drove with Peter to the Wisconsin Dells to visit our daughter Julia. She was working there in an evangelistic outreach program to international students who work in the amusement parks during the summer. Peter had been growing increasingly quiet around Duane and me, which is characteristic of boys his age. At the time I didn't realize that was part of natural development. I didn't know what was going on in his life. He seemed remote, but I decided not to push him to tell me what was going on. I missed the relationship I had had with him as a little boy. He always had been my pal and chum and chattered easily on long car trips together. So I was rather ill at ease during the seven-hour trip together to the Dells. Peter wasn't very talkative, and I was at a loss for small talk. When we stopped at a rest stop to eat the lunch I had packed, I took a leap and asked him if he had given anymore thought to what he "wanted to be when he grew up." The last I heard was a surgeon or sports medicine doctor for a major league baseball team. His answer was, "Can't you tell? Isn't it obvious?"

I replied, "No, what do you mean?"

He said, "Well, with all the mail I'm getting from schools, I thought you'd know. I want to be a pastor or chaplain."

I about fell off the park bench (in my mind), but said, "What made you change?" I don't really recall the exact answer, but Peter indicated that he wanted to reach out to people spiritually and didn't want to waste his time with other things. My mind was reeling. My bright, brilliant son a minister? To be the smartest pastor ever known? Was he really forgoing the life of wealth and luxury he had wanted for a life of sacrifice and austerity to serve Jesus? He seemed determined about it, so I didn't question him about his motives. The rest of the trip was interspersed with Peter looking in his cellphone for everything he could find about Moody Bible Institute and other Bible schools he could go to. We talked about pros and cons and the differences between the majors he could pursue. The sports ministry major was particularly appealing. My heart could hardly keep it inside as we drove, wanting to tell Duane about Peter's change of heart and plans as soon as possible.

About two months later I went with the Boy Scouts on a five-mile hike. Peter had to go along and stay with me to abide by the 2-Deep Boy Scout Policy, just in case I got separated from the other leaders and was with a group of boys alone. We had a good hike, with Peter encouraging the younger boys to keep going and talking with them. He was setting a good example as the oldest Boy Scout. The younger ones were obviously looking up to him on the hike. I was enjoying just being with the kids and my son. The conversation turned to what people "wanted to be when they grew up." The usual types of grandiose careers surfaced from the boys. Then they asked Peter, "What about you?" I held my breath. Questions raced through my mind as I felt my son's faith and testimony were being tested. Would he make something up that would sound cool to them, or tell them what he had decided? Was he proud of his decision and his God, or had he changed his mind? Was he going to state his previous career choice of being a physician when under some peer pressure from the boys to do something prestigious and lucrative? Or would he stay firm in the calling Jesus had made on his life?

Then I heard him say it, loud and clear, "I want to be a pastor or chaplain for a team."

Wow, it was out in the open, proclaimed for all to know. To my surprise the boys responded, "Wow, that's cool," and wanted to know a little more about it. I was so proud of Peter that day. He really was set on pursuing that dream, and was proud to let everyone know it. He still wanted to serve Jesus in that manner despite his first test from people who could have ridiculed him. He really wanted to show athletes the Truth and help them spiritually by being a chaplain.

Peter joined the cross-country team when he was in seventh grade. Although he was still pretty short and small, he worked hard at running. Guys can run faster as they grow and develop and usually do better and better with each year they run. But his small size when just thirteen years old wasn't going to hold him back. He applied his determination to running; he was going to run fast! He was the alternate for his team at the state cross-country meet when he was in eighth grade. He was driven to excel. But he also wanted his team to be the best. He learned through his coach Matt Coy that although cross-country seems to be an individual sport, it's also a team sport. The coach stressed working together with the other runners in the team (the pack of Beresford Watchdogs) to excel. It was the collective points from each runner that determined the team score. Peter had a natural leadership ability and was able to make all the runners want to excel and do their best. They looked to him to set the pace. They strove to keep up with him, no matter how fast he ran.

Peter also had lots of fun with the runners on the team. One day I picked him up after a workout at his best friend's house. He had a silly grin on his face when his friend's mother opened the door. He gently positioned his backpack on his shoulder rather than swinging it on with the usual bravado. The backpack didn't look very full. I suspected something. Then a faint "meow" sounded from behind Peter. He looked pretty sheepish and out came the kitten he had tried to hide and smuggle home. Everyone dissolved in laughter, and Peter pled with me to allow him to take home the kitten he had hidden inside the backpack. Apparently the team had run past a cornfield during their practice and heard a kitten crying loudly. They retrieved it, realized it had probably been abandoned, and Peter carried it as they completed their run. Knowing I'm a sucker for any stray animals (I've brought home a rooster, cockatiel, donkey, two neutered and declawed cats, and four goats from people at work who needed homes for their critters), he didn't think it would be any problem to add a stray kitten into the number of farm cats. It wouldn't even be noticed. The kitty eventually became a pet for another one of his running buddies, but Peter saved the day initially while the team looked for another owner.

Peter not only demonstrated good sportsmanship and a team attitude with the runners from his school but also with kids on other teams. The mother of one boy from Sioux Falls Christian School, with whom he competed, wrote to us, telling us that Peter prayed with her son before meets. He was admired by all who knew him. At one meet he was standing at the notice that was posted after the race, looking for his time and score, when Peter saw in the list of runners that a boy on a team from another school close to Sioux Falls had the same last name: Auch. Just as he was discovering that fact, the boy standing beside him said something about someone having the same last name as he did. It turned out to be Peter's third cousin. Those two became good friends, and Duane and I were able to get close to his parents. Alexander became an outstanding runner as well. Alexander really is a puzzle piece of God's providence. He planned that we could follow Alexander's progress in running and experience the fun and excitement of following the sport for two years after Peter was gone. Alexander helped to fill the void in our heart with some of the fun we missed at races after Peter died.

Peter was determined to make sure the whole team went to the state meet in 2013. He didn't want to get the glory and qualify just by himself. The qualifying meets for the conference took place in Lennox, SD, that year. The team had never come in first, and struggled to be in fifth place at several meets, so Peter wasn't sure they would make their goal to go to state together. His usual strategy at meets was to run near the middle of the pack at the beginning of the race and then pull ahead as the runners tired out. He usually came in about ninth or tenth. At that rate the team probably wouldn't make it to go together to compete at the state level. So the day of the qualifying race, he started out nearly in the lead and pulled ahead to the front of all the runners. The others on the team knew they had to keep pace with Peter, so they ran harder, too. I drove to the race from work, speeding all the way, so I could watch them. I didn't make it in time to see him leading everyone. He had never run so hard in his life. He tired out and dropped behind two or three guys. When I got to the finish line to watch, he was coming in, as usual, a little behind the fastest runners. But the rest of his teammates came to the finish line ahead of their usual places. I didn't realize until later that Peter had been the one who pushed them all to reach their goal. They were going to state together! The pictures of the team are priceless. Peter, a head taller than everyone by this time, grinning from ear to ear with his friends, rejoicing that they all had made it.

At the 2013 State Cross-Country Championship in Rapid City, Peter ran with the other six members of his team. He was determined to come in twenty-fifth or less and receive the coveted medal. He used his usual approach of starting in the middle of the 100+ runners, picking up steam and running harder as the race progressed. He passed up one runner after another to reach his goal. And he came in faster than he expected: seventeenth place. The team came in as a whole in sixth place. I had never seen him so happy and proud. He wore his neon green sweat band like a wreath or crown that day. His hard work and perseverance had paid off. None of us had any clue that within the next month he would receive the crown of life, a bear hug from Jesus, and the pronouncement: "Well done, thou good and faithful servant, enter into the joy of the Lord."

TRAGEDY

Preparation

God is so good to prepare us for some of the hard things that He knows will happen in our lives. He cares that we aren't totally emotionally smashed unnecessarily by circumstances that He foresees. He often puts us into situations to help us spiritually grow or to form relationships that we'll need in the future. That's evidence of His providence and loving-kindness working together. Looking back now, I can see God strengthening me for what lay ahead. These verses come to mind from Psalms:

> **"Oh taste and see that the Lord is good. Blessed is the man who takes refuge in Him!"**
>
> PSALM 34:8, ESV

> **""Many, O Lord my God,**
> **are the wonders you have done.**
> **The things you planned for us**
> **no one can recount to you;**

Were I to speak and tell of them,
they would be too many to declare."
PSALM 40:5, NIV

As I've been looking back over my life these past years and reflecting on events, God has helped me to discover things He did to show He was personally thinking about us. What an amazing thing to be in relationship with the sovereign God who is in control of all this! These preparation puzzle pieces, when laid side by side, demonstrate God's love, and they are dear to me.

My brother-in-law Jim Tebbe, came to speak at a missions conference at our church many years ago. My kids ranged between five to twelve years old. I usually do not remember specific sermons people preach for more than few days or weeks. However, Jim's message has stayed with me for many years. I believe that God used it to prepare me for the difficulties our family faced. It also gave me a perspective regarding one of the reasons God allows us to face unusual, painful, and detestable circumstances.

Jim preached from Acts 10 regarding the apostle Peter going to Cornelius's house. He saw the vision of the sheet containing many different unclean animals. Peter heard God's voice telling him to, "Rise, kill and eat." Peter was horrified at the thought of eating anything that was considered to be unclean by Old Testament law. However, God told him to give up those restrictions. God told Peter a second time, "What God has made clean, do not call impure" (or detestable). Because the apostle Peter was willing to give up what was comfortable to him and do something that didn't feel safe, and something considered to be gross and repulsive, he was able to go to the Gentiles to preach the gospel. Then God caused the Gentiles to turn to Jesus because of Peter's obedient witness. Jim applied the principles to us: at times God puts us in very uncomfortable, awful circumstances. We are forced to rub shoulders with people who are not like us. In these times relationships can form with people with whom we normally would never talk. He stressed that God may be giving us trials, because in the process we will have the opportunity to share Jesus with people who may never have anyone witness to them otherwise. God calls us to "rise, kill and eat" by embracing the tough times and looking for new people with whom we can share Jesus. His Kingdom spreads mightily when we are willing to use the detestable times in our lives for His purposes and glory.

Around the time of the mission conference, my sister Ruth was going through chemotherapy. She needed infusions every week. She demonstrated to the family how Jim's message could be applied. She joyfully went to her appointments and used the time waiting for her procedures to get to know others waiting for cancer treatments. She was able to share Jesus' love with many people. I was challenged by Ruth's example of making something good come of the trials she faced. She was keenly aware of the role to which God called her in establishing His Kingdom. Her approach to her terminal condition planted in me a vision of what God could do through tragedies that come into our lives.

Due to all the appointments we were having with counselors and therapists for Jonathan at this stage of our lives, we came in contact with many new types of people. We met many therapists and people working at group homes with whom we never would have had any contact otherwise. Jon's treatment wasn't something I'd ever choose. Those encounters and the stress of all his therapy were to me like what the apostle Peter faced when obeying the command to deal with the unclean animals that were too gross to kill, cook, and eat. But God was calling us to this situation for His purposes. I didn't follow my sister's example very well of verbally telling people about Jesus, but I understood one of the possible outcomes and reasons for the problems Jon had. My eyes were opened to one of God's purposes in our trials: it was so that we could show Jesus' love to these people who cared for our son.

Years later, when Peter died, God called us to meet and rub shoulders with many different people. Both Duane and I knew that one reason for the situation was to make sure Jesus' love was demonstrated to them. We understood the principle, because God had taught it to us many years previously, of "rising, killing, and eating" during the tough times so that the gospel could be spread. How loving of God to prepare our hearts for all that happened!

A few years before the accident one of my good friends, Charlotte, asked me to be the speaker at a ladies' Christmas event at her church. I agreed. God had been teaching me some things, and I had a topic in mind immediately: "God's puzzle." As I put my thoughts together and spoke to the ladies, things became clear to me. I could see how He had been working in my life, putting together circumstances for His glory. The ladies were kind and appreciative. But I gained far more than they did, for God was giving me a framework for understanding His work in my life and how it could be used for His glory. It was this understanding that God gave me that caused my faith in Him to develop. He was preparing me for what lay ahead.

A few months before the invitation to speak I had heard the song about God putting the puzzle pieces of our lives together. This was the first time the idea of God as our puzzle maker came to me. Up until then all the events of my life seemed like a jumbled-up mess. It all made so much sense when I applied the puzzle metaphor to my life. God was putting things together His way for His glory. The picture on God's puzzle is the Kingdom of God. I started to reflect on my life to see God's sovereignty in how things had occurred: how I met Duane, what He had done to protect me during my miscarriage, how He planned for us to adopt Jonathan, the incredible miracle of the two babies He gave us by birth, His protecting us from the fire, and His provision of our business. All of this was clear evidence of God making details work out for His plans. I could view these events in retrospect as pieces of His Kingdom puzzle. I could see how He was changing my heart to take control of my life and be Lord. My trust in God increased by leaps and bounds. If He was so personally involved in my life up until then, I could trust Him for anything in the future.

I started from then on to refuse to see anything in life as a coincidence. It became an exciting adventure to give God the credit for His actions. As I sensed a new trial beginning, I could relax and view the situation as the next puzzle piece God was putting in place. I could see that there could be pain initially, but God was good and had His purpose behind it all. With perseverance, good would come of the situation. I learned that the sooner I submitted to the process of fitting the pieces together, the less painful the experience would be. Once I started looking for God's plan being put into action, I could see how masterful God was in making the pieces of my life fit with those of my kids', others at church, and people in the community. God was preparing my heart to fit into a huge part of His Kingdom puzzle. Remember, the picture on God's puzzle is the Kingdom of God, which Jesus is forming in the hearts of individuals around the globe as we yield to Him being Lord. Eventually we will all join together in worshiping the King of Kings in heaven for eternity. It's a glorious puzzle He's putting together!

One of the things in retrospect that I could see God doing was to give me a patient to work with who had had a severe accident that caused a brain injury. He was a middle-aged man. I had taken care of his tube feeding needs for six years. There never seemed to have been any evidence to medical personnel that the patient had any brain functioning. It was very hard to observe the family go through the whole thing. The emotional and financial toll on his wife and kids were horrific. At the same time there was a big effort to get people in our medical system to understand the importance of getting advanced directives written and completed so the family would know what medical help and treatment you wanted or did not want if you might not be able to make decisions for yourself. Duane and I had discussions and the kids passively listened in. We all came to some agreement. I had our advanced directives notarized and distributed as needed to the doctor, hospital, and family. I am so glad we thought through the issues then. It made it much easier when our emotions were raw to do what we had decided upon. God was good to coordinate all those things in the context of my professional job in order to prepare me.

In the spring of 2013, my friend Shellie in Beresford started a ladies' study to read and discuss several books. Many women from the community came together. I was able to meet lots of people from the town where my kids went to school, who I otherwise never would have met. That was a blessing in itself. One of the books we read alongside the videos was Ann Voscamp's book *1000 Gifts*. From reading that book, I began the practice of finding three things daily to thank God for, no matter how insignificant they seemed at the time. I found that the more I thanked God, the more I loved Him and understood His profound love for me. God knew I'd need that skill!

This aspect of God's preparation may seem like a strange one, but God knew I needed this one to be prepared for what lay ahead. My father, living in California, had been failing in health for several years due to melanoma cancer. I was able to visit him and help him move to a care center a month before he finally passed away in 2012. I returned with my sisters for a memorial service at the chapel. Prior to this, as a child and adult, I had never touched anything dead besides a bug. While growing up, I had been repulsed by any dead animals in the back yard. I didn't have any childhood curiosity to look at a bird that had died. All I felt was disgust. In high school I had made it through anatomy labs and the dissection that was required without ever actually touching the animal's body. (I had very understanding lab partners who agreed to hold the critter down if I'd do all the cutting!) After my dad's death my sisters and I went to the funeral home, and there I got up the courage to touch my father's chest and lose my fears and repulsion. That may seem like a weird thing, but I needed to have all that squeamishness resolved before I had to face it with my own son. God was so good to make it possible so I had less emotional baggage to deal with later.

For some reason, in the spring of 2013, when he was still a freshman, I felt compelled to start working on Peter's scrapbooks. I knew it would take me about two or three years to get prepared for his graduation if I worked on it regularly. I hadn't done anything to organize all the things he had saved. Peter had me save every single picture, worksheet, and paper he did at school from the time he was in kindergarten. We also had many snapshot prints of him. Having had to get ready for Matt's and Julia's graduations, I realized I needed to get all his photos in a digital format so they could be used for his graduation display, invitations, and various events. I took two days, standing at the scanner at Walmart for four hours each time, to get them all onto a Zip disk. How grateful I am that God prompted me to get that done. We never would have been able to have the pictures we needed for his funeral later that year if He hadn't pushed me in His loving-kindness to get the tiresome task done.

God prepared Matt ahead of time by prompting him to go to Peter's state cross-country meet in Rapid City on October 25, 2013. Matt was in the last semester of his college. It was a very busy time for him, and not something that he could do very easily. It involved traveling to the opposite side of the state, taking off a day of classes, and driving there with us. He really hadn't had any chance to see his little brother run at previous events. This was the last one of the season and a very important race. Matt was there to see his little brother come in seventeenth in the state. It was a precious thing God did for Matt to give him that gift of celebrating Peter's success and creating good memories.

After the state cross-country meet Peter asked me one day if he could go with his friend Jake to another race. I didn't know his parents at all, but they seemed like safe people with whom he could spend so much time. I agreed. Jake was fourteen; Peter was sixteen. A special bond between those two boys formed that weekend. Peter didn't do well in that race, but they had a very good time together. I had no idea how Jake and his family would become amazing parts of the healing process of our grief in the future. God knew I'd need their love, and He opened the door to my heart to form a friendship I would need. That's His providence at work!

After the state cross-country competition Peter's circle of friends wanted him to play basketball with the team that season. He was one of the tallest guys in the class, so they valued him as a potential forward or center. Peter wasn't planning to go out, but he joined the team to please his friends. He started working very hard to sell tickets for the Booster club, as required of the athletes. His time at workouts increased after school. But in comparison to the tension he felt during the cross-country season to excel and meet his goals, as he was training for the basketball season, he was more relaxed. Those were a few weeks of Peter being his sweet, smiling, quiet, kind self around us when he was at home.

I took Peter shopping for basketball gear and shoes the week before the accident. I recall he really wanted a Superman shirt. He tried one on, but the shirt was too small and expensive to fit into his budget. It was my last time shopping with him, and a precious memory. We had spent so many hours shopping together throughout his life as a child and teenager. He had to tag along with me everywhere I went for many years because he was the little kid who couldn't be left home alone. He was my little buddy. This trip seemed just like any of those other trips, just a happy time between the two of us. I'm glad God etched that time in my heart. He knew I'd need this sweet memory.

I had grown more comfortable with Peter's quietness. He didn't talk much when driving together unless he had something pressing on his mind. He didn't share much about his relationships or feelings as a general practice. But on the way home from that shopping trip he had something pretty important on his mind. He asked if a person could major in biochemistry. I sensed that that he wanted to change his career from being a pastor to something else. He agreed that was true. I asked if it had something to do with the debate tournament he had in which his team lost four rounds and won only one round. It had been pretty rough on him. He said he realized then that it would be hard to be a pastor because of all the talking he'd have to do. He thought it would be OK if he could read all his sermons, but throughout the week he would be talking all the time—extemporaneously—and just couldn't do it. He said he liked science too much and wanted to go on to med school and become an orthopedic surgeon. He seemed to be telling me, as I listened to his heart between the words he was verbalizing, that he wanted to make the best use of all his abilities. Doing as much as he could with the talents God had given him was what he felt God was calling him to.

Death

God put down many pieces in His Kingdom puzzle on Friday, November 22, 2013. He was getting set to work in the hearts of many people by showing them His glory in the midst of a tragedy. For those of you reading this who participated and observed the events first-hand, your memories may be very different from mine. Here's what God was doing in our lives then.

I had a relaxing day on that Friday. I went to Walmart in Vermillion to get groceries and the things Peter wanted me to get him for activities he had planned for the weekend. He texted me to make sure I had meat for the event at church that night. I got home and plunged into baking cookies for Christmas. I needed to get several batches done for the Christmas decorating party at church, which would be the week after Thanksgiving. I had fortunately planned ahead and had chicken stew in the crockpot so I wouldn't have to cook and bake at the same time (normally we wait until about 9:00 p.m. to eat). Peter worked out with his friends after school and came home hungry. He ate two chocolate crinkle cookies and complimented me on them (which is touching, as I found out later that he joked with friends about how hard and overdone my cookies usually were). He noted that, "These are really good, can I have another one?" Then he ate a package of Ramen noodles, a bowl of chicken stew, some yogurt, a banana, an apple, and an orange. He was planning to go to a youth group crazy night of making cardboard and duct tape armor to have a battle, followed by eating a stew made from the ingredients each kid brought. I gave him cut-up pork to take. He was frustrated that I was only sending a half pound rather than a big amount. That was my last conversation with him. I didn't notice him take off in his maroon Grand Am.

It was precious that God gave me a good memory of being a normal mom to Peter that day. Looking back, it was the only time I remember being at home when Peter got home from school. Usually I picked him up at day care when he was little or I was at work late and he was already home, or we were at a cross-country meet with him and got home together late in the afternoon. To be at home, ready for him with freshly baked cookies, was just the classic mom I had always wanted to be to him. Somehow that's been a huge comfort to me.

After filling up his stomach, he went out to Duane's office off the garage and asked if there was something he could use to cut cardboard. Duane had just bought a new box cutter. He smiled and handed it to him. Normally such a request would have caused a search for a few minutes to find something suitable, or even a trip to the machine shed to rummage around for a while. Peter was happy he didn't have to delay and could just take off so he could be on time. (That small detail affected the split-second timing of what was going to happen.) He said "good-bye" and smiled and left. It was about 6:15 p.m. when he left the house, which would be plenty of time to get to church for the event at 6:30.

At 6:50 p.m., Pastor John called and asked if Peter had left our house yet. The trip to church usually takes about ten minutes. He hadn't gotten to church by the time the pastor called. Duane told him to call Peter's friend Mike, to see if he was going to his house first to pick him up. I then tried to call Peter, but there was no answer so I left him a text message to call back because people were concerned he hadn't arrived. There was no response. I wasn't too concerned at the time; maybe he was still driving and wasn't answering his phone. Duane and I ate our supper and then decided to call Pastor John back to see if Peter had arrived at church. Pastor John then told us that there was a big accident between our house and the church and they were afraid that Peter was in it.

We decided to take off then to look for him. My mind frame switched into the emergency high alert mode. I didn't feel alarmed or numb. I felt like a robot, just focusing on the most important tasks that had to be done. I reprioritized everything, leaving dishes undone, the house a mess, the cookies out on the counter, and the lights on all over the house. Just in case he really had been in an accident I gathered things I would need to be prepared to stay in the hospital for a few days with him, should the need arise.

Just as I was taking my bag out to the car, the sheriff drove up and told us that our son had been airlifted to Avera McKennan Hospital (the Catholic hospital in Sioux Falls). He told us that there were three cars in the accident and a total of four people. The others had minor injuries in comparison to Peter. It appeared to be a head-on collision due to someone passing a car and hitting Peter. Then the car that had been passed hit Peter's car as well. We started driving the forty miles to Sioux Falls right away. I called a guy from church on the ambulance crew to see if he knew anything about it. He was away from home but had already heard from his wife, who had talked to another EMT, that Peter had a head injury. (So much for confidentiality!) But at least we knew the possible seriousness of the accident because the ER personnel wouldn't tell us anything over the phone. I was pretty jittery on the way, but we prayed for peace and the ability to handle what we'd find.

We got to the hospital and found that Peter was out of the ER already and was going to intensive care after having a full-body CAT scan. We waited in the hospital lobby until a chaplain arrived to take us up to intensive care to wait for the neurosurgeon to evaluate the CAT scan results. The chaplain, sensing that we had some degree of faith, made us aware of his evangelical beliefs in the elevator. He was with us throughout the night. God used him to make us feel very peaceful through it all. I was so blessed that God sent that man to minister to us when we needed to feel God's presence and peace with us. Duane called his mother and brothers, telling them about the accident but expressing that we weren't too sure yet regarding the severity of the injuries. I called Matt to get him to come to Sioux Falls from Brookings right away. We couldn't get Julia to answer her phone and called Matt again to look around the campus to find her before he drove the forty-five-minute trip. It was quite a search for her.

The surgeon came in, a fifty- to sixty-year-old short, stout guy. He told us that Peter had a severe head injury, and that there were three problems. There was severe swelling under his skull that was putting pressure on the brain, which would cause all his organ systems to eventually shut down if surgery was not done. There was an extensive blow to his head, leaving only his brain stem functioning; all his cognitive processes were most likely gone. In addition the first responders had so much trouble getting him out of the car wreck that he was without oxygen for a long time. He suspected there would be significant brain damage from that alone. The trauma doctor told us he had a crushed pelvis on one side, a punctured lung, and possible injuries to other organs in his abdomen. He was bleeding internally and they were having difficulty locating the source of all the blood loss.

By that time Pastor John had come to be with us. He had to leave for a minute for a phone call at the same time the doctor asked us if we wanted to do the surgery to relieve the pressure on his brain. I was feeling like we shouldn't do it, and asked the doctor directly whether he would have it done if it were his son. He said he wouldn't, as his son wouldn't want to live being unresponsive and unaware of his surroundings, totally dependent for the rest of his life. I had a premonition that Peter would be brain dead forever even if we tried to keep him alive. Knowing Peter got very frustrated if he couldn't be the best in everything academically and in sports, he wouldn't be able to cope with such an impaired life if he was cognitively able to understand his surroundings at all. The doctor said we would have to make a decision in about fifteen minutes so they could get the OR ready before it was too late to make any difference. The swelling in the skull was doing more and more damage the longer we waited.

We prayed together with Pastor John and the chaplain for God to give us a clear answer—fast. A nurse came into the conference room and told us that Peter was settled down in his bed in the intensive care room. We could come and see him before talking to the surgeon again. I asked what I'd see, and they forewarned me that there would be a hose-sized tube down his mouth for breathing, lots of blood, IVs, and no response to us. We walked up to the bed, and immediately noted that the left eye was very swollen and blue and shut, his whole face was swollen, his right eye was open, which didn't blink, and there was no response at all. Blood was pooling under his head and gurgling from his mouth. We decided then that it was pretty clear that he was virtually brain dead, and gave the staff the answer that there would be no surgery. Duane called his mom and brothers to come quickly because Peter wasn't going to make it very long.

They asked if we wanted to talk to the organ donation organization to make plans for them to come, and we agreed to do so. Initially the surgeon thought he would last two to three days, which would give the organ transplant team plenty of time to get there so they could harvest as many organs as possible. I recall it was then that Duane asked Pastor John to pray that we wouldn't feel self-pity about all this, as it was clear then that Peter would soon die. So after the consultation with them, we returned to a waiting room while a chest tube was being put in to replace the hose down his mouth. The nurses needed to be able to suction him more easily. I really didn't want to leave him for a second, but they convinced me I wouldn't want to see them working on him. Finally we were allowed to return to him.

In the hallway on the way back to his room, I had second thoughts. Pastor John was there. I asked him if we had done the right thing by not giving approval for the surgery to relieve pressure on his brain and preserve his life a little longer. Pastor John answered, "If God wants him to live, He can do a miracle without the surgery now. It doesn't take a surgeon to save his life." That answer helped me so much to lay it all in God's hands to control. Maybe that was the instant at which my choice to believe in God's sovereignty in the situation was made. I don't remember making any other conscious decision to choose to believe and trust God in that moment, but in my heart I had done this. Duane had expressed his trust by his prayer not to become full of self-pity. His prayer was one of putting the focus on God, not himself and our loss. For me, after that moment of needing reassurance, trusting God was the only thing that could be done; He was my only option for coping. God had proven Himself to be with us in the past in the miscarriage, failed adoption, and difficulties with Jon. I knew He would be there. It was kind of an automatic response, based on my confidence in God and His wisdom. Somehow all I recall is being totally surrounded in His love. His glory was tangible. It didn't feel like we were living in a dream or something surreal. It was totally real. But

God was supernaturally filling our hearts and minds with the ability to think and stay calm. There are two verses in the psalms that describe the strength God gave us to go through those hours at the hospital and how He guarded our hearts and mind:

> **"He is not afraid of bad news. His heart is firm,**
> **trusting in the LORD.**
> **His heart is steady, he will not be afraid..."**
>
> PSALM 112:7–8A, ESV

Within minutes of returning to Peter's side, they began frantically working to get internal bleeding stopped. He had big gashes on his neck and across his left cheek that went from his mouth to his ear. They had used up many units of blood and nothing would coagulate. He had had massive amounts of IV fluid to keep his blood volume up. Many units of Heparin were given to clot his blood, and they were trying to pump in as much vitamin K as possible to stop the bleeding. They were desperate. By this time it was clear that Peter wasn't going to live much longer. I told the three nurses that they didn't have to try to save Peter until the organ harvesting people got there. We had decided not to have that surgery done while he was still alive. I requested them to just try to keep him alive for an hour until Matt and Duane's family could arrive. I remember the quizzical, relieved looks on the faces of the nurses. It was as if they couldn't believe I could be so calm and honest and considerate of the trouble and stress they were facing. I had some clue that it was God giving us the strength to demonstrate the peace He had given us. It seemed curious to me that other people would consider it to be a strange reaction to just rest in God at that time. Then the nurses contacted the trauma doctor, who gave them orders to stop efforts to stop the bleeding. This decision allowed Peter's blood pressure to drop as he lost more blood internally. The doctor explained that eventually his heart would not be able to compensate with the low blood pressure and would stop. It was just a waiting period from then on.

Duane's family came, and Pastor Dave, the assistant pastor from church, arrived so Pastor John could go to get Jonathan from the group home where he lived in Sioux Falls. Finally Matt arrived, having given up a terrific search for Julia on campus at SDSU. When he finally learned that she was in Aberdeen (four hours away) at a dance, he rushed to the hospital. He was nearing the completion of getting certified to be an EMT, so he was comfortable with seeing trauma. But seeing it in your little brother is much different!

Matt read scriptures to Peter. One was the same verse Peter was in the process of memorizing:

> **"I have been crucified with Christ and I no longer live,**
> **but Christ lives in me. And the life I live in the flesh,**
> **I live by faith in the Son of God, who loved me**
> **and gave Himself for me."**
>
> GALATIANS 2:20, NIV

What a comfort to know that in those very moments Jesus was living in Peter, though his body was fading away. He was living his last minutes by faith in his Savior. All the family, the pastors, and chaplain sang hymns to him and said what we needed to say as "good-byes." We worshipped together as we imagined Peter seeing Jesus very soon, entering heaven and eternity. It was a precious and glorious time. God felt so close then—my son was going to hug Jesus any minute! God was almost tangible, as if we could touch Jesus because we were holding our dying son's hand.

Several years later I passed by the same room where Peter died, when I went to visit someone in that ICU. I expected to feel God's glory emanating from that room again. But there was no feeling of God's presence there at all. It made me acknowledge how awesome God was that night, loving and encouraging us and sustaining us by His presence. Peter's blood pressure kept dropping, but due to his long-distance running, his heart was so strong that it kept beating and beating and beating. He didn't give up easily. It took about an hour for his heart to finally fail. He died at 12:11 a.m. on November 23, 2013. Julia found out about it fifteen minutes later, when she eventually answered her phone when the dance was done. She was shocked, as she hadn't heard anything about it previously or hadn't yet looked at all the texts we had sent. All I recall her saying to me was, "So my dreams came true." Then she told her friends and drove back home to Brookings. I didn't understand what her comment meant at the time. What she told us later is that she had had recurring dreams for several weeks of Peter being in a car accident. She never told us. But God was precious to her, preparing her mind and heart to hear the horrible news. He cushioned the blow by giving her those dreams. I found it very comforting to know God was taking care of my daughter's heart in the same way He had been preparing me.

Pastor John took Jon back to his group home in Sioux Falls for us because we didn't have access to any of his medications for him to stay with us overnight. We stayed in the hospital awhile longer, thanked the staff, prayed with the chaplain again and Duane's family, and decided to go back to Brookings to be with Julia when she arrived from Aberdeen. We decided to try to sleep overnight together at Matt's apartment.

In the waiting room outside the ICU where we had been with Peter, our good friends Charles and Linda Glanzer were waiting to see us. He had been a pastor and had also worked for Duane. When they arrived at the ICU waiting room they didn't know yet Peter had died. They just heard he had been in a very serious accident. They drove up to Sioux Falls to be with us and support us in whatever we were facing. What an example of what to do for grieving people. They said very little; they just listened and cried with us. They were there at 12:30 a.m., despite work they had to face the next day. They suffered with us, and loved us just by their actions. We told them the whole story, and then left the hospital and took off for Brookings to find Julia. We cried and sobbed with the kids into the early morning and finally dozed off to sleep.

Whirlwind

The next morning we got up and stumbled into McDonald's for breakfast. Fortunately there wasn't anyone else in there that I could see. I couldn't make my brain think to order any food. No one else was very interested in eating, it seemed, but I knew it would be a very long day ahead. We had to go to the funeral home, make lots of calls, get the obituary written, and the like. I couldn't even focus on the menu board. I finally told the clerk at the counter that my son had died a few hours before. "I can't decide what to eat. Just give us four of anything." She selected breakfasts for us and didn't even charge us. What a gift! I had my first indication of how profoundly grief can affect your ability to think and function, and how reliant grieving people are on those around them for help. People call this the "freeze response." Grief can be paralyzing. You cannot fight or flee. You freeze in place, unable to do anything productive or rational at all. Your mind and heart are so overwhelmed with emotion that routine tasks can be impossible.

My mind was full of questions regarding Peter's influence as we drove home that morning. By then we had some suspicion that everyone in the Beresford community knew about his death. I didn't have any sense of how people would take the loss. I feared some negative feelings from people. Peter had become very quiet at home as the fall progressed. Aside from being more easygoing and slightly more talkative for a few weeks after the cross-country season ended, he generally just conversed with us once in a while, having discussions with Duane about baseball and football and politics. He never told us much about school. When he did say something, he portrayed it to us as a totally dull place. Duane and I had gotten rather worried about him that fall. Although we knew he was wrestling with his career choice, we didn't notice much outward evidence of his faith, especially in the way he related to his brother Jonathan. He just sat through family devotions but didn't participate much. And I had had an ugly experience with him after a cross-country race in which he was very rude to me when I was trying to be supportive. I thought that maybe he was acting that way to other people, too. He seemed to be engrossed in who-knows-what on his phone, and isolated himself in his room much of the time. He was uncooperative when I asked him to do chores, putting them off until I was angry at him. He talked to me a little on shopping trips, but kept to himself otherwise. Peter was extremely smart and number one academically in his class. Due to the way I had seen him ignore his brother Jonathan, I feared he was seen as an arrogant jerk at school. He only talked about one friend, and if he said anything about other kids it was in frustration at how they were just wasting their time and not doing much. I was fearful that in addition to all the horrible things you have to do to get through a funeral for a child, it would be a really awkward experience to face nice people who were masking their distaste for my son.

With that in mind, as the family traveled home from Brookings I made a call to Peter's friend Riley. I knew Riley pretty well from taking him with us on a mission trip to Haiti a few months before. Peter ran with him, usually neck and neck, for the cross-country team. I assumed Riley would know what Peter was experiencing at school that he wasn't telling us. Riley was the student body president and had his fingers on the pulse of his classmates. His parents were influential and knew the opinions of many adults in the community. My first concern was how the Beresford community and his classmates were reacting to the news. What news was known, and what rumors were spreading? I needed to know some things that were going on at school so I could be prepared emotionally for what I'd encounter from all the people we'd face in the next few days.

So I asked Riley four questions:

- What was Peter like at school?
- If Peter saw a kid hurting and alone, what would he do?
- Was he dealing with his problem of arrogance?
- Did people see Jesus in Peter?

Riley assured me that Peter was one of the most well-liked kids in the high school. He was cheerful and reached out to smile and love kids and encourage them. He motivated his peers to try to keep up with him in the tight race to be valedictorian. He helped kids all the time with their homework. Riley thought he had a large group of girls who had crushes on him. Although Peter had problems with pride, he and Riley had discussed this, and it was something that Peter acknowledged, had assessed with respect to his actions, and was working through. It can be hard to maintain a Christian identity consistently throughout life, and this pursuit can become even more difficult in a school setting. From Riley's point of view, though, Peter's actions could frequently be traced back to the foundational hope that Peter had in Christ. His faith was certainly evident.

I didn't have much time to process Riley's answers before we reached Beresford to face all the decisions for the funeral. But in those last miles on that trip from Brookings, my mind turned around 180 degrees in my understanding of my son and who he really was. Duane and I were so wrong about how we viewed him! I was stunned to find out the influence he had on his peers. How had we missed seeing this side of him? Was he just so emotionally wrapped up in his friends' needs that he didn't have much left for us? God obviously must have been at work in his heart in profound ways, to which we were blinded. While we were pretty oblivious God was accomplishing His purposes in Peter's heart, causing tremendous spiritual growth and fruit.

With that information to embolden and strengthen us, we went to the funeral home and made plans. We were in autopilot, just making decisions that came at us. It was a whirlwind of emotions and things that had to be done quickly. We look back at those few hours and just see that God was carrying us through the "valley of the shadow of death." He was enabling us to do the next thing, the next task, that had to be done.

It was Saturday afternoon by now, and the funeral had to be on Tuesday because Thanksgiving was just two days later. Many people would leave the community on Wednesday afternoon to travel to see relatives. We knew that there would be lots of kids; it would be a big funeral. There wasn't much time to get it all organized. Eventually we all agreed that the funeral had to be in the high school gym, and the prayer service would be at our church on Monday evening. We picked out the coffin. We decided to give out the teen Gideon version of the gospel of John to all the kids, as we had a large supply of them at church.

We then headed straight to church. It was about twenty-four hours after the accident by this time. Pastor John asked us to stop by and visit with the kids. There were many who were torn up at the loss of their friend and needed to process it. We thought it would be just the high school youth group composed of about twenty kids. But when we drove up to the parking lot we saw about forty or more cars parked outside. We walked inside the Fellowship Hall door to see a sea of about one hundred or more kids around tables, all crying and in shocked grief. There were twenty parents or so who stood by the back door. The parents kept offering their "condolences," whatever that means. (I had never heard that word used before that night.) All I could see were the hurting kids.

I was dead tired by this time. All the trauma of the night before and activity and emotion of the day were crashing over me. Pastor John asked me to talk to everyone. I asked him, "What can I say?"

He just shrugged.

I started greeting all of them from close to the doorway, and then someone told me to walk across the room to the microphone. As I was walking between the tables of kids, the only thing that came to my mind was to mention to the kids that Peter had told me the kids teased him that I was his grandmother (due to my grey hair). The kids snickered. I felt a little more at ease then and words started coming to mind. I told them that Peter must have been very different at school than at home. I had heard that he was always singing at school. They nodded in agreement. The tension was loosening then.

I felt I should share about how we got Peter. (There was an uncomfortable look on their faces: "Is she going to tell us about the birds and bees?" was written all over their expressions.) But I told them about how we couldn't have kids, but God gave us Jon, Matt, and Julie, and then surprised us completely with Peter when I was pretty old. He was a miracle who was totally unexpected. I told them that I asked God many times why He decided to give us Peter. We were satisfied with three kids, so why did we have another one? I had never had a clear answer. Then I told them that Peter didn't have many friends at all before he transferred to the Beresford school system. He felt he was used and shunned because he was smart. His impression was that the kids were too jealous of him to be nice and accept him. I thanked the kids for being Peter's friends and told them I was overwhelmed by their love for him.

Then it just came out: my deep concern that they could be in the same situation of dying unexpectedly but without Jesus. I told them they needed to be ready to die. I had had so much experience in that year with AWANA, sharing the plan of salvation and teaching the kids methods to use in sharing the gospel with their friends, that it was pretty natural to share Jesus spontaneously.

Pastor John prayed with them, and the sniffles diminished. Matt then stood up to talk with them. He asked them to journal and write down all their memories to help heal and deal with their emotions. After that the kids ate snacks and started telling us their memories of Peter. It was precious. Their fondness of him was so clear. As they shared memories and funny stories, their tears turned to smiles and laughter. That Saturday night we began to have faith that God would use Peter's death to influence many kids, and we started praying likewise.

Very early Sunday morning, I went to work to get urgent things done, and I went to Walmart to get supplies we needed for the upcoming events and family coming to be with us. I checked my email in my office at work, and was so comforted to find that Kristie Mompremier (the missionary we knew well in Haiti) had heard about the accident and had their congregation of hundreds of Haitians praying for us. I emailed her and asked her to get the church to pray for the services that were to come. Haitians can really pray! I was anticipating seeing all those wonderful Haitian people four weeks later on an upcoming mission trip. I was seeing clear evidence of God's hand in placing this puzzle piece in His Kingdom picture. He was caring for me by letting me see the encouraging email, and using this in a more global way for His glory, as I found comfort from my brothers and sisters far away. This encouragement bolstered my strength to face more plans and decisions.

We went to visit Duane's brother's church the next morning and stopped by my mother-in- law's house. In the afternoon, we picked out the grave site in our church's cemetery and went home to start to select a picture for the bulletin cover for the funeral with Bible verses, write the obituary, and put together a slideshow of Peter's childhood pictures to show at the prayer service. There was so much to do! There was no time to really rest or sleep or cry or reflect or think. I just felt like a blur of total stress. The whole time was unusually compressed due to Thanksgiving on the Thursday later that week. Kids had to be free to take off school Wednesday afternoon, if necessary, to travel with their parents. There was no way to take it slower to get the funeral done without as much stress.

Goals

The blessing of that Sunday was Matt's finding a notebook in Peter's room. I had purchased it before school started. It was the only thing he said he needed for school. God can take things we think are inconsequential or insignificant and make them into something significant for the Kingdom of God. This blue notebook stood out to me when I bought it, because it was the first time I didn't have to pay a fortune for school supplies since my kids started school many years previous. But to God this turned out to be a big part of the story of His glory in Peter's life.

There wasn't anything related to classes in the notebook. Instead he used it to write his goals for his life. Matt ran into the living room, brandishing it. What a find! As we looked at it together, we were in awe. His determination to follow Jesus was astounding. He wrote his personal mission statement across the top: John 3:30 – "He must increase, I must decrease." We found out later that this statement was his *Twitter* ID. All the kids at school knew his purpose and motto. They knew Jesus was first place! It was at that point that we started to understand that God had something big in mind that was going to glorify Himself through Peter's life and death. This wasn't going to be just about a good kid everyone loved who died tragically. God had a plan.

Peter had goals for his spiritual life, mental and school life, physical fitness, and social life. Here they are as recorded in his notebook:

GOALS

"He must increase, I must decrease." John 3:30

Spiritual
Make Christ the Center of my life.
Become a spiritual leader in youth group and FCA
Memorize 40 verses and 10 chapters
Be ready to counsel this summer
Decide if I really want to be a pastor and if God is calling me to it
Read Bible Doctrine
Increase in spiritual wisdom
Be baptized
Find my spiritual talents

Mental/Social
4.0 – At least 4 100%s, no A-
Less than 3 missing assignments
Improve testing skills
Become a better speaker
Better common sense
Improve memory and speed
Read for 30 minutes /day
Find my talents
Become an Eagle Scout

Physical
Break school record in 5K, top 25 at State
Get a six-pack
6'3", 175 lbs.
Get rid of scar
Dunk a basketball
Qualify for State in track – place?
Mile: 4:40, 2 Mile: 9:55, 800: 2:05

Have a 25" vertical
Bench 180 lbs.

Social
Make 6 new friends
Respect teachers more
Less socially awkward
More outgoing
Ask Steph out on a date or two – maybe
Have 1 social outing per month
Be a waiter for Prom
Give two compliments a day
Show sportsmanship at every race.

Home
Think Win-win
Make deposits into PBA
Schedule the whole week on Sunday
Keep phone time to –1 hour
Job at Fiesta (or elsewhere)
Save $4,000 in bank account
Learn to play guitar
7 Habits
Set goals weekly, prioritize in planner
Procrastinate less
Shoot a nice deer and turkey
Make my bed every day
Buy everyone a Christmas present
Put the phone down
Get 8-9 hours of sleep
Monitor what I eat
Be a better hockey, soccer and track fan
Rubik's cube in sub 1:00
Books: Cross Centered Life, 7 Habits of Highly Effective Teens"

We needed a picture of Peter running to insert in the bulletin for the funeral service. That wasn't easy! Usually runners are so intense that they have pretty fierce looks on their faces as they are running, which wouldn't be appropriate for this situation at all. But it seemed like a huge blessing, after searching several hours through all the pictures people kept emailing, to find a good, thoughtful picture.

Empowered by what we were learning of Peter's witness, I wrote the obituary with the help of the family.

HEBREWS 12: 1-2

". . . let us run with perseverance the race marked out for us. Let us fix our eyes on Jesus, the author and perfecter of our faith. . . ."

"He must increase, I must decrease" John 3:30

Peter Benjamin Auch

Arrangements made by
Wass Home for Funerals
Beresford Alcester Centerville

1997 - 2013

Peter Benjamin Auch was born September 19, 1997 in Vermillion, South Dakota, to Duane and Mary (Rea) Auch. He died on November 23, 2013 in a Sioux Falls hospital due to injuries sustained in a car accident on November 22nd near Beresford. He was sixteen years, two months, and four days.

Peter was raised on the family farm southeast of Centerville with his two brothers Matthew and Jonathan and sister Julia. He attended grade school in Centerville, middle school in Beresford, and was currently a sophomore at Beresford High School.

Peter accepted Jesus as his Savior when he was four years old, after watching the JESUS film. His quiet love for God made him determined to make sure he did not "waste his life." He found that the two mission trips he took to Haiti and Pine Ridge were defining experiences that shaped his values. He attended the Brooklyn Evangelical Free Church and was active in the youth group and Bible studies, and served in various capacities.

Peter was passionate about running with the cross-country and track teams for Beresford High School. He set clear goals for his life and strategized to work toward meeting them. He loved sports, science, history, and politics. He was working on his Eagle Scout project for Boy Scouts, Sioux Council Troop 11. He was involved in student council, debate, oral interpretation, FFA, and Fellowship of Christian Athletes and basketball. Peter was known to mentor and encourage his peers to excel in academics and athletics. His warm smile, concern for friends, and fun-loving nature will be missed by all who knew him. He is survived by his parents Duane and Mary Auch of Centerville, brothers Jonathan of Sioux Falls and Matthew of Brookings, sister Julia of Brookings, and his grandmothers Elaine Rea of Los Angeles, CA, and Luella Auch of Menno, SD. Also surviving are two uncles, Steven J. (Anita) Auch of Yankton and Dennis R. (Joann) of Menno; two aunts, Joy Rosendale of Pittsburgh, PA, and Elizabeth (Jim) Tebbe of Lahore, Pakistan, and ten cousins and numerous friends.

His grandfathers John Rea and Eugene P. Auch; one aunt, Ruth Donan; and a cousin, Michael Auch, preceded him in death.

The next morning, on Monday, the *Argus Leader* and *Sioux City Journal* gave the account of the investigation done regarding the accident. The article described details of the accident that we hadn't yet heard from the highway patrol. We learned the names of all involved in the accident, how it happened, exactly where it occurred, and how long it took to clean up the highway.

On KELO-TV, the news had the same story. Many times, regarding the deaths of other people in accidents, I had seen those grim details posted on TV. It's totally different to know that on that blue screen with white print is the news everyone will see to learn of the loss of your own son. It didn't seem real. But at the same time I was overcome by how many people were able to find out about the loss.

All of us went to the funeral home on Monday to see Peter one last time. Julia hadn't seen him as he was dying, or afterward at the hospital. We had to decide for sure whether the casket would be closed for the funeral. One look at him and it was clear that it should be a closed-casket funeral. Duane, Matt, and Jon couldn't do much more than take a glance. The undertakers had done as good a job as possible considering the head injuries, but no one would have wanted to have that sight as their last memory of Peter. However, Julia needed to process that he really was gone. She tussled with his hair, smudged his makeup around to make it look better. We went back and forth with how we should leave his hair, kind of goofing off with him one last time. It didn't really look like Peter much. The gash on his face was gruesome. I felt his arms and chest, just like I had with my dad. He was hard. He really wasn't there at all. He wasn't alive at all; he was gone. It helped to touch him to say good-bye. I was glad his classmates didn't have to see him like that. The situation for them would have been far worse.

Selecting and assembling the pictures for the slideshow for the prayer service on Monday night was a horrible job. There were about a thousand pictures of his childhood years and all his sports activities to put in some order. People were sending us huge files of pictures to use, and we couldn't just leave them out as it wouldn't look very grateful. We had to get it done by 6:00 p.m. Monday. It was Sunday night when we started working on it, and by Monday morning we hadn't made much progress. By the time we returned from the funeral home I realized the whole public event for the funeral would start in less than six hours. Nothing worked well with it. The computer was slow; we lost files of pictures. I was pretty crabby. I had barely slept since the night of the accident. I was operating on empty, on the exhaust fumes of my emotions. No one seemed to be cooperating with my agenda. I was frantic. I'm sure they all had their things they needed to do to deal with their grief. To me it was a horrible to-do list with a deadline that couldn't be put off. There was not a spare moment to procrastinate. You can imagine what was happening: I was getting everyone mad at me. My controlling, take-charge nature resurged. I wasn't effective at motivating anyone to work at my speed. I left for the prayer service with Jon and Julia, leaving Matt and Duane to finish the slideshow. I hoped they'd arrive before it started! We needed a miracle to be ready.

Monday at school, teachers let kids just journal and process the whole weekend's events. The loss had impacted the entire Beresford High School, including teachers, administration, and the kids. Kids started using their Bibles to look up verses to write in their letters and journal entries to give to us (they made a wonderful binder of memories of Peter.) Kids were getting excited, reading and hunting for verses to get printed on a tee shirt to remember Peter. Kids who had never read the Bible were joining other Christian kids in reading and searching the scriptures. Kids were writing Bible verses on the blackboards in their rooms. The teachers stood by, letting the kids do what they needed to do, not violating any laws by leading the activities, but definitely not stopping their actions.

Here are some of the memories and tributes his friends wrote that day that have been very encouraging to us:

> Peter, you were such a role model to everyone around you. I praise God every day for your life. Thank you for being such an example to everyone and showing us how a godly man should live. I can't wait for the day when I will get to see your smiling face in heaven.
>
> Peter, it's amazing how much one person can influence so many people into following Christ, as you did. Not everyone is capable of such a task. You succeeded because you are pure and one of the nicest, most thoughtful people I have ever met. You're also

competitive, determined, and have perseverance. I am so glad I was lucky enough to have you in my life even for a short while. Thank you. You really did change my life for the better.

Peter, you were the coolest ever and you were the best youth group friend we ever had.

Petey, you are such an amazing man. What you accomplished in your short time will be with me forever. You changed my life and you are such a good friend. I love you, Pete, and I will always be thinking of you.

Peter, thank you for being the person you were. We all hope to spread the Word of God just like you. I'll miss Mrs. Corlew getting after you for finishing your worksheet before we got our notes done ☺. Cross-country won't be the same without you. Keep running, Bud. Miss you.

Peter, you truly taught me how to love Jesus. You were such an example to me, and I am so thankful for the blessing you were in my life. I will see you in heaven! I miss you.

Peter, I am so glad you finally get to be up with God, where you always wanted to be. I miss you so much. I feel selfish, but I really want you back. I want to live my life like you did. I have never seen a faith as strong as yours. I would give anything to have half the faith you have. I know you are still with us, and you don't want us to be sad. I'm trying. I have finally found peace! You taught me that someone can live life for Jesus. Keep running.

Petey Boy! Always the last one on the bus, but kickin' it on the course. I don't think I know a more gutsy, hard-core, go get 'em, eyes on the prize man! I love ya, Buddy!

Peter, your love for Christ was so powerful and evident. You were an amazing person, athlete, friend, and classmate. You will be forever missed. I can't wait to see you again someday.

Peter, you were an amazing friend and a great role model. Everyone looked up to you. You were so smart, nice, and funny. I will never forget the memories we shared walking through the halls together, and study hall. We all love and miss you. Keep running.

Peter is an inspiration to us. He was an amazing athlete, friend, and teammate who felt like a brother. We will never forget his smile, or the way he pushed himself every single day. He is a great role model, and every day we strive to be a little bit more like him. Peter will always be a part of our XC family and we'll never forget Peter or all the memories we made with him. We miss Peter so much, but we know someday we will be together again, and we will go on many more runs together.

Two hours before the prayer service was to start, in the middle of the picture hunt and terrible tension, Darlene, the lady who had been in the accident in the car that had been passed, came over to talk to us. I had wanted to meet her and let her know she was forgiven, and that we loved her and felt so badly that she was hurting so much about it. I'm so glad she came. I needed some closure with her. We prayed with her and it was a good, peaceful time that refocused my mind for the evening. God settled my heart by her visit, took my eyes off the pressure, and refocused my eyes on Him. She came at the worst possible time by my plans, but just at the right time by God's plans to comfort us.

About 400 people showed up at our church for the service Monday night. There were kids who had run with Peter in races from many schools around in the region, as well as his classmates and best friends and their parents. It seemed everyone who usually attended the church came. It was packed. Kids and adults shared their funny stories about Peter. Duane shared about how Peter read the book by Piper, *Don't Waste Your Life*, and had Duane do a Bible study with other guys with the same book. It had made a huge impression on Peter and caused him to change the focus of his life from just making lots of money to serving Jesus with his whole heart as a pastor. Then Pastor John shared the gospel. It was the first time I saw him do an altar call. Four girls came forward to accept Jesus' gift of salvation. Afterward many adults shared with us how Peter's life challenged them. Jake, who had taken Peter on the race after the state cross-country meet, had gotten so excited about reading a tiny *Gideon New Testament* at school that morning that Pastor John gave him a new ESV study Bible. He was so delighted to have one to read easily.

We gave out Gideon copies of a white gospel of John for teenagers. It was curious, as Duane's cousin had a dream the night he heard of Peter's death, of white Bibles being given to other kids at the funeral. We wondered what God had in mind with all this. We went home that night with hearts full of praise at what God had done. I don't recall if we had much sleep.

Funeral

The next day, Tuesday, was the funeral. Matt had decided he wanted to talk at the funeral. He was very concerned that people would just be comforted at it and go on with life, not being changed by the events of the weekend. Unless they were rescued by God, they would someday face a much different fate than Peter did. We were feeling that if this funeral didn't have any long-term effect on kids, he would have died in vain. Our hearts wanted clarification regarding the purpose of his death. It wasn't spoken between us in the family, but we needed to see God's heart in gathering Peter to Himself. So Matt prepared and wrote and wrote and worked on his speech. It was cutting it very close. I was too tired to feel panic when I saw him in his pajamas when it was time for us to leave him behind as we left for the funeral. I breathed prayers he would finish his speech, get it printed out, get dressed, and get there on time. God did another miracle, and Matt did arrive twenty minutes before it started.

As a family tradition we sang the hymn "He the Pearly Gates." It was sung at my sister's and father's memorial services. In my quiet time that morning I had read this verse from psalms:

"I proclaim righteousness in the great assembly;
I do not seal my lips, as you know, O Lord.
I do not hide your righteousness in my heart.
I speak of your faithfulness and salvation.
I do not conceal your love and your truth from
the great assembly."

Psalm 40:9, NIV

I felt compelled to help proclaim God's goodness and faithfulness to us to everyone who would come to the funeral by helping to lead the singing. I recall walking into the gymnasium. All the bleachers seemed to be down to make as many seats available for people to sit as possible. It looked like the whole town and school had shown up for the funeral. There was a great assembly of people in the high school gym—about 700 or more people. Somehow God gave me the strength to walk to the platform. The song has a very clear cut salvation message in it. The words to that song are:

Chorus:
He the pearly gates will open, so that I may enter in;
For He purchased my redemption, and forgave me all my sin.

Verses:
Love divine, so great and wondrous, deep and mighty, pure, sublime.
Coming from the heart of Jesus, just the same through tests of time!

Like a dove when hunted, frightened, as a wounded fawn was I;
Brokenhearted, yet He healed me, He will heed the sinner's cry.

Love divine, so great and wondrous! All my sins He then forgave,
I will sing His praise forever, For His blood, His power to save.

In life's eventide, at twilight, at His door I'll knock and wait;
By the precious love of Jesus, I shall enter heaven's gate.[1]

Riley, the student body president, spoke to his class using the four questions I had asked him about Peter. He challenged the kids to examine their lives. Riley was powerful in speaking to his peers. (See Appendix: Funeral Speech)

Then Matt spoke. He wasn't forceful at all in his demeanor or the delivery of his speech. I recall him looking small, worn out, speaking in a thin, quiet voice. But what he said was VERY powerful. People were shaken. The Holy Spirit took over and spoke to all of us through him. People I had prayed to come to hear the gospel showed up. Other people I hadn't had the courage to pray about came. Our doctor dropped all his appointments to be there! My CEO and all the administrative staff from the hospital came, as well as many nurses and other staff.

In Honor of Peter Auch:
His Life, His Death—What It Meant, What It Means
(Matt Auch's message at Peter's funeral)

November 26, 2013

I am Peter's brother. I think you'd all believe me if I said this is the hardest thing I've ever had to do. It is. But I also am convinced that speaking to you here is perhaps the greatest thing I've ever done. I pray that the words I have to say to you will be truly significant. That they will define the impact that Peter Auch made during his life and set the stage for the impact his life will make even after he's dead. For as Maximus Decimus Meridius said in the Gladiator, *"What we do in life echoes in eternity." We comfort ourselves by saying that he is with Jesus. And he most certainly is. That kid had a passion for the Lord; it drove everything he did. But even though*

---

[1] "He the Pearly Gates Will Open," Frederick A. Blom, 1917. Public Domain.

so many of you have comforted me, my family, and each other, even though it has truly touched me deeply and I appreciate it so much, what I am here to give you is not comfort. I hope that what I say will not be comforting, because I believe there is something more important. I am here to honor my brother. I am here to honor my Lord and my God, Jesus Christ who saved both Peter and myself. I am here to stir your hearts, not settle them. I am here to make you honor Peter's life by considering your own. By letting the tremors of this tragedy shake the foundations of your life by asking, "What am I living for?"

I am here with a rare opportunity, the opportunity to speak on behalf of the dead, to speak what he can no longer say for himself. Not all of you saw very much of Peter's life, not enough to really understand him. I want to interpret to you the words Peter spoke with his life so you will know what they meant, so you can understand, so the meaning isn't lost on you. Many of us are asking why Peter was killed. Why would God take him from us when we loved him so much and he had so much potential for his life? This isn't supposed to happen. People aren't supposed to die when they are sixteen years old. When I have to explain to my professors that I won't be in class and I see the words typed, "Because my little brother Peter was killed in a car accident," those words seem absurd, surreal, like my life got switched with some hellish alternate reality. I'm thinking this doesn't make sense and I'm asking, "Did this really happen?" But it's true. This is reality. And when I accept that, it might surprise you, but I'm not asking, "Why did this happen?" I know why. I hate it; I would have never have done it this way. I wish God had chosen another way, never would have put any of us through this agony. But I know why: it was for you. For you who knew him, for you who would hear of him. It was so you would understand and love the gospel. It was so God could show you His love, and sovereignty, grace, and glory. So God could show you Himself in ways that were impossible otherwise. I know why Peter died because I know what he was living for.

As Peter lay there dying in Avera McKennan Hospital and I stood by his side, I read this to him from Philippians. This passage defines my life. It defines his life. Paul wrote, "But whatever gain I had, I counted as loss for the sake of Christ. Indeed, I count everything as loss because of the surpassing greatness of knowing Christ Jesus my Lord. For His sake I have suffered the loss of all things and count them as rubbish, in order that I may gain Christ and be found in him, not having a righteousness of my own that comes from the law, but that which comes through faith in Christ, the righteousness from God that depends on faith - That I may know Him and the power of his resurrection, and may share in His sufferings, becoming like Him in his death, that by any means possible I may attain the resurrection from the dead. Not that I have already obtained this or am already perfect, but I press on to make it my own, because Christ Jesus has made me his own. Brothers I do not consider that I have made it my own. But one thing I do: forgetting what lies behind and straining forward to what lies ahead, I press on toward the goal for the prize of the upward call of God in Christ Jesus" Philippians 3:7–14, ESV.

When Paul said, "whatever gain I had, I counted as loss for the sake of Christ," he spoke about everything that he had done in his life that he thought was worth something, everything that he had given his life to before he came to know Christ. Paul was one of the elites, a leader in society, respected in the temple for his zeal; he had a flawless résumé. What about Peter? What was his gain? You all know he was a standout kid. Everything a high schooler could be. From cross-country, basketball, track, Boy Scouts, FFA, student council, to debate, he was in it. Everyone looked up to him; you all liked him. He loved life and wanted to get as much out of it as possible. We enjoyed being with him because he was not at all afraid to loosen up and have a great time, and we all loved that about him.

But at the same time he was such a driven kid, driven like no one I've ever seen. He knew what he wanted out of life, and everything he did was to meet that end. He pursued excellence in everything, and his goal was not just to excel, but to challenge others to excel. A true leader, he led by example. It might have seemed like he was naturally gifted, but the truth for him was 1 Corinthians 15:10: "But by the grace of God I am what I am, and His grace toward me was not in vain. On the contrary, I worked harder than any of them, though it was not I, but the grace of God that is with me."

But as great as all those things were that Peter involved himself in, to him they were losses. Compared to the surpassing greatness of knowing Jesus Christ, everything he did, to him was nothing. Yesterday I found a notebook in his room that had a two-page list of goals for every major area of his life. It included things like "break the school 5K record," "finish my Eagle Scout," "make five new friends," "get top 25 at state," "no A minuses," "get a six-pack," "be less awkward." These goals shot high, but I believe none was a stretch. But for all the worldly goals he listed, you can see on the back of your program in Peter's own handwriting the words he had written at the top of the page before listing a single goal. The words of John 3:30: "He must increase. I must decrease." Then after he had written that, the first goal he had listed was "To make Christ the center of my life." For him everything he did was never about the glory he was going to get from doing well. He was living for something more than himself. He pursued excellence because he was convinced that to settle for anything short of it was to rob God of glory.

Peter was over at my place once, scanning over my bookshelf. He pulled out one book that had really changed my life when I read it freshman year of college. If you were there last night, my dad and Pastor John talked about it. It was Don't Waste Your Life *by John Piper. He sheepishly asked me, "Can I have this?" I said, "Only if you read it." He read it all right. In a lot of ways it changed his life, or maybe it would be better to say it summarized a change that God was working in his life in many ways. A lot of days when I was home for the summer, I would go into his room and he'd be there sleeping. Dad would have work for us to do so I'd wake him up by saying, "Are you just going to lay there all day, or are you gonna get up and do something with your life?" You know, I had to give a hard time; it's what brothers do. I think that egged him on. His passion was to make his life count for something. He did not want to waste his life. I knew he wouldn't. I was so impressed with the way God was shaping him. I'd look at the books he had lying around his room. I'd see the way he interacted with his friends. I'd hear about everything he was involved in and taking the lead in. I'd watch him run, train, and workout. I would look at the way he approached and examined his life, the way he invested in people, the way he invested in what he had set his mind to do. He had confidence; he had a serious but fun-loving spirit. And I was absolutely sure that he would grow up to be a great man, a truly great man. He was in it for the long haul. He was on fire but not the kind that lasts for a minute; the kind of fire that sustains itself and burns for a lifetime. But I was wrong. I was wrong that he would grow up to be a great man. I was wrong because he already was.*

As soon as I got to the ICU and I stood by his broken body lying there on the bed, I held his big old hand, pulled out a Bible, and also whispered these words to him from Philippians 1:20–23: "It is my eager expectation and hope that I will not be at all ashamed, but that with full courage now as always Christ will be honored in my body, whether by life or by death. For me to live is Christ and to die is gain. If I am to live in the flesh, that means fruitful labor for me. Yet which I shall choose I cannot tell. I am hard pressed between the two. My desire is to depart and be with Christ, for that is far better."

Before Peter died I asked him, "What is it like? What is it like to see our Lord?" A part of me wanted to be in his place; I was envious of him with every fiber of my being. It seemed so natural, yet so strange, to die. I couldn't have imagined the trauma to his face with the injuries he had sustained, but there was something beautiful in those last moments that drew me to him. I stroked his hair and his face; when blood drained from his nose into his swollen eye and ran out the corner like a tear, I wiped it away. He was so incredibly bashed up, but somehow he still looked so much like himself. I couldn't help but think that Jesus did not look much different at all as He hung there on the cross, as He took his last breath and said, "It is finished." He had done what He was born to do; so had Peter. We think of all the great things that Peter could have done with his life and it seems that his life was cut short. But that thought is just an illusion. That's how it seems, but it's not how it is. The reality is that Peter did everything that he was destined to do. For Jesus, death was not the end; through His resurrection Jesus overcame death and the grave so that as Peter died we could say, "O death, where is your victory? Grave where is your sting?"

Death is gain because Peter is in the presence of God, enjoying Him and His glory forever. But there is another reason Paul could state so confidently that "to die is gain." It is a paradox. Death is the loss of all the future you were looking forward to with that person. Every time I think about all the things I wanted to do with him that I now can't, I start shaking. I collapse to the ground, curl up in the fetal position, and just sob. And it's only by the grace of God that as I've seen a lot of you and as I stand here that I can be strong. God has given me this to say, so He gives the strength to say it. I wish I could go skiing with him and Jon over Christmas break, just brothers, like we had planned, go backpacking through every national park in the southwest US, like I promised we would the last time we took a road trip. I promised we would come back and really dig in and see everything. I wish I could be at his graduation, to see him give the valedictorian speech, because you all know he was gonna beat you out. That was his goal, and he did what he said. I wish I could move him in to his dorm room. I wish someday he would call me up and say, "So, there's this girl." I wish at my own wedding I could look to my left and see him standing there with his sheepish grin. But I can't. He is dead. And somehow his death is gain. His death is gain because all those things he did in his life, he did for you. He wanted to lead you and he knew he could only do that through being an example. He wanted you all to be the best that you could be, to know the same sense of purpose that he felt. He wanted you to know Jesus the way he knew Him. And though Peter did not intend to die, I am convinced that his death is gain because through death he has impacted us deeply. Through death he will secure those dreams he had for you more surely than he ever could by living. He had to die to point you to the Savior who died so that you could live. There were things he wanted to get started, things that he was passionate about that frustrated him. He was frustrated because he wanted to see the same drive and sense of seriousness, the same passion in all of you who he lived with. He wanted to see that in the youth group, in a Bible study brotherhood with a few guys, in FCA, in the "Don't Waste Your Life" study he asked my dad to lead. But as much fruit as there was in those things, he wasn't satisfied. He dreamed of more. But those dreams are not lost; whether they will be realized is yet to be seen.

He had lived well. He was free to die well. "What we do in life echoes in eternity." This life for Peter is closed. He lived for roughly 5,904 days, but for how many more days those days will echo is yet to be determined. It's up to you. Don't pray for me. God is keeping me strong. Pray for yourselves. Don't be comforted. Be changed. Don't kill the pain. Dig into it. In this moment our hearts are burning red hot like an iron. Don't quench it just yet. Not before you have been shaped, not before you have been refined. Examine your life. Consider what Jesus said: "If anyone would come after me, let him deny himself and take up his cross daily and follow me. For whoever would seek to save his life will lose it. But whoever loses his life for my sake and the Gospel's will find it." If you don't know Jesus, then take a look at your life and ask, "Am I satisfied?" Ask, "Will I be able to face my own death with confidence that I had not lived for myself, but that I had given my life to follow the one who died to give me life?" Peter's life was not wasted because that's what he lived for. His death is not wasted because you are all here. What would comfort me would be that you would honor him. What would honor him would be to see you light ablaze with a passion for Jesus Christ the way my brother had. Peter did not waste his life. Now I would ask you not to waste his death.

We sat there stunned, unable to shed tears, with our hearts on fire with God's message to us. When Matt was done, Julia sang the "Lord's Prayer." While in high school she had sung the national anthem before games many times in that gym. It was so fitting after Matt's powerful message. It was a benediction to all he said, giving people time to let his words sink in. It was very healing for the community to hear her sing for Jesus and her brother. It felt like God was touching us with a blessing of His peace that comes when we submit to His plan and reach out for His help. Pastor John then spoke about running the race of the spiritual life, including the start of the race when you become a Christian and continuing on no matter what, "looking unto Jesus."

It had snowed and become bitterly cold between the time of the accident and funeral. Few people went to the internment due to the weather. I dreaded that part of the whole day more than anything. It would be so final to see his casket beside the gaping hole and realize I would never see my baby in person again. He'd be gone physically forever. The finality of it is so horrible that it still brings tears to my eyes as I write this. But God is so amazing to shield us when we just can't take anymore. I got out of the car right near the gate of the cemetery. Three of Peter's friends came running right up to me. They were giggling and wanted to know how Peter got the scar on his cheek. They meant the one he had under his right eye. I stopped to tell them how he had banged into a metal trunk when he was eighteen months old, and how two weeks later it broke open again when he ran into me. They told me all the goofy stories he had told them, about a cow kicking him and chickens pecking his face and leaving the dots (where the stitches were). The girls got me laughing so hard at how silly he was, that I could hardly focus on the final prayers under the dreaded tent. God helped me with humor to be in a positive frame of mind to talk to everyone waiting for me in the Fellowship Hall, where they were gathered. In His providence He knew what I'd be feeling and put those girls there with what many would consider as inappropriate behavior, just when I needed to be protected from my dread being played out.

Matt's speech was a very important puzzle piece in our lives and the lives of many other people. God sovereignly spoke through him to work on forming the Kingdom of God in the hearts of all who heard him speak. Very quickly we found out that people were powerfully affected by what Matt said. He clarified for all of us God's purpose for the difficult time we all faced. Many people wrestle with the "why" of the death of a loved one. To me it seemed that Matt answered the question before most of us had time or the emotion to put a voice to it. Moreover the dramatic circumstances surrounding Peter's death provided an obvious answer to the question, which is different from the bewilderment triggered by most grief situations. Matt proclaimed to all of us, "I know why. It was for you. For you who knew him, for you who would hear of him. It was so you would understand the gospel. It was so God could show you His love, and sovereignty, grace, and glory. So God could show you Himself in ways that were impossible otherwise." Matt set the tone for the community's healing. I have rarely heard people ask since then, "Why did God take Peter?" They knew it was because Peter made them aware of Jesus. His life displayed Jesus to his peers. His death proclaimed the gospel to all of us. His life had purpose, so his death reflected the same. He was part of God's glorious puzzle.

Most people who lose loved ones struggle with the why question. A premature death just doesn't make sense. Usually there isn't a clear answer why God gathers someone to Himself before their life is fully lived by our standards. Why would a sovereign, powerful God, who has the complete ability to stop someone from dying in an accident, or a God who has the power to heal a fatal disease, or a God who has the power to rescue a small child from death, not use that power to preserve life? It's OK to ask God why He took our loved one. It's very important to be honest with God and lament and cry out to Him with all our raw complaints and hurts. We need to feel free to tell God, "I don't understand what You are doing!" "I hate what's happened!" The psalms show us that we must "pour out our hearts" to God, as He patiently hears our cries, before He bows down to compassionately answer us. If we cry long enough and honestly enough, God will show up to meet our needs. When we lament we are telling God, "I know You're sovereign and can do something about my pain; I trust You to meet me where I'm at and comfort me." Our lament is an expression of hanging on to God. It indicates that He is a God worth clinging to, and in return He holds us closely to Himself. Those who pour out their grief to God grow to know God's heart. The hopeless person gives up on God and never communicates with Him, and gets hardened and falls away from their faith. But those with faith accept that their plans are not God's plans and His ways are not their ways. Eventually, as they pour out their hearts to God, they join Job as he indicated that now his heart knew God:

"My ears had heard of You, but now my eyes have seen You."

JOB 42:5, NIV

And that is the answer to the why question for most of us: the reason for the loss is to put us in a circumstance in which we are challenged to grow to know God. God dearly wants us to know Him, not just know about Him. He faced horrendous pain to enable us to reestablish a relationship with Him in sending Jesus to die to ultimately save us and make us right with God. He may have to use extraordinary means to make sure we draw near and don't stay aloof from Him, wandering in a dessert of dry, dreary, religious experience. That's a harsh thing to admit, especially when it hurts so much to lose someone we love. But God desires our communion with Himself much more than He wants to make and keep us happy in a life free of troubles.

Faith realizes that God gives us the information we need regarding the reason for the death of someone we love. Some people have more revealed to them than others. Even knowing why won't change the day-to-day problem of dealing with loneliness and emptiness. Even though we know the big picture, we will still hurt and grieve. Jesus grieved for His friend Lazarus, to the extent that He wept despite the fact that He knew why he died. Jesus knew of God's resurrection power and the miracle God was going to do, but still mourned for the trouble and emotional pain the death caused to Mary and Martha, who were the sisters of Lazarus.

Understanding that God is big enough to have a purpose for the death of those we love is a comfort in itself, even if He keeps the purpose hidden from us. We can rest in God with that understanding. He didn't just let Peter die randomly. He doesn't let others die without a reason. If nothing else, we can trust that our loved one is part of the puzzle that He's putting together and that He will be glorified in some way. If nothing else happens besides our relationship with God deepening, our trust strengthening, and our understanding that God is still good, He is glorified.

The funeral became a line in the sand in my mind regarding my trust in God. It was clear that He deserved all the praise and honor and credit for the amazing things He had done in my life. He was a God who could be trusted to be with me in a wide range of trials and joys in life. He was my rock and the one who was using events in my life for His glory. I had seen signs of His loving-kindness and tenderness when I was at the bottom. He had become a God I could trust even in the terrible pain of Peter's death.

I have concluded that one of the major purposes for the loss of my son was because the grief period deepened my relationship with God in a way that nothing else could have done. The grieving process was the time period of my life when my love for God increased. If Peter did not accomplish anything else in his life and death, what he did do was to catapult his mother into learning to love and understand God more profoundly.

Simultaneously God proved to me in new, amazing ways the depth of His love for me. Receiving His love enabled me to respond in love to Him in new ways. Processing my grief enabled me to grow in this new relationship. Jesus said in Matthew that the first and greatest commandment is to:

> **"…love the Lord your God with all your heart and**
> **with all your soul and with all your mind,**
> **And a second is like it: You shall love**
> **your neighbor as yourself."**
>
> MATTHEW 22:37, ESV

That verse is a good road map for the grief journey. I had to accept my loss, find strength and comfort from Him in His Word, and respond to Him in faith and love Him with all my being. Only then was I ready to begin to focus outward to develop a new normal pattern in life, find joy in my new identity in Christ, and move forward to serve others in the Kingdom of God. God had to sovereignly put many puzzle pieces in place to accomplish this in my life. He was continuing to include me in His glorious puzzle of shaping us to be like Jesus so His Kingdom would be spread.

PART 2

Grief Recovery: A Context for Growing in Love

SHOCK

G rief for a person who died suddenly is often intense and chaotic. There is a feeling of shock. It is harsh. Nothing is normal. It feels like our lives have been shattered. The puzzle of our lives that was put together, in neat order suddenly gets dropped and the pieces are scattered so far and wide that we can't pick them up to put them back together. We can feel as if we are losing our minds because grief consumes every aspect of our self. Grief may feel like arrows and barbs of many disjointed, painful memories or problems being hurled at us from every direction, with no shield to protect us.

Grief is the price we pay for loving someone intensely, the degree of our grief often being measured by the depth and closeness of our relationship. Grief is unpredictable and everyone experiences it differently. Despite the fact that two people in the same family are grieving for the same person, they may have a difficult time relating to each other since their reactions are so different. Grief sometimes shatters close relationships with living loved ones, too.

Grief may be experienced as waves in the ocean that come crashing in over you. You unexpectedly get swept under the wave of intense emotion, struggling to keep your head up, gasping for breath. Triggers of intense reaction surprise you when you think you are in control. It can be humiliating to suddenly dissolve in tears in public just because you saw something that reminded you of the person you lost. In the early days of grief, you may do things that you never expected.

One of the most troubling things Christians face is that God may seem very far away. People often do not feel His presence at all. The truth is that He is with us and promises to comfort us. Grief can be a time of drawing near to Jesus and growing in love for Him, or it may be the opposite. Satan is a thief who has as his purpose to steal, kill, and destroy, and if allowed, the time of grief can be the means he uses to destroy a Christian's faith. Grief is a big puzzle piece in each Christian's life; it reveals the extent to which we are allowing God to control our lives and be Lord of the situation.

Over time and with lots of hard work to deal with the grief, the tide of grief goes out and the waves of pain are less intense. When there is a low tide the waves still lap at your feet, but they aren't as bothersome and don't sweep you under where you are gasping for air. The puzzle pieces of your life start to get put pack into place. There may be some gaping holes left from the pieces getting damaged when they crashed apart, but those are spaces through which Jesus can shine through us to bring light to other hurting people.

Just like a person who puts a puzzle together, working on one part of it then jumping over to another section, then to another and back to the first area, people learning to deal with their grief jump from one task of grief to another. When I led a grief recovery support group (GriefShare), I developed an object lesson that illustrates this. Picture a ball made of various colors of rubber bands, all wrapped around a core. Each color represents one task of grief: acceptance, finding comfort in God and His people, finding a new normal and identity, and moving forward and eventually finding joy at the core. As you deal with your grief you take off one rubber band at a time, each one representing one of the tasks that need to be done. You usually can't accomplish all there is to do in one of the tasks at one time. Similarly with the rubber band ball, you work on a little of the issue of acceptance, then work on developing a closer relationship with other people, find yourself functioning better in life, and so on. Then you return to these issues again as you progress, gradually removing all the colors of the rubber bands. At the center is the new life to which God calls you. There is joy along the way, but at the core the predominant feeling is a restful peace in God, with a heart welling up in praise for His presence and comfort.

These grief tasks don't happen in a nice consecutive order. As God puts the puzzle of our lives back together, He works on one part, then another, then another until finally we feel whole enough to move forward into a new life and area of service. In the following chapters, for the sake of being coherent, my story is organized by topical sections instead of chronological occurrence. But I didn't experience the puzzle pieces in nice, neat topics; I didn't finish one grief task and then move on to the next. Everything occurred in an unpredictable fashion, sort of in a jumble. But I believe it was all put together just as God intended.

Much of my grieving was intense internal drama. Outsiders couldn't see the massive overhaul of my heart taking place as I walked through the valley of the shadow of death holding Jesus' hand. It is common that after a funeral, grieving people turn inward. On-lookers may think they are handling things well. However, there is an intense internal struggle to make sense of the tragedy and loss and to allow God to conform thoughts and desires to ones that bring wholeness and healing.

Coping

In those first few days I found a great deal of comfort in imagining what Peter was doing in heaven. I was so grateful for the assurance that Peter was in God's presence. I imagined that he had met up with his grandfather, my dad. He was challenging him to go out jogging with him to get in shape. I was troubled about Peter having to wear some sort of confining robe in heaven, until I remembered the *Chariots of Fire* movie. The runners in that movie, depicting the Olympics in 1924, wore off-white colored shorts and shirts. I imagined that God let Peter wear what he was most comfortable in: running gear. Then my mind was drawn to imagine Peter racing Eric Liddell, the runner in those Olympics who refused to dishonor God by running on Sunday, forfeiting the possible gold medal for the team and USA. I envisioned Peter looking up the forty heroes of the faith that we had read about in family devotions. He must have been so happy getting to know them in person! I had a picture in my mind of Peter relaxing, sitting with my father (his grandfather), discussing all his Bible questions.

I was on an adrenaline high for the first week at least. I had boundless energy. Noting God's grace and goodness in working in the hearts of so many people kept me going. I wanted to help other people who were feeling the loss; it was a way I could deal with the pain without having to concentrate on my own feelings. That would come later. We were supposing Peter's immediate friends were experiencing lots of pain. The day after Thanksgiving, I felt compelled to bring some clothes of Peter's over to Jake, with whom he had run in cross-country. His mom was putting up Christmas decorations. Any thoughts of the upcoming holidays hadn't entered my mind since the afternoon Peter drove off to the youth group event, never to be seen alive again. I was baking Christmas cookies when my world was forever changed, but Christmas was the furthest thing from my mind from then on. I was surprised that life was going on as usual for other people. My world had turned upside down. Time had stopped in my mind. Her son, the one who had been given the Bible after the prayer service, was in his room, and hadn't left it much at all since the funeral a few days previous. He wasn't talking about what he experienced. But that kid turned to Jesus in his grief. He read and read and read his new Bible. He grew in his faith like I've never seen before. I've never seen anyone devour the Word of God like he did. That kid was transformed. God plowed up the soil of his heart, making him accept the seed of the Word of God. He's grown and matured in his faith and is still serving God full steam ahead, bearing fruit that glorifies God wherever he goes.

The day after the funeral I stopped in the clinic to see my doctor. I needed to distribute funeral flowers to people and decided to give some to him. He had delivered Peter, and has been our family doctor for all of our kids' lives. I knew he would be hurting that he had lost his little patient. He had encouraged Peter in his running, being an athlete himself. I remember going to his office, handing him a bouquet of red and white flowers. He hugged me as I was telling him about the message Matt had given. I was so surprised when he said he had been there. I was so grateful to God for allowing our doctor to hear the gospel and see God's power speaking through Matt and singing through Julia.

The Saturday after Thanksgiving we went as a family to the body shop in Beresford where Peter's Grand Am car remains had been taken. It was terribly cold. The car was covered with a blue tarp, to protect kids from seeing and imagining the trauma of the crash. We were horrified as we looked through the smashed car for his belongings. We envisioned what he had experienced in the last seconds. Although hard, it was good to see the car to begin to accept his death and face my grief.

In the first few days after Peter's funeral somehow God started filling me with gratefulness. I was so thankful that Peter's death didn't seem in vain. So many people had heard of Jesus and had been challenged to think seriously about what they were doing with their lives. It was so clear to me that God was glorified by everything that happened at the funeral. I was seeing everything through a lens of gratitude and joy. My feeble heart could reach up and love Him for giving Peter's death a known purpose.

Muddle

Besides gratitude, what I experienced in the initial days was an intense fear that I'd forget all of Peter's mannerisms, the way his voice sounded, quirks, things he said, and things we experienced together. This came to a head when I found six half-consumed glasses of water around the house, in the bathroom, his room, the kitchen, living room, and the like. As I dumped them all out I recalled how determined he was to keep hydrated so he could run well, but that he was pretty poor at keeping things neat and organized. I felt that if I wasn't careful all my memories would be poured down the drain, just like I had poured out his water glasses and washed away all the traces of him. Fear was invading my heart.

I have a poor long-term memory, and I knew how many of the cute things from the kids' baby and toddler years had vanished from my memory. I was terrified that if I let Peter's memory die he would be totally gone from my life and I'd forget him. I started writing any memories that surfaced whenever I could to avoid this. Pictures helped a lot, but they were stagnant and still. They seemed to scream that Peter was dead. What meant much to me was a video that his cross-country coach made of the trip to Rapid City for the state meet. I could see Peter moving and in action and hear his voice. It was precious to me and I watched it over and over. It kept him alive in my heart when I wasn't ready to let him go.

My brain was so totally full of things about the funeral, trying to figure out how the accident happened, trying to remember all I could before it was too late, and trying to handle all the details of taking care of all the legal issues, that I must have been totally worthless at work. Duane was bearing the brunt of the aftermath of his son's death, but the discussions together about issues were exhausting. I took off work for just one week before returning to my job. All my outpatient nutrition counseling had been cancelled for a month. But I had to do the routine things required for caring for the long-term care residents and hospital patients. No one else could fill in my place. Fortunately it was the holiday season, so the hospital census was low. I was very inefficient. I could focus slightly on what I was doing at my desk, but just under the surface of my thoughts were Peter and all that happened. My attention wandered away; part of my job is to look at what a person's weight was between various dates to assess their nutritional health. Peter's death date was always the line drawn in my mind when determining when any weight change occurred. Did it happen when he was alive or afterward? My office was far removed from the rest of the hospital, on the third floor where hospital staff seldom came. No one else in the facility came up there except for some occasional training classes down the hall. I was alone and could deal with things by myself. How good God was to keep me there in that solitude, when I needed it so much! I've moved to eleven different offices in the thirty years I've worked in Vermillion, but that office was just where I needed to be then. God is sovereign even over our office space! How often I felt His love surround me as my mind wandered and He encouraged me with verses that came to mind.

Going back to work quickly was good for me, possibly because it was a health-care setting where death is commonplace conversation. No one seemed uncomfortable with me being with them and talking about whatever came to my mind. They didn't seem to grope for what words to say. My friends at work were amazingly open in letting me blurt out anything about the dying process, funeral, organ tissue donation, Peter's life, my feelings, and so on. They seemed to want to talk about what they had observed and heard at Peter's funeral and their feelings about valuing their kids. God blessed me so much whenever I'd go to work. They acted as God's love personified.

Exhaustion

Many people have noted how exhausting grief is for them. I, too, felt totally worn out each day once I started back to work. Being vulnerable to people, even if they are helping you, is exhausting to a person in grief. I could muster enough energy to go to my desk and just do the basics. I found that walking on my treadmill each morning as I watched GriefShare videos helped to give me some energy to get going. But if something would trigger crying or even a few tears, it felt as if all my life was drained out of me. Many grieving people avoid situations that trigger tears or strong emotional reactions. I didn't really have that luxury. Things happened at work that couldn't be avoided. I had to face things and muster strength to get through it. I stuffed my tears, allowing myself only to get choked up when waves of emotion surged over me. But when driving, it felt dangerous when a wave of grief would hit. Grief captures all your concentration, and if this happens on the road it may leave you too weak to respond quickly when you most need to be alert. God protected me as I drove back and forth to work.

I when I returned to work after Thanksgiving, I turned my flip-type calendar back to November 23 to see what verse was printed for the day. The reference was from the psalms:

> **"Those who sow in tears will reap with songs of joy.**
> **He who goes out weeping, carrying seed to sow,**
> **will return with songs of joy, carrying**
> **sheaves with him."**
>
> PSALM 126:5–6, NIV

God gave me that verse to treasure and claim as a promise. I had sown in tears, watching my son die. But God was starting to give me assurance that Peter's life would have a great impact on others and that it would bring great joy to us and the community. When I felt really down and sad as I worked, I often turned to November 23, read the verse again, and worshiped God for His promise. This morning I read a quote from C. S. Lewis that reads, "It is in the process of being worshiped that God communicates His presence to men." As I look back on those days I felt God's nearness as I praised Him. The more I praised in my pain and brokenness, the closer He was. He was with me as I sang at church, no matter how many tears streamed down my face. The more I worshiped Him, the bigger God got in my mind and heart, and the smaller my grief seemed. Praise magnifies God in the place of our hearts so that He is big enough to take care of our pain.

There was an enormous task to face in writing thank-you notes for all the plants, flowers, help, and money people had given. I imagine it amounted to around four hundred notes. The task was overwhelming, to put it mildly. My sister Joy, who had flown in the night before the funeral, offered to help write them. I let her do some. But by the time I got into the task I realized how beneficial it was in my grief process to write them myself. I really resented her doing any of the thank-you notes because I couldn't feel the benefits! I wanted to finish all the notes before Christmas. Right after the holiday we were taking a mission trip of seven people to Haiti. I really needed to get them done so I'd be free to do the final organizing of the trip. So I set a goal to write ten notes each morning for a month before leaving for work or the day's activities. If you know me, or maybe you've guessed, I'm kind of wordy. My notes were kind of long. I have small print, and if I write the common two-sentence thank-you note, it looks rather dumb on a card. Besides that I really felt grateful for all the amazing ways people I hardly knew blessed us. So as I wrote, the gratitude welled up in me. God supernaturally gave me joy and a grateful heart each morning. It became a powerful way to see what God had done to shower us with His love through so many people. It became another form of worship. God was so near to me every morning as I wrote those notes. I felt His comfort through each person. I realized that God was blessing me over and over with all these precious people I hardly knew. The thank-you-note stage of grieving became one of the most therapeutic and healing parts of that early grief process. When the last note was done, shortly before Christmas, I was honestly sad because that powerful trigger to praise and worship God wasn't available any longer.

Denial

Right after Thanksgiving, Matt and Julia had to return back to classes at SDSU and prepare for finals. Jon went back to his group home, and my sister Joy returned to her place. Duane and I were left alone. I noticed that food piled up in the refrigerator because Peter wasn't there to eat huge amounts anymore. The house was pretty empty. However, because all the other kids had gone back to school, my brain, in some self-protective mechanism, told me that Peter was just away like they were. He'd be coming home for Christmas after final examinations, just like the other kids. The first task of grief recovery is to accept the death of the person you love, to really understand and feel that they are gone for eternity. It took a long time, over one or two years, for me to get to this place of acceptance. I was so full of denial that I got to the place I even denied his existence. We had family pictures in our bedroom of the first three kids before Peter was born. It was very easy to just pretend that Peter hadn't been born when I saw those photos on my dresser. The pain was too much to take sometimes, so I just blocked it all out with a lie. Grief blurs our perception of reality.

I realized I had to face reality or I'd get stuck in denial and really be a mess. I had taken a picture of Peter in the ICU, just a minute or two after he died. I looked and looked at the picture on my phone, absorbing every detail of the gruesome sight to get my head back into reality when the denial would take over. Finally the phone needed to be replaced, and the picture wasn't loaded up in a predominant place on my new phone to see it routinely. By that time I was ready to let it go. Acceptance was sinking in. But when death happens suddenly, the enormity of it all is overwhelming and a person's mind cannot fathom the loss all at once. Acceptance happens gradually over time.

Matt graduated from SDSU in civil engineering two weeks after Peter's death. How he ever took finals and got through those hard weeks are only by God's grace. Matt's best friend Kyle had recently lost his father and was a huge support to him. We knew Matt was planning to go on a six-month trip to Africa as a type of missions engineering internship in January, in just thirty days, or a month away, but the location hadn't been determined. We were chatting about his plans with friends after the ceremony. Matt mentioned that the organization had made the decision to send him to South Sudan. At that time that country was a very dangerous place. Many Africans had been killed in the warfare between the north and south; it wasn't a safe place for expatriates, either. I sucked in my breath when I heard him say where he was going. My heart cried out to God in pain, *God, you just took one son. Are You going to take another, too? Do I have to give up two sons for You?* I was rather horrified at my attitude toward God that I wasn't willing to suffer for Him as much as He had suffered for me. As it turned out the organization switched the assignment to

Uganda. But Matt decided he needed time to grieve and heal. He couldn't face such a big task so far away from home right away without the support of his friends. He stayed home with us instead for a semester. During that time he changed his plans to go on staff with the Navigators (a para church college campus ministry) for the following year and spent most of his time raising financial support.

Support

A big concern we had just after the funeral was for all the hurting students at Beresford High School. They had been so sweet to make big banners for us with their memories and kind words and Bible verses. But they were hurting. Duane called his college roommate who worked with GriefShare in Orange City, Iowa, to come to Beresford to meet with the kids. Ken and the coleader of the support group, Mary Block, and my niece met with the kids one evening. The students didn't say much at all. I learned through that experience that when a classmate dies, kids react differently than adults. Kids need tangible events and tasks to process their feelings. They need an experience to be arranged for them, at which they can do something to give voice to their feelings. We had a lantern launch on Christmas night for that reason. Many kids braved very cold weather to send up lanterns into the night air. It was a way of releasing their pent-up feelings. Kids had taken things from the wrecked car at the body shop. They needed items to hang on to when their friend seemed so far away. I had been angry about the pilfering, but those kids needed what they could find in the car to get some comfort. They appreciated the tee shirts of Peter's that I gave to them as a means of feeling close to their friend.

Matt's graduation was on the first Saturday of December. That is the traditional day we went together as a family to a Christmas tree farm to cut down a tree, get it set up, and put the lights on it. The other kids had drifted away from that tradition due to being in college, but Peter had done it with us and without them for several years. I just had no idea

how to handle facing that tradition or any aspects of the Christmas celebration so soon after the funeral. I didn't have any interest in celebrating
or any energy to expend in the process at all. We had talked as a family,
and having the house totally decorated as usual was very important to the
three kids. They needed that comfort and security to keep it from being
a terribly sad time. They were used to me doing it all so they could just
come home and enjoy the holiday ambiance. A precious friend at church
asked me on the Sunday after Thanksgiving what she could do to help. I
knew she meant it. I told her that I just had no idea how to get the tree
decorated for the kids. The worst part to me at any Christmas is the fight
with the string of tangled lights to put on after Duane gets the tree in the
stand. My friend assured me she'd take care of it for me. When we came
home from Matt's graduation late that night, we drove up to the house
and saw through the patio door's windows a beautiful live tree, decorated
and glowing with the lights. What a huge blessing! I will never forget
the love my friend gave to us that day by that great act of kindness. It
was the most beautiful live tree we ever had for Christmas. Jesus met my
need when I was totally unable to meet my kids' need for comfort. God
is so good!

Right after New Year's, we took a small group of people and our
daughter Julia on a mission trip to Haiti. There was no way to back out
of the trip due to all the money everyone would lose on tickets. It really
wasn't too wise to do something so stressful so soon after losing a loved
one. I don't recall much about that trip except that it was very hard due
to the communication barrier. If you haven't been through the grieving
process for someone close to you, you may not be aware that a grieving
person often has a need to tell their story over and over and over and over.
It helps to diminish the intensity of all their emotions to a level where it's
not so overwhelming and consuming. I had a huge need to tell Peter's
story repeatedly. My friends at work listened every day. People at church
helped to process my grief as well. But in Haiti, although the Christians
in the church had prayed for us in the days just after his death, they had
no idea what to say and couldn't understand anything I said in English. I

had pent-up feelings that just had no possible means to be expressed on that trip. By the end I felt like I was going to explode. The takeaway from that experience is that if you are a friend to someone who has lost a close person in their lives, let them talk and talk. You don't have to say much. Just ask a simple question to give them the freedom to open up, then listen, even if they say the same thing over and over. You are helping them. Don't be afraid you'll make them cry if you ask questions. They need to express it. Keeping it all inside is very painful. Grieving people often feel like a volcano ready to erupt if there isn't a way to express themselves. Giving them a safe place to cry with you drains out the intensity of their pent-up emotions.

PURPOSE

Magnet

When Matt came home after he graduated, he was determined to help us figure out how to break the password/code on Peter's cellphone. He needed to figure out the four digits that would enable us to look at anything he had stored in it. Matt asked Peter's friends what code he could have used. No one had any ideas. So Matt methodically started trying every number possible, beginning with 0000. On January 10, 2014, my journal records states that he finally found the number. It was 1123. There is absolutely no significance to that number except the date of his death, 11/23. We have no idea why Peter chose that number. He didn't seem to do things at random; they had a reason. There were some texts there. He didn't save much. I was the last person he texted that afternoon, as I was shopping. He hadn't been looking at his phone at all when he was driving. How we thank God for that. He was innocent. He had three last sweet texts to his best friends. He pointed them to Jesus in those texts, encouraging one girl that despite her feelings that she wasn't smart enough to make it in school, she should keep on studying and trying, and that she could do it. He lived out his mission to the end. What was in his phone confirmed that he was a magnet for Jesus in his everyday life.

Cause

Right after Peter died the question of why silently reformed in our hearts. We didn't voice it out loud because Matt had answered that question eloquently in his funeral speech when he proclaimed that Peter's death occurred to proclaim God's glory and compel us to decide how to live our lives. But like other parents, I too needed my son's legacy to continue in some positive manner, for his death to make sense. Without a cause, a child's life seems to have been totally wasted when they die prematurely. If some good can come from their death in terms of preventing the same experience and pain that you've had, then it feels easier to cope with the loss. To leave a legacy, parents who lose children often focus their efforts around a cause that pertains to their child's death. After a period of grief, they plunge into supporting organizations that promote suicide prevention, fight drunk driving, prevent farm accidents or texting while driving, promote gun safety, or stop bullying, school violence, or SIDS (for infants). Devoting their lives to fighting the injustice or preventing the same suffering they experienced gives meaning and some way to deal positively with their terrible loss.

For us, there was not one of these usual types of causes to support. All we had was the knowledge that God called Peter home so He would become famous because of the life of my son. It was God's purpose or cause to transform the lives of people for the Kingdom of God. Therefore, I had the compulsion to see evidence of that spiritual growth in people in the community and beyond. There was absolutely no sense to Peter's death if there was no obvious change in people's lives. I was desperate to hear people tell me that they understood the gospel and loved Jesus as a result of Peter's example and death. Much of my grief journey revolved around this cause.

Split-Second Timing

We had lots of questions about the circumstances of the accident. We had to know whether Peter was at fault at all, by being distracted or speeding or breaking the law in any way. It all seemed too preposterous that the accident could have taken place in the manner it occurred. We got answers as Duane worked on insurance and communicated with law enforcement personnel.

It was determined that neither Peter nor Derek[2] were distracted by texting while driving. Jared[3] the passenger, told me later on that he was looking at his phone as he sat on the passenger side until an instant right before the accident occurred. There wasn't any alcohol or drugs involved in the accident. The black box in the cars revealed that Peter had been traveling sixty-six miles per hour in a sixty-five-mile-per-hour zone when he was hit. He hadn't put the brakes on. Derek was driving seventy-eight miles per hour. It appeared to be a case of reckless driving. We were very relieved to find out Peter hadn't been speeding. If Peter had been at fault in some way, the outcome would have felt very different to us. Once again we were privileged to see God's hand in the situation. He was making this horrible event as easy on us as possible.

As Duane had several conversations with highway patrolmen and the ambulance driver, and read the formal report from the law enforcement office, he pieced together a picture of what happened that night. Peter was heading east on Highway 46, going down a small hill. He had traveled that route thousands of times since he was born. He knew every inch of the way. He would have been totally aware of the creek that crosses under the road just before you reach the Greenfield Road intersection. He knew about the guardrails on either side of the road right there and the big drop off into the creek bed. As he drove down that hill he would have seen two vehicles approaching him. No big deal. But just as he was right at the

---

[2] name changed to protect identity

[3] name changed to protect identity

place where the guardrails started, with the drop off on either side, the second car suddenly started to pass and veered into his lane, coming right at him. Other students in Peter's drivers' ed class, those who practiced driving with him, said that they had discussed what to do when someone comes right at you: you drive into the ditch. But he was trapped. Peter couldn't avoid the accident. He had nowhere to go. He couldn't plunge into the deep creek bed because of the guardrails at the edge of the road. All he could do was face a head-on collision. The driver of the car tried to correct the bad mistake he had started when passing, and veered so that he would hit the passenger side rather than hit head-on. That car with Derek and Jared ended up in the ditch, farther up the road to the west. No one saw their vehicle until later. After taking the blow to his passenger's side, Peter's car spun so that his driver's side was in the opposite lane. Darlene[4], in the SUV that had been passed, barely had any time to put on the brakes before she crashed into the driver's side of Peter's car.

When we realized all the timing involved in how it occurred, we had to decide that it was God's supernatural timing. He was sovereign in every tiny detail of gathering Peter home to Himself. If Peter had been traveling just a little slower, it wouldn't have happened—he would have been able to drive into the ditch. If he had lingered at home a few more minutes looking for the box cutter, it wouldn't have happened—Derek would have passed Darlene and Peter wouldn't have been in his path at all. If Derek had been driving slower after getting off the interstate, it wouldn't have happened—Peter would have been past the guardrail area, and would have been able to drive into the ditch. If Derek had realized that he was illegally beginning to pass at an intersection, it wouldn't have happened— he wouldn't have passed at all. But it did happen. Our family had a choice. We could either become bitter at God for allowing the tragedy or accept that God has millisecond timing in sovereignly putting down this puzzle piece.

We chose to accept that God was somehow accomplishing His glory

---

[4] name changed to protect identity

in the way the accident occurred. It took steeling our minds to focus on God's plan rather than pitying ourselves.

This verse from Psalms became a reality to us:

> **"My frame was not hidden from you when I was made
> in the secret place.
> When I was woven together in the depths of the earth,
> Your eyes saw my unformed body. All the days
> ordained for me were written in your book
> before one of them came to be."**
>
> PSALM 139:16, NIV

As we let God's Word sink into our spirits and the reality of the facts of the situation, it became clear to Duane and me that Peter had only been designed to live sixteen years. He only spent the number of days on earth that God had ordained him to live, and not a millisecond more.

Paul's writing to the Ephesians took on new meaning to us:

> **"We are His workmanship, created in Christ Jesus to do good
> works, which God prepared in advance for us to do."**
>
> EPHESIANS 2:10, NIV

God made Peter with specific good works planned ages before he was born. He was God's masterpiece. He molded Peter so that he would walk in the way God had planned. He lived his sixteen years and did exactly what he had been created to do. When I'm tempted to wallow in self-pity that I won't be able to see him go to university, get married, have kids, and the like, I have to remind myself of this verse. God never purposed Peter's life to continue to old age. Peter lived the number of days God ordained, and that is good.

Even though all of us as parents think that we should be able to see our kids grow up to adulthood and outlive us, it may not be what God plans. He may have vastly different purposes for our kids than we have. When I hear people say, "Your kids aren't supposed to die before you," I cringe. Do we really have a right to expect God to keep everything comfortable, happy, and perfect in our lives? Who am I to determine what purpose God has for my kids? Can I decide how my child can best serve God and glorify Him? It's painful to let God put puzzle pieces in place for the purpose of establishing His Kingdom in the hearts of other people, especially when it involves our kids' safety and lives. It hurts to think that God would take our loved one and use it as the means by which someone else would enter the Kingdom of God. Do I love other people enough to make that sacrifice? But as I grew in my love for God and my eyes opened to see the needs the kids in the community and other people in the world for His salvation, my need for security diminished. Peter was gone; I couldn't get him back. But there was an enormous solace that God was in control and bringing good out of the pain. I rejoiced that my child had a part in God's sovereign glorious puzzle.

His Sign

The first year after a death of someone close is filled with tasks that have to be done. There isn't much time to really absorb what the loss means for the rest of your life on an everyday basis. We had many tasks to complete: insurance settlement, legal issues, and designing a tombstone. We knew amidst all these pressures that a sign would be put at the site of the accident as a reminder to other drivers. In South Dakota, a sign is placed in the ditch along a road where there has been a traffic fatality. One side says, "Think," and the other side says, "Why Die?" We drive by the accident site multiple times a week. We'd have to face this emotional reminder over and over while trying to cope with everything that needed to be done.

I knew it was coming. A friend was in contact with the highway department and told me the sign would be put up soon after the ground was thawed in the spring. Then it appeared ahead of me as I was driving to AWANA at church after a very stressful day at work. From a distance

I saw the shape at the area of the highway where the accident happened. I was confused for a second; it was on the opposite side of the road from where Peter's car came to a stop, but close to where he was hit first. Yes, they did put it in the right place, just at the spot Peter would have been looking when he had his last sight of earth. Just then, in the tears that flooded my eyes and heart, I read, "Why Die?" Bitterness welled up in my heart and I silently screamed, "Yeah, why did my strong, handsome, awesome son die? Why him? Why my baby and pal who was right by me for sixteen years?" Peter had tagged along with me everywhere until he could drive by himself. He was part of me. I cried out, "Why did the fun in my life have to die?"

Then a thought crossed my mind, from God's own heart. "My Son died so Peter could be in heaven with Me forever and not face eternal separation in hell. I know what it's like to see a son die. My Son died for everyone who's ever lived and will live." The rage in my heart calmed, but the tears came again. Peter had wanted people to know how wonderful his Savior was. He wasn't very good at verbalizing it, but somehow the message was lived out at school. My trembling stopped but the tears continued, as I was being made aware that the huge gap left behind, evident by Peter's absence, had a reason in eternity. There was a good answer to the question on the sign, "Why Die?"

As I drove on, I couldn't see the "Think" on the other side of the sign, but I knew it was there. How appropriate that word was: "Think." Peter wanted people to stop and think about what they were doing with their lives. It made him frustrated and mad to see his peers wasting their lives, pursuing hollow things to waste their time. Looking in his room after he died, I found the books he once read: *Do Hard Things, 7 Secrets of a Successful Teenager, and The Cross Centered Life.* As we considered how quiet he was at home in the last few weeks, Duane and I came to understand that he was apparently thinking about what he should do to use the time he had on earth to his full potential. He was probably wondering, *What is the "hard thing" that I can do for God?*

Returning back home on that road that night, I could see in the dark the word, "Think." I paused to remember that Peter had spent time reading the Word and found John 3:30, which he made his life verse. "He must increase, I must decrease." He knew his faults: he could easily act proud of himself and take credit for his success in life. But he thought about it and determined that he needed to give all the glory to God, rather than take the credit for himself. Jesus needed to take over in his life so that people would see Him rather than Peter. The example of my sixteen-year-old made me think, *What am I doing with my life?* Sure, Peter had a Type A personality that was good at goal setting and being focused. But can I follow his example just being the personality I am? After his death I had it on my to-do list to figure out what my life verse was. I needed to figure out a succinct statement of purpose for my life. It wasn't an easy task.

Driving east again several days later, the sign loomed up again in front of me. "Why Die?" An idea crossed my mind that the sign should say, "Why Live?" Not in the sense that life is worthless because of the loss. But rather, what makes life worth living? Is life just a senseless, empty effort at trying to become as comfortable as possible? That's the underlying worldview in the USA. What does that pursuit lead to? A house and yard full of things to spend time taking care of. What's the purpose in that? It's not worth much to work so hard for stuff just to feel and look good. Life might just as well end now if that's true. Whatever I live for must be worth dying for, or it's worthless. What is so worthwhile and important that I would gladly die because of it?

I thought about my life. Why could I go on living with the huge hole in my heart left by my son's absence? What could be worthwhile now? The answer flooded my heart: the only joy in my life that came since Peter's death was seeing faith grow in his friends' lives as they learned to follow Jesus. I had attended an event at the high school the week before the sign went up, at which there was a halftime show put on by the dance team. They danced in honor and memory of Peter to Matthew West's song "We Won't Be Shaken." Hearing and seeing them declare to their peers and the community that despite the loss, their faith in God wouldn't waver was what made life worth living then. I knew that many of Peter's friends sought the answer to the question, "Why Live?" They were discovering and were confident that the answer is to follow Jesus. Their lives, just like Peter's life, were given to them to glorify God. As time went on they moved on to college. I didn't see them much anymore to get encouraged by what was going on in their lives. But God was going to show me a new purpose, maybe one even bigger, for living. He caused the spiritual significance of the sign to point me in a new direction.

After Peter's sign was put up, I noticed many other similar signs at dangerous places on roads. As I drove I wondered, *Are all those people with Peter in heaven, or lost for eternity? Are those people glorifying God forever as they were meant to do? Were they given a chance to hear what the purpose was for their lives and make a decision to follow Jesus?*

Peter's sign was a reminder many times each week, as I passed it, that Jesus died for all of us, so that we can be in heaven with Him. We will see Peter someday. He sees the angels in heaven rejoicing when someone from Beresford and elsewhere accepts Jesus as their Savior, and joins in the excitement. The sign still reminds me of the challenge to think about what I'm doing with my priorities. Am I making Jesus first place today? Have I thought about how I can serve Him today? Am I making it a priority to enable people to come to know Jesus today? The sign, when I see it even now, with its two statements, "Why Die?" and "Think," keep causing me to focus on my reason for living: to make God's glory known to others so they can know Him, too.

Later in the year after the sign was put up, a friend of ours had an experience that shook him. It shook us, too, when he told us. I remember when he stopped us in the church lobby to tell the story. I heard him and was shocked. Then I grabbed a bulletin to scribble down the words so I would quote them accurately and never forget. At times our friend audibly hears God speaking to him. Perhaps God's voice to him is like very strong thoughts that are so overpowering that they seem audible. He didn't want to dwell on how God speaks to him, only that he knows for sure when God does speak. When this took place he hadn't heard from God for a long time. Every day he drove past the sign on the way to work; he had seen it dozens of times. One day he looked at the sign, and in frustration said loudly to himself, "What a waste!" He meant, what a waste for a talented person like Peter to die in a senseless accident when he could have done so much with his life! Then he heard God say, "Didn't I ransom Peter?"

He responded, "Yes."

Then God spoke clearly again. "Then don't I have the right to do as I see fit with that ransomed life?" God had purposed to use Peter's life and death in a very special way. He had it planned from the time he was conceived to have his life glorify God. God had the rights to Peter's life since he had given his heart to Him.

Duane and I were deeply affected by what our friend told us. It's an incredible feeling to realize that God spoke audibly to someone else about your child. He really notices us! It felt like a direct message from God, telling us two very important things: Peter had been ransomed by Jesus, and he definitely was in heaven with God. There was no doubt about his salvation. Secondly, because of the supreme cost of our salvation, we have no rights to how God plans our lives. God uses us for His glory. He has total rights to us once we decide to follow Him.

Our minds were blown by God's providence and purpose for our "little" boy. It remains a mystery why God chose us to be his parents. And it humbled us that He used our family to raise Peter so he could do what God wanted. It became so clear why God had decided years earlier to cause me to have another miracle baby. It was for God to be glorified. The words of a song are so true: "From life's first cry to final breath, Jesus commands my destiny." All we could do is humbly praise God and submit to His plan, being grateful for what He had told us.

This experience compelled me to choose not to dwell on the things I was missing with him being gone. So many parents who lose children grieve over the things their child never will be able to do, so many things they will miss out on. I chose to rest in the fact that God had purposed Peter to live exactly the number of seconds that he did. It wasn't as if God's plans were ruined because Derek smashed into Peter. God wasn't grieving and feeling disappointed that Peter couldn't excel as a runner in high school, graduate at the top of his class, go to college and be a witness there, and go on to medical school and eventually become a wonderful doctor. No, God was delighted that the little boy He ransomed at age four had learned to know Him, follow Him, and was willing to do His will. God was pleased that Peter's total reason for living was to let Jesus increase and for him to decrease in significance. His death wasn't a mistake at all. God comforted both Duane and me so much through this understanding.

Article

The months of facing the loss of our son moved on. There was less new evidence of what God was doing in individuals' lives, which would have given me purpose for my pain. I started dragging through the experience. I couldn't see much of any change that God was making in my heart either. Things were pretty bleak. God's purpose seemed to be diminishing. Therefore, I was quite surprised one day when Peter's coach contacted me to see if it would be okay to publish a story that had been written about him. Duane and I realized that it was a big deal he had run so well at the state cross-country meet in the fall of 2013. We knew he was a leader on his team, someone to whom his classmates looked for inspiration. We knew he had been kind to runners from other schools against whom he competed at races and that they loved him, too. But we really had no idea that God was going to use Peter's life on a broader scale to impact other athletes outside the region where he had competed. My awe of God increased and I felt overwhelmed that He was using my little boy, my "Peter Pumpkin," in a more public way.

The cross-country coach's brother Andy Coy was impressed by the story of Peter's running and the impact he had on the team his brother coached. He worked very hard to write an article that was posted in running websites and printed in periodicals. (See the Appendix: Ready to Run.) We were stunned to see the impact of this article making Peter's priorities to focus on Jesus clear.

Comfort

While dealing with many issues common to those who grieve, I was moved over and over again as I saw evidences of God's love. He used these experiences many times to cause me to draw closer to Him. My love for Him grew through the comfort He gave, as I saw His tender loving-kindness demonstrated in many ways. As I worked through my grief I learned lessons about how to know God. Jesus Himself promises:

"Blessed are they who mourn, for they will be comforted."

Matthew 5:4, NIV

Somehow I realized that comfort would come from a firm belief that God would keep this promise. The question was, "How would He comfort me?" Without any clear answer I returned to my previous means of coping with difficulty, by looking for evidence of God's providence and sovereignty. I had learned to trust God before by looking for how the Kingdom of God was being established in my heart. By this time it was a natural reaction for me to look for the puzzle pieces God was setting in place though circumstances I faced. I had learned that He demonstrated His love for me in showing how He was putting events in order, in His timing to bring good in situations. God hadn't changed at all, despite my world being turned upside down after the accident. I just had to learn to see Him at work through eyes that were often full of tears.

Dreams

I must admit that at night, when I was trying to sleep, I envisioned the accident over and over. I couldn't see how Derek could be so stupid as to begin to pass when Peter's car was obviously right in front of him. My rage started to build inside toward Derek. But I was also very troubled about what Peter experienced in the second just before he was hit, when the headlights were coming right at him in the dark, and he realized he had no way of avoiding the crash. I recalled how distraught he was when he just sideswiped the pickup before the prom. He was a mess from just a little accident. What terror did he feel? Many nights I couldn't sleep for hours, troubled by the mental torment my son felt. Peter always had total disdain for people who drove badly, and how upset he'd get at close calls when I'd drive. I can just imagine him saying as his last words, "Oh my God!"—a real prayer for sure just before the impact.

One night I had a dream. In the dream the whole family was in a lodge. It was a dark room, but Peter was there. He was grown up; he looked about twenty-five years old. We understood he was just visiting from heaven (not that I believe this happens in real life). He was very involved in catching up on what the family had been doing. He really didn't say anything about heaven. We eventually knew it was time for him to return. Peter stood up to go, and Matt stood up, too. Matt asked him to let him look at him. He wanted to look at his face, to make sure it really was Peter, his brother. He had to see if there was a scar across his left cheek from his mouth to his ear where it had been nearly cut through in the trauma of the crash. The scar was there. It was Peter.

As I was hugging him good-bye in the dream, I told him that I had one question, which was, "Peter, all I want to know is what happened that night. How did the accident happen?" I wanted to glean anything possible regarding his emotional state as he was driving and realizing he was going to crash. Was he panicking? Was he frantic? Was he terrified?

Peter responded to me, "I don't know, Mom. I just hit the car that came right at me."

I asked, "What about the other car (Darlene's)?"

He looked at me like he didn't know what I was talking about, and said, "I don't know."

That response was so characteristic of how he'd answer me. But this time it was very comforting. Then he calmly left and the dream ended. God helped me with that dream, and from then on I could sleep. It seemed that God must have calmed Peter in His loving-kindness in that last split second, so that he was free of terror and panic. He didn't suffer at all. He just hit the first car and was unaware of the second terrifying impact. God had taken care of Peter for me in his last moment of awareness and protected him from the emotional trauma.

A man at church shared a dream he had several months after the accident. He didn't know Peter well, but shared it with me as a means of comforting us. In his dream he saw Peter from the back view. He was on the porch of a building with stone pillars. Peter wearing a short, white robe, similar to those that people wear when doing karate. He was putting a slipper on his foot. Two little kids ran up to him and called, "Peter, Peter, come on! It's time to see the King!" Peter ran off with them, playing and skipping with them as they took off across the beautiful green field with flowers. My friend wondered what kind of slipper Peter could possibly be wearing. It seemed so odd for a guy to be wearing those types of things on his feet. A few days later he went to his granddaughter's dance recital. She was wearing the same type of slippers as she danced. He realized that in his dream Peter was going to dance with Jesus and celebrate! When I heard his dream I wondered who the two little kids could have been. Later it came to me, as a comfort: one was the child we had lost in the miscarriage, and the other was the son that Duane's brother and his wife had lost right at birth, Michael. We could imagine that Peter had found both of them to play with and love in heaven.

I realize you can't make too much of dreams; they aren't actual manifestations of the person's spirit. God's Word is the truth, and God's Word speaks life to us. However, dreams can be tangible ways God comforts people in grief, putting new ways of thinking about issues into our minds to change negative patterns that drain us. Dreams can confirm what God is telling us as we spend time in His word. As Psalm 127:2 says, "God gives to His beloved, even in his sleep" (NASB).

Journaling and Writing

Journaling became a big part of my healing process. It brought comfort to write. I didn't write regularly, but it was the place where I expressed my sadness when I needed to. One of my entries in January read, "Leaving work each day is so hard, seeing his picture on my desk, and letting my mind think about not having him home again tonight. There won't be any phone calls tonight on the way home: 'Uh, Mom, have you left work yet? Could you stop and get some _____ food or deodorant or body wash?' (Peter was always hungry and wanting to be clean.) I miss being needed by him so much. It's hard to find some purpose as a mother now. The older kids don't need much physical attention or help. That role of being a mom, active in my kids' lives, is so engrained." My purpose was wrenched from me, and I struggled to find a new identity. I felt worthless without a defined role. My older kids weren't at home anymore. We were thrust into having an empty nest prematurely. I really didn't know what I could do with all the free time. What was my role to be now? What was my purpose going to be? What could possibly fill that void?

Gradually, as my heart started to heal, I found that writing my thoughts and posting them on Facebook or submitting them to the church newsletter helped to put order and meaning to what I was experiencing. These articles are in the Appendix. As I wrote, God spoke to me regarding the truth of what He was doing in my heart to heal my brokenness. He showed me that one of His purposes for our grief is to enable us to bring comfort to other people in similar circumstances. As

I turned to His word, I was able to write the long booklet, "Press On" for Peter's classmates for their graduation, God comforted me, giving me one last chance to exhort them to follow Jesus and not waste Peter's death. Writing became a way to release pent up feelings to give voice to them in a positive manner.

For many people, writing down emotions, no matter how jumbled they may seem in grief, is a key to being able to sort through the mess. Writing enables you to record facts and feelings, so they aren't lost completely. But in the process you can let those thoughts go so that your brain isn't so cluttered with everything to think about at once. When you write down the jumble of thoughts, they are preserved. There is a terror grieving people feel, that if you stop thinking about memories and emotions and let them go they will vanish just like your loved one. Then there is more to mourn: the loss of your memories of the person as well as the person themselves. Writing preserves the memories so they aren't gone for good. You can return to them when you need to remember. But you're freed of the pressure to hold on indefinitely, letting them churn around in your mind. Once your brain is able to let go there is a freedom to allow in new thoughts that may be positive. Or there is the possibility of being able to think clearly to improve in functioning in day-to-day tasks. The memories are liberated from your consciousness, so you are free to function on what's important at the moment. Give a journal to grieving friends at the funeral; they don't have the energy to get organized to shop for one themselves. They'll be able to begin writing and processing their emotions right away.

Drawing Near

I have frequently heard grieving people say how hard it is to feel that God is with them. There is a terrible struggle for some people to feel close to God. When your schedule is totally interrupted and all your habits of daily seeking God are disrupted and you can't focus on His Word, you can feel abandoned. Verses people give you in cards are comforting, but the extended times with God seem impossible to attain. The ideal times with God seem to me like what it felt like to be with one of our pets in the past. We had a cat at one time that gave me a good metaphor for how to find comfort in God. She would jump up on the bed near my feet every morning between 5:30 and 6:00 a.m., without fail, and curl up and purr. She just stayed there purring until I woke up and hugged her and let her cuddle for a while. That's what drawing near to God feels like. He enjoys it when we initiate spending time with Him, just enjoying His presence. The ideal is to be like my sweet cat, drawing near to God in praise and thankfulness, and talking to Him about what we're feeling and what's on our heart. I loved that cat more, patted her more, and hugged her more than any of the other cats we've had (who were the aloof-type of beasts). And in the same way, I found that God showers His love on us when we spend time regularly with Him in prayer and praise, and listen to Him speak.

When that sweet cat died, Julia found a little long-hair farm kitten to become our house cat. That kitty was sickly and never developed good muscles to jump. Now she's rather disabled and can't get on anything higher than eighteen inches by herself. She has a nearly inaudible meow and is barely able to communicate with us. (Actually those are really good traits in a cat!) The cat is so like me in my relationship with God in my grief. I'd like to say that after Peter died I could curl up with Jesus and spend a lot of quality time with Him, talking to Him, drawing comfort and strength like my healthy cat. But I was much more like our disabled cat. If the door to the bedroom is open, she'll come in at any time of the day or night, looking to see if we're there. Then she'll stretch up, paw at me, as if she is asking me to pick her up. When I lean over to help her up, she'll start to purr. But she just can't settle down for more than a few moments before she scampers off the bed to do something else. She'll come back in a few minutes, repeating the process until I get up. I was like that cat most of the time as I tried to look to God for comfort. I, like other grieving people I've talked to, knew I needed to draw near to God. I'd reach up to Him with whatever strength I had whenever my emotions overwhelmed me, day or night, read what I could focus on in the Word, and meditate for a bit of time on what I read. My prayers were disorganized, formed from whatever popped into my mind at the moment. Most were silent, unformed thoughts aimed at God, pleading for help. There were too many things swirling around in my head to focus at all in the initial days after the accident. But God fulfilled His promise, drawing near to me when I'd do my feeble part to reach up to Him, clumsily pawing at Him. God responded back and drew near to me by picking me up and reassuring me through what I read in the psalms and other scriptures. Despite my inability to focus, God honored my effort to draw near and He would comfort me. As the apostle James wrote:

"Draw near to God and He will draw near to you."

JAMES 4:8, ESV

The truth I found is this: God is the same, regardless of how I come to Him. He just enjoys it when we "purr" with Him, enjoying His presence. The extended periods of time spent in Bible study are very beneficial, but He gave me comfort even in the little spurts of finding truth from a card, verse calendar, a sermon, or something on the radio. God loved me, even in my emotional disability and distress, when I drew near to Him. He responded whenever I could muster the energy to paw at Him, like my cat does to me, asking for grace and love.

Brokenness

A year after Peter's death I was at a "Surviving the Holidays" event, put on by GriefShare in Iowa, struggling to even want to think about Christmas that year. It was the second Christmas after Peter died. I thought it would be easier the second time. But when the small group leader opened the discussion by asking us all to share where we were last Christmas, I couldn't remember a single thing about the day. It's as if it didn't happen. I knew I decorated the house, but that's about it. My brain was still such a muddle that I couldn't remember my friend decorating the tree for us. Facing Christmas this second time was going to be a challenge, one I wasn't interested in experiencing. To me the season seemed about as bleak as the snowless brown landscape outside. How in the world could I have the energy to do all the needed things to prepare for this season? Who cares about all these traditions? What's the point of it all anyway? Yes, it's Jesus' birthday, but my meager celebration for Him would be rather pathetic in comparison to the wonder of what's going on in heaven, so why bother to try?

A statement made in the video I watched at the "Surviving the Holidays" event pierced my numbed mind: "There is no need for Christmas if there is no pain and suffering and sin. Jesus came to end it all, to end brokenness. This is the sufferers' holiday. Christmas guarantees that God is there for me and others with losses." God spoke to me in the midst of my grief lethargy. He reminded me that broken lives from any loss through death, violence, injustice, or negligence are the reasons Jesus came at Christmas to live among us. Jesus Himself declared this to be His mission at the start of His ministry, when he quoted from Isaiah:

> **"The Spirit of the Sovereign Lord is on me because He has anointed me to preach good news to the poor, and sent me to bind up the brokenhearted, to proclaim freedom for the captives and release from darkness for the prisoners...to comfort all who mourn and provide for those who grieve in Zion – to bestow on them a crown of beauty instead of ashes, the oil of gladness instead of mourning, and a garment of praise instead of a spirit of despair. They will be called oaks of righteousness, a planting of the LORD for the display of His splendor."**
>
> ISAIAH 61:1–4, NIV

Jesus reminded me that morning that He came as Emmanuel, "God with us." Jesus was there with me, helping me face my grief during that

Christmas season. I recalled as I sat at the GriefShare holiday brunch that the previous night, Duane and I had gone back to the Avera hospital for an event. It was the first time we had returned to the hospital where Peter died. As I glanced around the lobby I realized that it was the place where I first understood on the night of the accident that Jesus was going to be with us through the whole ordeal. It was a sacred place, one where His presence was felt, and where He picked a person to begin binding up the wound in our lives. The chaplain had met us in the ER and took us through that same lobby to go upstairs to the ICU. It was in the lobby by the elevators I felt God reaching out to us in our broken state, through that man, to tell us that He was with us. He had not abandoned us, letting us break apart and become unfit for His use. Yes, we were broken, but He had come to bind up the wounds that had split open and had been bleeding all year. He was there to begin comforting us so that we would be able to feel His "oil of gladness and put on a garment of praise instead of a spirit of despair." I had faith then that because He had started the healing process, and because He was Emmanuel (God with us), He would finish the healing process in my heart. What an amazing, wonderful Christmas present it was from Jesus! Jesus showed me that my brokenness and the brokenness of other people are the whole reason for Christmas. His gift for me was the promise of wholeness again.

Tombstone

Getting the tombstone designed was a difficult thing for the family. Tensions surfaced as we tried to come to some agreement regarding the design. We all agreed that a big boulder would be fitting for Peter's grave. His name means "rock." Furthermore we just couldn't fathom him liking a smooth, polished marker with flowers or some other design. We knew we wanted his signature on the stone, and "He must increase, I must decrease. John 3:30" etched on it so his passion would be proclaimed for many years to come. We found a person who was able to make a design to our liking. She suggested adding in a photo of Peter as well. I gave her his sophomore school picture. Finally the day came to bring home the tombstone. We shared Peter's story with the lady as we paid for it. Then Duane and I got it loaded in the back of the pickup and started home. She had given me a replacement picture in a packet, to use just in case the one affixed to the stone became damaged. I casually opened the packet a few miles out of the town, and gasped when I saw the picture. Here's why: his scar was gone!

Peter was about eighteen months old when he fell in the basement and hit his cheek on the side of a metal trunk that didn't have very smooth polished edges. It split his cheek open, and he needed about five stitches. It seemed to be healing nicely, but a week after the injury I was in the public library with him. He was looking around by himself, curious as usual. When it was time to go I called him, and he came running to me. I had my arms out, ready to catch him. But he ran faster than I anticipated and my left thumbnail hit him in the cheek, right where his stitches were. It split the wound open again. We hurried off to the clinic to get it closed again. But this time the surgeon said that he would be left with an obvious scar. Too much scar tissue had formed in the wound already, and he couldn't get it shut well again in the same spot.

The scar was obvious, for sure. It was an inch long directly under his right eye. It had little dots on either side where the stitches had been. Once he became a teenager he let us know how ashamed he was of that scar. He hated it. It wasn't masculine looking, especially with those dots. He wouldn't tell anyone the truth of how it happened. On Peter's list of goals, in the column under physical goals, he listed: "To get rid of scar." Just like he was diligently working at all the other goals on his long list, he was working toward this one as well. He had tubes of Scar Gel in the upstairs bathroom, downstairs bathroom, and beside his bed. He was determined to use it several times a day to get the scar faded away. It didn't work at all. It remained red, ugly, and plainly evident. Peter didn't know at that time in his life that scars tell a story of the healing God brings in our lives, turning an open wound into a healed scar that pro-claims His loving-kindness. He had no idea that God planned that wound to bring Him glory.

So when I causally opened the packet the lady gave us after the stone was loaded up, I was overcome with amazement. I caught my breath. There was no scar on his face in the picture. It was as clear and perfect as the day he was born. She had photoshopped it out, thinking we wouldn't want any imperfections to be so obvious forevermore on his memorial stone. His face was just as he had always wanted it to be, whole once again, as if it had never happened. He had gotten his wish, and he had achieved one of his goals. He "got rid of the scar."

God blessed me so much on that painful ride home, assuring me that He loves me in the midst of our grief and pain, to the extent that He would have a lady take care of such a small detail to bless us. He is certainly the God who said, "Blessed are they that mourn, for they will be comforted." Without the scar on Peter's face I wouldn't have known this evidence of God's loving-kindness to me. My grief would have been more painful to work through. God is amazing in the very intricate details of how He demonstrates He loves us. He was working behind the scenes many days before I would need some special encouragement to make this blessing possible. How my love for God grew on that long ride home with the tombstone!

Cleaning Up

Dealing with a person's things is a time when a great deal of healing can happen. Memories return and feelings surface that may have been stuffed away. Letting yourself feel the pain and then storing the things you want to remember is healthy. It's also a time of letting go of things that can bog you down. As I've often said to grieving people, "tears drain away the grief." A lot of comfort comes from the process of cleaning up.

Our family took a long time to deal with Peter's things. We still haven't changed much in his room. Each of us have a different rate at which we grieve, and being able to touch and see things to bring back memories is important. When a person's things have been given away or discarded, there's no way to bring back memories those things hold and to process them. I got rid of some of Peter's things too soon, and it really hurt my kids. They hadn't had time to say good-bye to the things that held memories they treasured. So I had to learn to just wait. At times I went into his room just to look around, to reminisce about what he was like.

One day I was looking in Peter's room and opened his copy of *Our Daily Bread* to November 23, to the last day he possibly read it. He faithfully got a copy of the devotional from church to read every day, so it's likely he read it the morning of the accident. Perhaps those thoughts filled his mind, never knowing what would happen that evening. The devotional indicated that there are times in our lives when a sudden tragedy or turn of events or a death changes everything in our lives. This is what happened to Mary when the angel Gabriel came to her to announce that the Holy Spirit would come upon her to the end, that she would bear the Messiah. Mary reacted, not thinking of herself and the trouble she'd have, but of God's glory and power in the situation. She responded to the angel:

"Let it be to me according to your word."

LUKE 1:26–33, ESV

I was struck by the impact of those words. So many times in grieving I wanted to change the whole thing. I didn't want to submit to God's plan. I fought letting God gather Peter unto Himself. It didn't seem fair to lose him and let God have him. It was too painful to feel the gaping hole in the house. It was awful to think ahead to all the fun times we'd miss out on with him gone from us. God challenged me to respond like Mary, Jesus' mother, to "Let it be to me according to your word." I was learning then that loving God on a daily basis involved letting Him do His will. It meant submitting to Him, no matter the cost. It meant valuing His purposes more than my own. It was a hard lesson.

As I paused in Peter's room I thought about how God had changed Peter's heart in his childhood. I felt so treasured by Him. How many parents face terrible times with their kids falling away from the faith! How many despair that their kids have made bad choices for which they'll face miserable consequences forevermore. Many parents lose a child and there's no notoriety, or blessings, from the fame and attention of the community. The child dies and no one seems to remember. Why had God chosen to make it easier on our family? We hadn't done anything to deserve this loving-kindness; it was only God's mercy that planned it this way for us. Why were we so blessed? Why had God given us such an amazing son who had a heart for Him? I could only respond in love and gratefulness for His blessing in the midst of our pain.

I found a Post-it note in Peter's Bible, written many years ago by my father. He lived far from his grandchildren, but he understood the role he could play in their lives in pointing them to Jesus. So he wrote this note to Peter and included it in a birthday card when he was a seventh- or eighth-grader:

Dear Peter,

We are glad you are so interested in sports and so good in the games you play. Ask your mom or dad to read and explain to you Philippians 3:10–14 and 1 Corinthians 9:24–27. The apostle Paul surely knew about the sporting events of his day! God bless you and make this next year of life very productive.

I looked up the verses to which my dad referred. Here they are:

"Do you not know that in a race all the runners run, but only one gets the prize? Run in such a way as to get the prize. Everyone who competes in the games goes in to strict training. They do it to get a crown that will not last; but we do it to get a crown that will last forever. Therefore I do not run like a man running aimlessly, I do not fight like a man beating the air. No, I beat my body, and make it my slave so that after I have preached to others, I myself will not be disqualified for the prize."

1 CORINTHIANS 9:24–27, NIV

"Not that I have already obtained this, or have already been made perfect, but I press on to take hold of that for which Christ Jesus took hold of me. Brothers, I do not consider myself yet to have taken hold of it. But one thing I do: forgetting what is behind, and straining toward what is ahead, I press on toward the goal to win the prize for which God has called me heavenward in Christ Jesus."

PHILIPPIANS 3:10–14, NIV

I marveled at the prophetic nature of the verses my dad gave to Peter. He had no idea that within a year of his own death, Peter would be joining him in heaven. He had no idea that he gave Peter a clear spiritual mandate to press on and finish the race Jesus had for him for the prize awaiting him in heaven. Peter knew that his real reason for running—and the reason for his whole life—was to bring glory to God. How I thank God that despite the limited times Peter had with him, his grandfather, my dad, was able to impart this truth to him, to give him direction and purpose. His realized that Peter had to focus on Jesus while running the life of a teenager in order to get the prize Jesus had for him. God was good to let me see His sovereignty in preparing Peter's heart, as a young boy, for what lay ahead of him.

Impact and Community

The fact that God was being glorified as He transformed the hearts of people who had been touched by Peter's life and death was a huge comfort for us. I don't think I could have faced life at that time without the encouragement God gave us. As the year after he died progressed we continued to see evidences of God changing people, because they had been confronted with Jesus through Peter's life and funeral service. A mother of other cross-country runners started a study with her friends to read the *Don't Waste Your Life* book. That study has grown in numbers and has had ripple effects for the last five years. The family now fosters babies and children. Although her kids are grown now, she isn't wasting her healthy, strong years at all; she and her husband are giving of themselves night and day to take care of kids with huge emotional needs, who need to be shown Jesus. Her daughter led a Bible study at her college after seeing the changes in her mom's life. Many high school girls started meeting together for a weekly Bible study. Our son Matt and Peter's friend Riley led another early morning study with kids for the remainder of the school year after he died. Fifteen kids went to Hidden Acres camp one summer with scholarships from money donated in Peter's memory. It was exciting to see them grow in their faith. Many adults shared with me how much Matt's speech at the funeral affected them and made them think about the direction their lives were going. One girl who had gone to church with Peter from the time she was little, but strayed away from her faith, came back to Jesus, was baptized, and then served with Youth With A Mission

(YWAM) after graduating. A girl who Peter had encouraged daily in her spiritual life also served with YWAM for a year before starting to study at a university. A Boy Scouts leader who worked with Peter started coming to our small group Bible study soon after the funeral and has continued to grow in his faith since then. His daughter became a Christian through Peter's influence and the encouragement of her father. One of the most precious things that happened is that a lady told me that because of Peter's influence, she was able to turn to Jesus to get freed from an addiction to alcohol. God is so good to use this loss to establish His Kingdom reign in the hearts of people! They, too, are part of His glorious puzzle!

God brought me comfort through people in my life. One young lady, Breanna, was particularly instrumental in feeling the pain of Peter's loss with me. She had known him very well. Neither her mother nor I would let the two of them date, so they just remained very good friends. Peter had a great amount of respect for Breanna's love for Jesus, and Breanna respected Peter's faith and encouraged him in his beliefs. After he died Breanna frequently shared memories of him with me that revealed his character and heart. She shared with me her heartache and feelings, knowing we both missed him terribly. It was sweet Breanna who came to the cemetery just as we were setting up the tombstone and hung out with our family, treasuring the time with us at the place where her good friend was buried. It was precious.

A few months after Peter died Breanna decided to follow his example and turned her energies to befriend a foreign exchange student and show him Jesus' love. She decided that her goal for her junior year was to make sure this atheist kid from Germany heard the gospel and became a Christian. Sure enough, God answered her prayers and Anton repented, accepted Jesus, and grew in his faith before he had to leave Beresford to go home. She tells me that Anton is growing in his love for Jesus and goes to church in Germany. Breanna continues to share lessons she learned from her friend Peter with other kids, and in the process she lets them know how much Jesus loves them. She had been so encouraging to me through carrying on her bold witness. She is making sure that the ripples of the effect Peter had on her life continue to spread.

There is a tendency when grieving to be so self-focused that we become very selfish. I had to learn that seemingly everyone in the community was grieving in some way over the loss of Peter. Just because I was his mother didn't mean that I was entitled to all the grief, as if other people's pain wasn't real or deep. I had to choose to reject the thoughts that "I lost my child, so my pain is the only pain that counts." There was something extremely comforting in recognizing that all his friends, people at church, his coach and teachers, brothers and sister, and relatives were grieving, too. We were all in it together. We were all beat up together by the loss. As I recognized this I could open my heart to people who were hurting in their own way, but who still wanted to bless me. They sometimes did it in ways that made me feel uncomfortable and conspicuous. They stretched me. It would have been easier to hibernate in my own world. I learned from people in my grief support group that isolating oneself only leads to deeper grief. I found comfort in facing people who longed to care for us and bless us. As we healed together, joy returned. I found my heart growing bigger and more sensitive to other people facing the same losses. As I started putting others' needs alongside of my own, I found my pain lessening and a renewed sense of purpose developing. The hurting community was a huge comfort to me, because God blessed me over and over again by their kindness.

On my trip to Haiti in May of 2014, I was totally blessed by a guy named Fabeeze. He is the director of a men's choir that travels around Haiti, singing and sharing the gospel. Fabeeze's son was killed in the earthquake that devastated Port-au-Prince. One day I was in the church when Fabeeze was there, getting set up for a worship service. He could speak a little English and knows many of the same hymns to sing in Kreyol that we sing in English. Haitians focus on heaven much more than we do as Americans, and frequently sing about going to be with Jesus. He knew of Peter's death. He expressed some sympathy for what happened, identifying how hard it is to lose a child. Then without being able to say much more to each other, we both broke out in singing "When We All Get to Heaven" at the top of our lungs. It was so awesome to grieve together with this godly man, who had suffered so much but was able to praise God for the assurance of salvation and our future in heaven. What a comfort to know God is big enough to heal the pain of the thousands of families in Haiti who lost their kids. Singing and worship are such good tools to take the focus off our pain and transfer it to our hope, and when it's with others in the body of Christ it's even more powerful.

Another precious Haitian man, Dabu, lost his daughter suddenly to an infection. Daline was sixteen years old when she died. The repercussions of her death were just as significant in their Haitian community as what Beresford experienced with Peter's death. Dabu is a missionary who walks all over the mountains and the plateau in central Haiti, witnessing and establishing new churches. He is a precious saint and one of the godliest men I know. He and his wife were devastated by Daline's death. Soon after I heard about the tragic news, I had a dream. Peter was in heaven waiting for her and greeted Daline as she approached the gates. He took her with him and showed her around, introducing her to his new friends. It was a short dream, but when Dabu and his wife heard about it he was so blessed. God is so good to bring us comfort through other brothers and sisters in Christ. How amazing it is that the puzzle pieces of our lives touch those of others' around the world. God does work together with us when we love Him, to bring about what is good.

Inspired

The story that touches my heart the most is that of the mother of Peter's best friend. Cindy and her husband had brought their kids to AWANA at our church for many years. There, our Pastor's wife Nancy shared the gospel with Cindy. But she never made any decision to follow Jesus at that time. She and her husband started to come to Sunday morning services at our church right after the funeral. She told me later that she needed to find out what kind of God could be so great that we could trust Him and glorify Him through our son's death. She had been raised in a Christian home, went to church every Sunday as a child, but had become complacent as an adult. Until then her heart was cold, but now she understood her need for salvation. One day she and her daughter prayed together to repent and accept Jesus' offer of forgiveness and a restored relationship with God. I talked to her a few Sundays later, and I'll never forget her telling me, "Mary, I'm so terribly sorry that it had to take Peter's death for me to realize I needed to accept Jesus." I cringed, but God gave me the grace to respond, "Cindy, you're worth it." I hugged her and meant it. Yes, it makes it worth everything to see people accept Jesus and grow in their faith and follow Him. In those first years it was only seeing the fruit of what God had done through Peter's life that gave me the ability to come to terms with his death.

Cindy was transformed and inspired by her new faith. She shared with me how she told coworkers, at the devotional time at work, of her new relationship with Jesus. God started working in her, and desiring to use her skills she approached us about organizing a race in Peter's memory. She started the "Get Inspired Peter Auch Memorial 5k Race and Fun Run" that was held for four consecutive years. What a joy it was to work with a great committee those four years to plan the race and find speakers to share the gospel. The races were held at dusk, so that glow-in-the-dark shirts and gear would reinforce the theme of being lights for Jesus to carry on the inspiration Peter's passion for Jesus had given to us. God comforted our family to a great extent through the love of all who attended the races.

Donation

Another way God comforted me was through His providence that was demonstrated in events surrounding the donation of Peter's tissues. The story of Peter's donation actually began several years earlier. God knew He had to prepare us for Peter's death. God had His hand in all this, sovereignly planning how it would involve the lives of many people and glorify Him in amazing ways.

When Peter was fourteen, a teenager at our church needed a kidney transplant. Duane, being very healthy and having the same blood type, felt compelled to see if he could donate his kidney to him. We went through the whole physical assessment process, and it turned out that Duane was a perfect match. However, they overlooked one crucial thing—Duane was forty-three years older than the teenager who needed a kidney. Duane's kidney wouldn't last as long as the guy would need it. So they decided to use Duane's kidney only if they couldn't find another younger donor. As it turned out another guy in the church youth group, the son of our best friends, decided to be tested and also turned out to be a perfect match. Our kids watched us through that process and learned about the need for people to donate. They accepted our values. It was one of those "of course you'd donate" things in the family. We visited Alex and Sam after their surgeries in Minneapolis, where the transplant took place. Our boys had so much fun celebrating life together with them. It was the last time my three boys would ever be together, just goofing off at a Twins game and with their friends at the hospital. It was a precious memory for all of us.

Peter privately wrote many of his goals, but the goal that I was keenly aware of was his desire to get his permanent driver's license. The morning after his sixteenth birthday, he made sure we got to the driver's license testing center in Vermillion to get it, before school started. He wasn't about to waste even one day with only a restricted license. So we got to the testing place at 7:30 a.m. and were handed all the forms that needed to be completed. I remember realizing he'd never make it back to school on time, thirty miles away, if he filled out the paperwork himself—you get lots of experience filling out forms as an adult; it's a new and slow experience for a sixteen-year-old. The lady there was pretty irritated at me for doing it for him. I whizzed through it, checked off that he would be a donor in the process. I knew his feelings and could confidently answer the question. I may have casually asked him, "Peter, you'd be a donor, right?" and got a "yes" as confirmation. He got his picture taken, paid the fees, and tore off to school (within the speed limits). He was pretty happy to be on his own, driving without me with him from that time on. I had driven with him as he practiced so much that I was very confident he was a good driver.

The donation process became one of the huge ways God showed that He cared for us. He blessed us in the midst of the most terrible pain we'd ever faced. He didn't abandon us. That night after the accident, once we made the decision to let Peter die naturally, the ball for donation started rolling. We showed proof of his donation decision on his driver's license. We decided against donating his heart, because we wouldn't be able to be with him at his final moments if that surgery would be done. We agreed to let them take anything else that was useful.

The afternoon after he died the calls from the South Dakota Lion's Eye and Tissue Bank started. A very kind lady on the phone asked to clarify if they could harvest bones and ligaments and tendons. I said, "Of course!" The next call was about skin tissue, and she explained that because he was so tall (6′2″), there were so very many people he could benefit from skin tissue—lots of skin! Later she called, saying she was so terribly excited that he had such good veins. It was if she was saying there were miles of veins due to his long legs. They could use all those veins in a research project on human tissues that would be used for stents for heart patients. Her excitement and joy were contagious. She was so very delighted about the gifts our son could give to other people. She caused us to see there was good that could come from the tragedy. So very many people could benefit. She told of all orthopedic problems that he would help due to his good tendons and ligaments and strong bones. That made me start to smile and have some joy in the pain; Peter wanted to be an orthopedic surgeon, to help athletes with injuries. We just knew that he'd be delighted to benefit fellow athletes and others with his tissues. His corneas were a gold mine—he had perfect vision. Two people would be able to have good sight because of him.

So what was a terribly difficult day turned out to contain some joy, knowing Peter would be able to benefit so many people. With those calls God showed me His care for us, letting us know that this was one of the ways his death would help people and have an impact. His strong, healthy body wouldn't be wasted, the one that he exercised and nourished to be in great shape. There is a wonderful feeling when your loved one lives on in a small way in someone else and is helping them every day.

Peter was able to donate his corneas, various tendons, ligaments, bones, skin, and blood vessels. Within a few weeks the South Dakota Lions Eye and Tissue Bank told us that fifty-eight people benefitted, in addition to the tissue used for the research study. Three people wrote to us to express their gratitude for their sight and improved movement.

Each year the South Dakota Eye and Tissue Bank has a beautiful luncheon to honor donors and recipients. My experiences at the donor luncheons brought a lot of comfort. Recipients and their families meet donor families and share their stories and experiences. It becomes a tangible way to find hope in the loss. At the first luncheon I was so blessed when a friend of our daughter Julia, who was studying at SDSU, approached me. The girl said she had been there the night and day when Peter's harvesting surgery was taking place, assisting in the process. As she worked she came to understand that the body was that of her friend's brother. It was hard for her, but she was so honored to be able to help make the donation. She told me it is always a sacred, precious time, a time when the donor's body is treated with utmost respect. I was so relieved to hear that. Then I realized she was there behind the scenes of those phone calls I got that afternoon after he died, as they did the surgery, and found all the wonderful tissues that could be used. For me it was such an incredible, loving thing to discover. In my grief, how I needed some connection to a real person who was there and cared for my son after he died! Someone saw him, touched him, and demonstrated love and respect to him when I couldn't be with him any longer. It gave me a much-needed connection to him. It was one of those amazing ways God made it possible to feel loved by people in the middle of my grief. He had planned all the details necessary to encourage and comfort me long before the luncheon that day. His sovereignty in this experience made me feel so loved by Him.

By the time two years had passed after the accident I was starting to think beyond myself, and was understanding the purpose God tells us of regarding why we face trials and pain. We went to the luncheon again the next year to continue to work on our grief issues.

God spoke to me there, as I watched the event planner go from one grieving person to the next, encouraging them. It became a clear example of how Jesus can use a person to be His love in action to hurting people. With those thoughts in mind as we left the luncheon, we drove to a concert in which Julia was singing. The last number was based on the Prayer of St. Francis.

"Lord, make me an instrument of Your peace. Where there is hatred, let me sow love; where there is injury, pardon; where there is doubt, faith; where there is despair, hope; where there is darkness, light; where there is sadness, joy.

O, Divine Master, grant that I may not so much seek to be consoled as to console; to be understood as to understand; to be loved as to love; For it is in giving that we receive; it is in pardoning that we are pardoned; it is in dying that we are born again to eternal life."

I felt God branding in my heart the idea that the comfort He had given me was not to be kept for myself. He was calling me to use it for other people to bring them joy.

I listened to the words, knowing that in the midst of all the pain we feel, if our desire is to be an instrument of God's peace, then He is able to not only continue the healing process in our lives but also bring comfort to others. I was challenged to open my eyes with compassion to see others with the same struggles I've had in my life: infertility, miscarriage, failed adoption attempts, a special needs child, a child who has gotten in trouble with the legal system, a father and sister who died from cancer, a mother dwindling away in a care center, the death of a son, and the separation from family by large distances. People with similar issues are the ones I want to comfort, and God may give opportunities to develop sensitivity to people with other needs and problems as well.

STUCK

After we made through six months of grieving, things may have looked good on the outside to other people. It appeared that Duane and I were doing really well with our grief, but things weren't good inside me. I was pretty good at putting on a façade. But inside I was becoming consumed with anger. It was festering and sending down roots. I could praise God about the people who were getting inspired to follow Jesus, but my heart was rotting with rage. God had to soften my heart and get me to forgive. He needed to put a puzzle piece in my life in a dramatic way to get hold of my heart to remain Lord of my life. He knew that unless I forgave, I wouldn't be able to walk with Him.

There is a tendency for grieving people to get stuck in their recovery process. Getting "stuck" is different from having difficulty with grief surfacing with intensity at holidays and anniversary dates. Being "stuck" involves being trapped in harmful behavior and thought patterns that develop as a result of the circumstances of the loss. Often counseling is needed to hear the truth from God's Word and to apply it in the situation. Satan is eager to destroy us, and I've become convinced that people who are grieving are prime targets. If he can get people to be "stuck" in their grief they will neglect reading truth from God's Word to find comfort, and then gradually drift away from Jesus. If Satan can prevent us from moving forward to the new piece in the puzzle God has planned for us, he stops us from glorifying God. Since we are made to glorify God we feel miserable and wretched in our grief.

For me it was sin that nearly caused me to come to a halt in following Jesus through the grief journey. The verse in Proverbs says,

> **"In all your ways acknowledge Him, and He will make your path straight."**
>
> PROVERBS 3:6, NIV

Usually I've interpreted that verse to mean that we are to notice what God is doing and give Him the credit and worship Him for demonstrating His power and love. Then the verse promises us that He will be able to direct us in positive ways. However, to "acknowledge Him" also may mean listening to the Holy Spirit speaking to us, convicting us of disobedience and responding in repentance. Those sins create barriers to becoming Christlike, and they get us off in a side trail of some detrimental pattern of behavior. We may get stuck in that trail. The path God intended for us to follow isn't straight when we are not confessing the sin we are harboring. It may sound harsh for a grieving person to hear that God is using their grief journey to deal with sin. But I've seen repeatedly in other grieving friends that there is a tendency to wallow in thought patterns or behaviors that lead to getting stuck. Paul in 2 Corinthians 10:3-6 exhorted the believers to "take every thought captive to obey Christ." The work of grief recovery demands a great deal of controlling harmful thoughts. God is working everything together for our good, even in the midst of terrible loss. His goal is to establish His Kingdom or to make us Christlike. That process may involve exposing and dealing with patterns of behavior that will prevent us from following Him and finding peace and joy.

Rage and Pride

God forewarned me of the possibility I would get stuck in anger and rage. In His providence, about three weeks after Peter died, I had an encounter that alerted me to this pitfall. I was feeling a little more functional and was pushing myself to get things done as the holidays were coming and I had to finalize plans for the mission trip at New Year's. I still was feeling lots of support from people and focusing on God's goodness. Each year I organized the church's Christmas decorating party and brought many of the goodies. I was pretty tired, but I thought that with the help of everyone we could get the decorations up in the church by the end of the first week in December.

The day of the party, I remember leaving work later than I planned. I intended to briefly stop at Walmart for some things I needed for the evening. However, at one of the end aisles someone stopped me. She had worked at the health-care facility with me many years previous. She expressed her condolences, and then began to tell me the story of her son's death, which she pointed out was very similar to Peter's. I hadn't realized her son had passed away, so I felt pretty badly for her. She told me minute details of the accident. She animatedly told me about every possible thing every nurse and doctor did wrong. She expressed such bitterness toward her family for the way they handled the situation that she was red-faced and nearly shaking. It was appalling. Finally I jumped in and asked her when the accident had taken place. I was shocked when she told me it had been seventeen years since her son died.

God had that woman tell me about her grief and allowed me to see her reaction to alert me to what bitterness, anger, and an unforgiving heart can do. I needed to see an example of the long-term destructive effects of unresolved grief before I found myself in her place. I was generally in a joyful, positive, grateful mind-set and was unaware of the smoldering rage under the surface. God warned me through her, that I needed help to deal with my grief or it could fester just like it did in the life of this woman. God sovereignly arranged that encounter at Walmart to warn me that I could end up stuck, just like she did!

In the first year after the accident I had the feeling that people thought I looked strong and was doing very well. I wasn't grieving like they expected, so to them I looked like I was getting through the pain pretty well. Grief affects people differently. I didn't express much sadness and depression and withdrawal like you would expect. When I was around people, they energized me and God gave me joy through them. What few people saw, though, was the unforgiving spirit that was developing in my heart. I tried to mask it. In fact I don't think I knew that I was getting stuck in this sinful pattern.

I was full of rage at Derek, the guy who hit Peter's car and caused the accident. I played the accident over and over in my mind when driving past the site. How could anyone be so stupid to try to pass there in the dark? It should have been easy to see Peter's car coming on that long stretch of open road. How could he pass there? How could he not know he couldn't pass safely? I wanted revenge.

Duane talked to the state's attorney, and reckless driving was the only charge that was possible in the situation. No alcohol was involved, so vehicular manslaughter and homicide weren't options. I was so furious! We heard that the sentence could be worse than the typical fine for reckless driving, due to a death being the outcome. That was my only hope for revenge. He needed to sit in jail a long time and rot!

I went to the sentencing in February, wanting to watch Derek get all he deserved. I wanted him to suffer and be an example to all the other kids in the community: you are punished severely if you don't drive carefully and end up killing someone. I didn't want anyone to think that it's okay to speed and pass stupidly and selfishly and kill an innocent person—all you get is a relatively small fine and then it's over.

As I drove to the courthouse in Vermillion on the date of the hearing, I saw a billboard a few blocks before I reached my destination. Christians often put Bible verses on it. There it was:

"For God did not send His Son into the world to condemn the world, but to save the world through Him."

John 3:17, NIV

God said to me, "I don't condemn Derek at all. I intend Derek to be saved through all this." I felt God convicting me that I had to forgive Derek and watch Him work in the situation. It felt as if a toilet plunger had been used to free up the clogged mess in my heart. The rage and hatred suddenly began to drain away. I only had five blocks to drive before I would get to the courthouse, which was a short distance in which God purged my vengeful heart so I could forgive. As I drove, parked, and walked up the steps to the courtroom, it felt like God was using the toilet brush to scrub the corners of my heart to purge any spots of unforgiveness. His reproof was loving, but severe. I couldn't hang on to my stubborn, selfish hatred in front of a God who loved Derek so much. God knew that with my practical, prideful, controlling approach to life, He had to do something radical to transform my heart so I would forgive. This wasn't the time for God to be a comforting teddy bear. I had let sin take over in my life, and I had to let it go or I would get stuck in my grief and wouldn't be able to follow Jesus. God knew exactly what I needed.

However, in those minutes while I went up the stairs of the courthouse, as God was letting me feel the peace and joy of a clean heart, pride took over in the empty place. I thought it would be wonderful if I could make a very public display of forgiving Derek. If he was sentenced to prison I planned to plead with the judge on his behalf to delay the start of his sentence until the end of the semester, so his studying wouldn't be halted midterm. My "savior" tendency kicked in, wanting to get the praise and admiration of everyone for being so kind and generous. I had no idea if it would be possible to work out this deal for Derek, or how I could pull it off, but the idea was compelling. And the more showy the better.

Once inside I sat trembling while waiting for Derek's turn. It took about forty-five minutes for the judge to wade through the hearings of many others with various traffic violations. Feeling the rage and revenge get purged out as I let go of all the rottenness in my heart was amazing. Fighting the prideful thoughts that crowded into my brain became the new challenge. I was seated toward the back of the room. There were at least fifty people, waiting their turns to face the judge. Most were young people who were there alone. But across the aisle, about two benches ahead, there was a young man seated beside two people who seemed to be his parents. From what I could see of him, he looked like the pictures that had been in the newspaper, and I deduced he was Derek. It was so strange to see the person who had killed my son. He looked meek and fearful, as if he needed his parents' support to get through what he was to face. He probably had no idea what his sentence would be and its ramifications for his life. There was still a feeling in me that he would never feel what we did in the loss of our son. His situation wasn't good, but it couldn't be compared to the permanence of Peter being gone. It just wasn't fair at all. I still wanted to get back at him. Traces of my revenge still lingered.

Finally his name was called, and he walked up to the Judge. They were both far away from me, at the front of the big courtroom, so I could barely hear. I strained to catch every word. Although I realized that I was going to have to obey God and make a conscious choice to forgive, I still wanted to revel in hearing the charges first. I wanted some pleasure in seeing any shifts in his posture, which would indicate to me that he was squirming under the harshness of the penalty.

The judge charged him with reckless driving, asked if he pled guilty, which he did. Then she told him to go to the end of the hall, outside the courtroom, and pay the $300.00 fine and $84.00 court fee. "Bang" went the gavel and that was it.

I screamed inside: "Only $384.00 for the life of my precious Peter?" Only $384.00 as punishment for taking the life of a brilliant kid with so much to offer and so many abilities to serve God and help people? Didn't the judge realize he killed someone? She never mentioned it at all! All the rage poured back into my heart. What about jail? Sometimes people go to jail for reckless driving. Wouldn't Derek even do that much, even for a few days? The answer was "no." I sat there stunned. But there was no reason to stay, so I got up to leave the courtroom. It was there that God once again spoke to my heart: "Shut up and forgive."

This time, in the few steps it took to get from my seat to the door to the lobby, I surrendered it all to God. I felt as if I had been spanked, with no self-defense at all. I needed God's harsh confrontation to turn my behavior and heart around. I met Derek and his parents just outside the courtroom door as we were leaving. It was right then that I made the decision once and for all to forgive and love Derek. God gave me the grace and mercy to go up to him and hug him and tell him I had decided to forgive him. I quoted John 3:17 to him and pled with him to give his life to Jesus someday and get right with God. He blinked and nodded.

We talked awhile, getting acquainted. Finally I asked Derek, "What happened that night? What was going on? How did it happen?" He said he just didn't know. He couldn't remember anything. He had looked down at his gas gauge, realized he didn't have enough gas to make it home, and looked up to see Peter's headlights right there in front of him. He tried to avoid hitting him and swerved, but ploughed into the front passenger side. He didn't remember passing Darlene at all. He just couldn't figure it out at all and felt horrible about it. It was a mystery to him.

Derek was struggling with his grades, and was getting minimal sleep. He had flashbacks of all the lights coming at him and police cars. I told him we'd be praying for him. His mom was worried about him, as he had stopped going to church. His psychiatrist wasn't much help: he just told him to forget about it and go on with life.

After that day I kept in touch with Derek a little on Facebook. Julia met him at SDSU and talked with him several times. He was able to complete ROTC basic training and go back for his sophomore year at SDSU. I thought that was the end of the story.

A few months later, in August, I was at the veterinarian's office in Beresford with our new dog, getting his shots. In walked the judge with her dog. As we waited for our appointments I told her about my experience in the courtroom the day of the hearing and God helping me to forgive Derek. She stared at me, didn't say much, but did mention that she was not aware of any reckless driving case at that time that involved a death. I had the urge to ask her what Derek would have been charged with had she known about the death. She said she would have to look into it.

I wrote her a letter a few weeks later, reminding her to tell me what Derek deserved. I didn't want to do anything legally. I just wanted to know. There was still some pride left in me; I needed to know what penalty he had avoided by the decision that was made that day. I needed to know the extent to which my forgiveness had gone in liberating Derek to a free life. Possibly it would help Derek to more fully understand God's mercy in his life. I would be able to tell him and feel self-righteous. There were still a lot of rotten attitudes in me that needed to be torn out!

A few weeks later a letter came from the judge. In her judge legal jargon, she basically said that she had not been advised of all the facts in the case prior to the sentencing and couldn't comment on it any longer. You could tell she was rather disturbed about it, but couldn't do anything anymore. God had kept the judge from all the facts in the case. The lawyer who represented the state must have neglected to inform the judge of all the details. The lawyer left out the very important fact that the speeding and passing at an intersection resulted in a death. Something went very wrong from a human perspective. There was no justice, but it went very right from God's perspective. Why would God have the facts be omitted at the sentencing? What was His purpose? Why did Derek face such a minor penalty?

It occurred to Duane and me that God had to pick two or three people to be involved in the accident. God picked Derek and Darlene and Jared (the passenger) to be the tools for His purpose. In His mercy toward them, He didn't let the facts be made known to the judge. He didn't want Derek's life ruined by a jail sentence. He loved Derek and wanted to save him. He spared him all the legal trouble he seemed to deserve. God was merciful, kind, and loving, wanting Derek to seek Him and be made righteous before Him. He loved Derek so much He didn't want him to suffer all the shame a jail sentence would bring to him and his family. After all,

Jesus had been punished for his sin of speeding when He died on the cross; Derek didn't need to be punished again.

I also realized that God had to eliminate any possible way I could continue to seek revenge or glory in Derek's misery. The case was closed. I couldn't do anything anymore to get justice. I finally submitted to God and accepted the truth in Romans 12:19: "Vengeance is mine, I will repay, says the LORD." It was at that time when I was finally able to forgive and totally feel at peace. Joy started to fill up all the empty places where the rotten attitudes had festered.

That day at the vet's office, I was overwhelmed by the truth that God has the right to work in our lives, the wisdom to do what's best, and the power to orchestrate even the tiny details of our lives. He planned for the judge to bring her dog in at the very same time I was there. He worked out all the events that led to my final submission to Him. He made it possible for me to understand the extent of His control of all the aspects of the court case and the accident. Millisecond differences in what we do are planned and carried out to accomplish His purposes.

Fear

God not only dealt with my anger and pride but also lovingly dealt with my fear. My love for Him really soared when He orchestrated some events to calm the fear that was plaguing me. The high school students asked me soon after Peter's death if they could get a shirt printed for a school event to honor him. These were kids who were affiliated to some extent with Fellowship of Christian Athletes on the campus or part of other Bible studies. These were the same kids who had looked diligently for verses the Monday after he died. The shirts were to be sold and worn for the first time at a halftime show at a basketball game in Beresford. They intended to dedicate the game to Peter's memory since he wasn't there to play with them that season. Duane and I were to come to the center of the court to receive a large booklet of all their memories that they had compiled. Everyone was asked to express their support of us by wearing the tee shirts. The students wanted to print "DON'T WASTE YOUR LIFE" on one side and "I press on to the goal of the upward call of God in Christ Jesus" on the other. I agreed. The shirts are a distinctive deep purple with neon green large words. The "T" in <u>WASTE</u> was shaped like a cross. The shirts have been worn all over Beresford and the area; people can't ignore the tee shirt when they see it. It makes people wonder about the slogan and think about their lives and what they're doing with the time they have on earth.

After the event I saw more and more people wearing their purple and green shirts around town. I had a growing concern that we could be infringing on some sort of copyright laws by taking the name of John Piper's book and printing it on a tee shirt. I don't know much about the law, but it seemed like we had stolen the title and used it on a tee shirt without permission from the author of the book. I didn't want any legal problems! I didn't think that someone like John Piper would sue us or take us to court, but even putting him in a situation in which his advisors would pose the issue was terrifying to me. I quake and wilt in situations when an authority or influential figure is angry at me. This tendency is probably due to scars from the harsh verbal chastising I had as a child. I never learned how to stand up for myself when I was younger, and hadn't grown too much in that area as an adult.

My sister Beth encouraged me to be proactive, write John Piper, and tell him Peter's story to encourage him. She suggested I mail him a shirt to wear. I wrote him a long letter and mailed the shirt to him, hoping I had chosen the right size so I wouldn't offend him any further! I told him about Peter reading his book, influencing his peers, his death, and God's work in the kids' lives. I never heard anything again. I feared the worst. Any day we could receive word that we were going to face some ugly situation.

We started going to a new church around then, and we invited Pastor Steve and his wife over for lunch one Sunday. They saw a little memorial display I had in the dining area with a set of bright-colored miniature running shoes and Peter's picture. They asked what the shoes were all about. We told them the story of Peter's love of running and the *Don't Waste Your Life* book being such an important tool in Peter's spiritual growth. I told them I was concerned about the tee shirt and not knowing what was happening with Dr. Piper.

Terry, the pastor's wife, said, "Oh my! I was just in Minneapolis last week. My daughter and I went on a bike ride on one of the many bike paths in the city. A man came toward us, and after he passed my daughter stopped peddling and said, "That was John Piper." How did she know? The tee shirt he was wearing had the title of one of his books printed on it. Terry couldn't remember for sure when talking to us what the shirt that Dr. Piper was wearing looked like. So right then Terry took a picture of one of Peter's purple and green shirts and texted it to her daughter. Sure enough, Peter's shirt was the one her daughter remembered seeing!

How amazing! God knew I needed my fears to be calmed. He planned for Dr. Piper to be riding through a park, wearing the tee shirt at the exact time my pastor's wife and daughter would be riding the opposite direction toward him so they could see him very clearly. Then He led her to comment on her observation regarding name of the book title to her mother, who remembered it when she was talking with me, so we could put two and two together. Dr. Piper obviously liked the shirt. By wearing it in public he indicated to me that he wasn't going to do anything negative regarding the fact that we had used the name of his book without first obtaining his permission. All of this could not have been a coincidence! God goes to great lengths to work things out so He can lovingly work out His goal of drawing us to Himself. That puzzle piece boggles my mind!

Offense and Apology

Sometimes the puzzle pieces God wants to put in place in our lives must be reshaped until they fit into His glorious puzzle. It's as if God has to clip off parts of a piece so it can fit into His overall puzzle. He has to work in our lives so that He can be glorified. For me the painful process of letting God soften my heart to get me to the place where I could apologize for hurting someone during the grief process took a long time. He had to clip away at my bad attitudes over several years. Once His work on my heart was accomplished and the piece was reformed, it could snap into place so His glory could be evident.

This story began when Peter was fourteen. He was a Boy Scout, and being a Type A personality with long-range planning skills he began thinking of what he should do for his Eagle Scout project. Boys intending to get their Eagle Scout rank must finish their project before their eighteenth birthday. He got it into his mind and heart that he should work on getting a little rundown park in Beresford to be an attractive nice place for kids to play. The park was located by the railroad tracks that ran through the town. It had an old swing set with worn-out seats, a well-used, paint-chipped merry-go-round, and a metal jungle gym. There was a small picnic shelter toward the back of the area. Many Sundays after church, Peter asked us to drive by the park so he could look at it and formulate a vision of what could be done. Duane and I thought that the park was so pathetic that it wasn't worth wasting any of our time and effort to encourage Peter regarding his plans for improvements. We tried to dissuade him and get him to consider other options. But Peter must have remembered that, as a little boy, he begged and begged to stop to play at any park he saw. He loved all the slides, climbing equipment, and swings. Fixing up this park was just what was in his heart to do, and we couldn't stop him.

Peter was quite shy despite his determination, and it took all the courage he could muster to contact the mayor of Beresford to discuss his vision as was required in the Eagle Scout project process. Eventually he did discuss it, and that set in motion working with his scout master Mike to get his project started. Mike loved the idea, and Mike loved Peter. Peter was one of his oldest scouts and was the natural leader of the group. The younger boys loved him. He set the standard the others tried to follow to get their badges done; he paid attention to the younger guys and encouraged them. To him scouting wasn't just about his own self-improvement. Then Peter died, and the troop was crushed. The memory of the sad sight of the honor guard of young Boy Scouts bringing Peter's casket into the church for the prayer service still makes me cry.

Mike took hold of Peter's vision for the park and saw it as a chance for all the boys to rally around improving it for Peter's legacy. It became known as "Peter's Park." We discussed and planned together. We met with the surrounding community members to find out their wishes for improvements. We set to work as a troop, painting and repairing the picnic shelter. Mike and I designed the landscaping for the park sign and a tribute to Peter's vision. Mike wanted to express his gratefulness to Peter for his leadership and envisioned a lovely memorial stone to be the focal point of the landscaping project. We worked together and got it engraved. We decided to rename the park "Eagle Park." Improving various parts of this park would provide many boys for years to come with opportunities to complete their Eagle Scout rank. Mike also worked very hard with the Boy Scouts to get the Spirit of the Eagle award for Peter posthumously. That is an award that can be given in memory of someone who deserved the Eagle Scout award, evidenced by their character and leadership. It was humbling to see all Mike did to bless us.

However, my emotions and pride got in the way, and I let Mike's very strong leadership start to really irritate and anger me. He had plans that were quite extensive and I just didn't have any energy to support everything he wanted to do at that little place. One day I drove by the park, and to my surprise the whole troop was working on the landscaping project. I hadn't been notified that they were doing the project that day. The way they were laying out the landscaping stones was nothing like the plans Mike and I had developed together. I smothered my shock and anger and hurt, and tried to look happy about it. But I drove off seething, because I wasn't informed of the changes; I wasn't allowed the chance to participate in this aspect of the project. I felt as if I wasn't in control anymore. I had seen myself as being an extension of Peter's vision and plans. When things happened that weren't done my way, I felt like my son's wishes were being violated. It was as if Peter didn't count in the whole thing anymore. To me it felt like dirt was being thrown on his coffin at the grave site (as was done in a funeral practice in the past), which I considered to be very insulting. I was hurt. When the landscaping was completed, with the beautiful memorial stone in place, I was horrified. It looked like a shrine to Peter. It made his own tombstone look kind of drab and pathetic in comparison. Being rather private and feeling rather overwhelmed by all the attention our family was getting, and wanting God to get the glory rather than us, I really hated the way it turned out. Mike called soon after that to discuss some issue and to get praise for his efforts. During the course of the conversation my anger swelled out of control. I verbally tore him to shreds. I was cruel and heartless in what I said to him. He hung up on me. The relationship between us was severed.

From then on the friction between us was terrible. Many people in the town knew of our falling out. I avoided Mike and stopped any involvement with the Boy Scouts. Further efforts to improve the park came to a standstill. The mayor tried to act as a go-between and bring some resolution to all the issues that Mike, Duane, and I disagreed about. I mustered support from others in the community to see things my way so I could turn them against Mike. The mayor had the landscaping reworked to some extent to make it easier for his staff to mow, which improved the appearance. That helped me a little, and I decided to be quiet about the whole thing and disengage from the park improvement efforts and the Boy Scouts. But my pride and resentment smoldered, destroying me from the inside out. I knew I had offended Mike terribly and needed to ask for forgiveness, but at the same time, I heard rumors from people in the community that he was very angry at me. I was terrified at facing a confrontation with him again. I feared making matters worse if I met with him to resolve the conflict.

My spiritual attitude got even worse. By four years after these events I started avoiding taking communion, because I knew there was sin in my life that hadn't been dealt with. I was delighted to lead the kids' worship service on communion Sundays because I could get out of the whole situation without anyone suspecting what was going on. At the same time, I was working on this book, and felt like a huge hypocrite, harboring this dark, horrible sin in my heart. Then Pastor Steve preached a sermon on forgiveness. God pierced my heart that morning and told me I had to contact Mike. Duane and I discussed it; he told me that I really needed to apologize to Mike before this book could be published. But a long time had elapsed and I couldn't remember the details of what I had done or all my problems with Mike to construct a good apology. I feared offending him more by omitting some offense he would remember. However, I had to use what I did recall and sent the following letter to Mike.

Dear Mike,

I've wanted to write this for a long time but haven't been able to put my feelings into words. I'm not sure now I can adequately put this into writing.

I have known for several years that I hurt you deeply and repeatedly regarding numerous issues concerning Eagle Park. It's so long ago that my memory fails me regarding details. I know I don't remember things clearly, nor do I remember them the way you do. I do know that your intention was to bless Peter's memory and to bless us with the park as a memorial to our son's character and involvement with the Boy Scouts. Your delight in working on this project was evident. It was an expression of love and comfort to us. The Spirit of the Eagle award that you sought to give Peter was a special tribute to him, and I appreciate how much you worked to obtain that plaque.

I want to thank you for envisioning the park and working with many people to see Peter's dream become a reality. It truly is a nice place now for kids to play. The improvements never would have happened without your leadership. The park is a special place now, especially with the rock and the memorial plaque explaining its history. It is an inspiration to children and families to work toward in raising their children. It is a beautiful means to glorify God by proclaiming His promise to us that, as we wait for Him, He will raise us up on eagles' wings so we can run without becoming weary.

I want to apologize for all the hurt and trouble I caused in the process. My most distinct memory is the phone call we had, at which time there was a sharp disagreement and I was cruel with my words. What I said was uncalled for, and the attitude I had was anything but Christlike. I am ashamed of myself and how I hurt you. All I wanted at that time was to get my way and maintain my pride. My lack of humility was appalling and led to the end of the working relationship we had had.

I'm sure there were other times that I expressed things that caused disagreement, frustration, and further pain. I know I have not been grateful enough and have been critical. Please understand that this most likely doesn't express all the ugly attitudes I had as you saw them; it is what I recall now.

I am sorry for all these things and would like to ask for your forgiveness. I do not deserve it at all.

Sincerely,
Mary Auch

About a week later a letter came back to us from Mike. He indicated that he understood that everyone gets angry. He had hoped for a long time that we could at least be able to smile or nod at each other to open a conversation that would lead to both of us apologizing for the wrongs between us. He noted that he had seen Duane in town that week, and realized because Duane smiled at him that there was the possibility for some positive interaction between us. Then he got the letter from me. He wished God's blessing on our family. Healing was possible now.

As I read his letter I felt God snap a puzzle piece into place. His Kingdom rule had been accomplished in this area of my heart. Due to finally obeying God and confessing my horrible actions, a peace and joy swelled inside of me that I hadn't experienced in years. The rage drained out. There was a calm, clean feeling inside me. Jesus' blood had cleansed this horrible, ugly, black sin, and I was freed of it. I was forgiven by God.

The grief process can reveal ugly areas of our lives. It is a time that Satan can use to get a foothold in our hearts, turning us away from God. If he can get us to focus on ourselves, we stop acknowledging God in all our ways. He gets us to veer off the straight path God has set for us to follow in our grief process. Satan would prefer that we get stuck in quicksand along the side of God's path, unable to free ourselves. If we don't listen to God's voice we can get trapped in sin patterns that lead to destruction. That's exactly what Satan wants to accomplish. He's a roaring lion, seeking to devour us. Grief is a prime time for Satan to work at getting our eyes off Jesus. How I praise God now, that by confronting my sin, obeying God, and seeking reconciliation, He pulled me out of that horrible place.

As I think about how merciful God was to get me unstuck out of the sins of unforgiveness, rage, pride, and fear, I remember this verse in psalms:

"If the LORD had not been my help, my soul would
soon have lived in the land of silence.
But the LORD has become my stronghold and my
God the rock of my refuge."

PSALMS 94:17, 22, ESV

What an awesome God to prevent me from wallowing in my sin! It took some sovereign actions on His part to draw me close to Him so I could repent and find Him to be my refuge.

New Normal

GriefShare

Years before the accident God started getting me ready for all the grief we'd face. He sent me on a mission trip with a retired missionary who had over the years lost every one of her family members. She had become very involved in leading GriefShare groups in Iowa. When Peter died I notified her as quickly as I could. Mary Block was very supportive, and helped Duane and me as we began our grief journey. She started a group in Beresford just for us and a few others who had lost their loved ones. Through the thirteen-week sessions we were able to share what we were going through, learn other ways of looking at issues that would bring healing, and find that joy was possible. The GriefShare program encourages people to find comfort from God through the Bible, and support from other people through whom He works.

There are six tasks of grief that need to be done to enable people to come to a place of joy. A person may work on a little of each of these at the same time, jump ahead to tasks at the bottom of the list, and return to work on the first steps—however God leads each individual person in their healing process. But eventually these are all accomplished:

- **Acceptance**
- **Turn to God/focus on the Word**
- **Share emotions**
- **Establish a new identity**
- **Create a new normal**
- **Move forward/leave a legacy**

The meetings helped me to accept the deaths of my baby, my sister, my father and mother, and Peter. The workbook exercises for devotional times enabled me to focus on verses that pertained to the comfort God offers available in the Word. It was a good place to share emotions with others experiencing the same thing. GriefShare encourages you to establish a new identity and figure out what a new normal looks like in your life. It enables you to move forward to the new purpose in life God has in store for you. Without that positive influence in my life, going through the valley of the shadow of death would have been very difficult.

One of the metaphors that GriefShare uses to help understand the grief journey is that of tangled mess of yarn representing our emotions: anguish, bitterness, depression, despair, fatigue, apathy, sadness, relief, panic, frustration, guilt, loneliness, worry, and so on. We may feel like a knotted mess of various feelings all at once. Grief recovery involves untangling the emotions and facing them, while allowing God to heal those hurt areas.

Later when I became a GriefShare leader, I used a ball of different-colored rubber bands to illustrate the recovery process. Each one of the six colors can represent one of the tasks of grief, as listed above. As people grieve they deal with acceptance to a certain extent initially, as if one of the rubber bands of that color is removed. Then they may find comfort in God's Word with certain verses of healing representing another color of rubber band. As they start to share emotions and memories another color band is removed. A new identity may be forming, the start of finding a new normal way of living begins, facing the tasks of living an every-day life becomes possible, and there may be glimmers of happiness, all represented by removing another colored rubber band. But the ball is dense with many layers of these colored rubber bands or tasks of grief work. You return over and over again to the same six tasks, getting deeper into the layers of hurt that have to be healed, removing the difficulties and pain as God brings healing. As each layer approaches the center of the ball the bands are stretched less tightly. There may be less intensity to what you experience. Finally what's left is the remaining task of moving forward in life to what God has planned for you to do in His Kingdom.

Discussions at GriefShare enabled me to deal with these tasks. It wasn't a smooth, continuous process. At times I was working on creating a new normal life without my youngest son to parent. At others times glimmers of what it meant to move forward to new areas of ministry were seen. Then I'd return to the first problem of acceptance and denial, realizing I still hadn't completely absorbed that Peter would never return. The times of watching the videos and sharing difficulties at GriefShare made me realize that I had to go to places that reminded me of my hurt in order to heal.

Duane and I purposefully started going to cross-country meets the following year to deal with our pain. I'm sure other parents wondered why we went. But there was comfort in being with them. We had a chance to relive events where Peter had been the year before and process that he was gone. Every time the kids would line up to begin the race, it would be glaringly apparent that Peter wasn't with them. I'd give up my denial a little more with each race. After parents got over the initial discomfort of knowing what to say to me, I brought up the subject and talked of Peter freely. Then these people became a huge blessing to us. Through facing the pain and realizing my son wasn't running with them, that he was gone, I was able to make steps forward in getting the healing I needed and to allow others to heal with me.

Acceptance

The Beresford Booster Club decided to make a special area at the edge of the golf course in Beresford for the cross-country team to begin their practices. It was to be a memorial as well as an inspiration to the team. The site has five metal silhouettes of runners who had been on the team the year Peter died. The art teacher, who is one of our closest friends, took photographs of the team members and reconfigured the shapes of the runners to a two-dimensional, flat form. It is masterful how she conveyed movement and emotion and personality. The figures evoke strong emotions as you view them. Although the forms were designed to be generic runners, the silhouette in the forefront clearly depicted Peter leading the pack of runners. He has his arm raised and index finger pointing to heaven. There are several meanings to that pose: that the team is number one, or that Peter's legacy is that Jesus was first place in his life, and in all he did he wanted it to be for the glory of God. The site, known as Runners' Point, is beautifully landscaped and a unique tribute.

It was at Runners' Point, one day, almost two years after the accident, that I finally accepted that he was gone. By this time I thought I had dealt with the issue. But grief is unpredictable. It blindsides you when you least expect it. One minute you can be happy and feel normal, and the next something happens to trigger a memory or confront you with your loss. When I was thinking I had made some progress, I was faced that day at Runners' Point that I was really back at the beginning task.

The statues at Runners' Point form a good backdrop to team pictures. After one of the races, the boys' cross-country team posed for a few shots. I watched. It was a happy time, reveling in their success that day. Then they asked me to come and pose with them, by Peter's statue. I stood beside the statue of my son, put my arm around its cold, hard, sharp shoulders. As I smiled for the photo I looked out at all the mothers taking pictures of their sons and the team. They looked kind of horrified; they could visually see what I hadn't grasped totally. Then it totally hit me. They had live healthy sons to hug and take home. All I had was a metal shape that resembled my son that would stay in the park forever. He really was gone. He wasn't coming back—EVER. I cried and processed that pain, and laid Peter to rest in my heart. I needed that day and painful experience to understand that I couldn't ever make him come back. I was able then to face reality so I could start to find a new identity and move forward. I got released that day in my grief. I was no longer defined as the grieving mother of the amazing cross-country runner. I could be set free to find joy in new things in life.

Everyday Tasks

Matt stayed at home with us for a few months after Peter died, working with the Beresford track team while raising support to join the Navigator's campus ministry full time in Brookings at SDSU. He periodically went into Peter's room to look and remember and learn as much as he could about his little brother. Matt had missed much, not being able to spend much time with him. He wanted to gather people's memories of Peter to piece together an accurate picture of who he was. One night he found the last assignment Peter did in school before the accident. We had been looking for a signature to use to engrave on the tombstone that we were designing.

It was the seventh month "anniversary" of his death, kind of a meaningful day for us. Matt looked in Peter's room and found his notebook with the school assignments he had been working on, hoping to find a paper with a recent version of his signature. I was brushing my teeth and washing my face when he showed me a paper. Without my glasses on all I could see was Peter's name at the top; the signature didn't look much different from the rest of those we had looked at on other things. Matt kept it in my face until I noticed the date at the top of the paper, next to his name: 11/22/13. It hit me: that was the last worksheet he did that memorable Friday. I felt like I was touching something sacred, a link to my son so far away—something precious and important. The worksheet was on Chemical Names and Formulas. All I focused on was the first section, "Naming Ions."

If you knew it was your last day on earth, would you spend time learning how to name ions and do a worksheet to practice it? It would be the last thing I'd think of! Maybe Peter would have done the assignment anyway, because he was fascinated with science and loved chemistry. If he knew the right terms he would be able to talk to Jesus better about the ions once he got to heaven, Jesus being the Creator of those ions. But would his teacher have let him out of the assignment if he knew Peter was going to die that night? What would he have done instead in class? I paused and wondered, *What IS important to do on our last day on earth?*

I looked at the paper more closely and noticed that Peter had finished it. Unlike all the other papers in the notebook, this one didn't have a grade written in red ink at the top. He had completed it in class and had it ready to hand in Monday morning. It hit me. He did an excellent job on the worksheet and had it finished so he could do other important and fun things that day. He was faithful in the little things. I found out later that he spent that class period helping other kids think through the questions to figure out the answers, because it was the hardest assignment they had had in the semester in that class up until then. He was doing what he often did: helping kids and challenging them to be their best. After doing the worksheet in class, he probably walked to the next class, smiling and cheering up people, and squirting them with water from his Gatorade bottle to let them know he cared about them. Then he worked out with his friends after school to get in shape for basketball and track. He never knew it would be the last time he'd see those kids, but he was happy when he came home because he had had a good time with them.

The fact that he spent his last day doing mundane things really struck me. In grief, one reaction I felt, which is common to many people, is to consider the common tasks of life to be a waste of time. In light of the fact that someone has died, and the foundation for your life is knocked out, does it really matter whether or not you do things like wash dishes, clean cobwebs, fold laundry, or rake the leaves? It's common to think that those things are a complete waste of time. Grief is tiring. Why waste energy on trivial things that have to be redone the next day or month? Furthermore why waste the tiny part of your brain that's free of grief on learning anything as seemingly useless as how to name ions? It's so easy to get stuck in this frame of mind. Life can really become a chaotic mess if this feeling persists. Furthermore, if stuck in this stage, grief becomes very selfish. Everything starts to revolve around you and your needs and feelings.

God spoke to me in my heart through Peter's example, saying to me that those small things are important if done for God's glory.

**"And whatever you do, in word or deed, do everything in the
name of the Lord Jesus, giving thanks to the
Father through Him."
"Whatever you do, whether in word or deed, do it
all in the name of the Lord Jesus."**

COLOSSIANS 3:17, 23, NIV

If I could do tasks around the house as unto Jesus as Peter did, it was worth it. Peter considered helping his classmates to be the way he could be the hands and feet of Jesus to those kids in his chemistry class. Those kids weren't annoying to him; they were what made life and going to school meaningful. I was challenged to look outside myself and my grief, and to stop looking at needy people around me as annoying interruptions in my grief. No, they were the means God used to take my eyes off myself and to look outward to others.

Heaven

Like many people who have lost loved ones, I developed a keen interest in heaven. I wanted to be with Peter so much, but couldn't, and was quite frustrated. I had an overwhelming desire to go to heaven, too. It wasn't a form of suicidal thoughts because I, like most people in grief, didn't want to act out my feelings or cause any self-harm. Many people have a strong sense that life on earth really doesn't matter anymore; the only reality is where their loved one is. For me I wanted to know as much as possible about this reality. I wanted to feel as connected to Peter as possible, so I sought to find out what he was experiencing in heaven.

This urge occurred concurrently with the publishing of many books about heaven: *Heaven is for Real, 20 Minutes in Heaven, My Time in Heaven, Flight to Heaven*, and the like. I bought every Christian book related to heaven I could find. The stories of near-death experiences, in which people described glimpses of heaven, were what I wanted to read about most. There are seventeen inches of space on my bookshelf with all these books. I delighted in the descriptions people wrote of approaching the gates to heaven, and experiencing vivid, loving, beautiful things before they were resuscitated and came back to live in their bodies on earth.

I tuned out many cautions other Christians gave about the veracity of these stories. They were so comforting to me! I was so happy when I read these, understanding what an indescribable time Peter and others in my family were having in their new home. I still do not doubt them. From hearing the reports two patients at work gave me who had to be resuscitated, what I read was very similar to what they experienced. My favorite book was, and is, *Imagine Heaven.* The author sifted through thousands of near-death accounts and found twelve common experiences that pointed to what scriptures say about heaven. He wrote about how these experiences illustrate scriptural descriptions of heaven, as if the Bible gives the outlines in a coloring-book picture, but the people who told the stories were filling in the colors between the lines.

However, as I read my library of heaven books, my delight in listening to God's Word and praying to Him started to wane. I've realized that getting my focus off the Lord and onto all these stories was becoming, for me, a form of idolatry. Others' word pictures of heaven were taking the place of my own relationship with Jesus. I wasn't delighting in Him much when I'd read those fascinating stories. The trend wore off, the fad diminished, and there weren't new books to purchase to keep my interest alive. My interest declined. When I stopped the unnatural focus on heaven, gave up trying to imagine each day what Peter was doing there, and just focused on Jesus instead, He could speak to me in my quiet times again. My love and relationship with the Lord had room to grow in my heart because it wasn't being crowded out.

There is one aspect of extensively focusing on heaven that became a major factor in propelling me to keep working through my grief. As I focused on the glory of heaven, where Peter is, the desire to make sure as many people get there as possible deepened. It became crystal clear to me that evangelism is essential. Obeying the Great Commission to go and make disciples became my passion. So many people are oblivious to their eternity, assuming they will "go to a better place." It's a terrible gamble to make that assumption. Being with Jesus in heaven is too marvelous to miss out on. The consequences of missing out—due to ignorance of the need for repentance, forgiveness, and following Jesus—are too dire. Because we know Peter is there, we have peace and assurance. It became clear to me that other passions and interests in life pale in comparison to the priority of making sure other people are convinced of their eternal future. The heaven focus deepened my desire to show others the way to Jesus, no matter the cost.

Empty

One of the ways Duane and I faced our grief was to continue to go to high school events. I think we were grieving the loss of the role of being supportive to our kids in the fun things they did. We felt that if we stayed at home, when our friends were enjoying the games and plays and concerts, the loss would feel more painful. Therefore we wanted to be involved in the graduation process. High school graduation signified the end of parenting children through high school. Peter was the baby of the family, so there were no others after him to support. Graduation would also most likely be the last time we'd see many of his classmates. It would be a chance to see what effect Peter had on the kids one last time. It was one last time to be comforted by the community.

One of the hardest lessons I have had to learn in my grief journey is that Jesus is the one who fills me up, not other people. I often looked to the kids in Peter's class to meet my emotional needs. I frequently felt disappointed that they didn't continue to tell me what God was doing in their lives as they grew in their faith and love for Jesus. I felt let down over and over. In addition, Duane and I dreaded the time around graduation. We felt we were missing out on all the fun things parents do to prepare their high school senior for the big day ahead. I also felt guilty about being relieved I didn't have to do all the work involved with a high school graduation, for what would have been the fourth time. We felt torn. We wanted to see Peter's friends on this very special day of their lives, but we knew the wounds of missing him would be reopened, exposing the loss once again.

I was trying to be optimistic, knowing I was doing pretty well in the grieving process, with only rare meltdowns. I had faced situations where the gap of Peter's absence was obvious and was doing OK at them. I had gone to the graduation ceremony the previous year to see what the ceremony would be like. This would help me deal with the loss and determine what the potential grief triggers would be on what would have been Peter's actual graduation day. Hopefully I could diffuse them ahead of time. I faced seeing the gym set up in the same figuration as it had been at the funeral, which had been in that same place. I teared up due to the memories that surged over me and felt the pain. I felt I had dealt with any potential triggers so the real graduation day wouldn't be a day of terrible grief and sadness. I felt so confident I even accepted the principal's offer to have us participate in the graduation ceremony to accept a gift from the class. I knew God would help us face it and we could do this.

However, the week before graduation I was pretty stressed out as I was getting ready to lead a mission trip to Haiti with Peter's friends three days after graduation. My to-do lists both at work and at home were miles long; I was overwhelmed. I was acting and feeling more like Duane usually does; Duane sees life as "half empty." I usually see life as "half full."

I woke up one morning thinking that there is nothing "half full" about your son dying and missing out on his high school graduation. I was living on empty. I felt less than empty. My son was gone permanently. I felt totally dehydrated spiritually and emotionally. I needed a drink to fill my heart to at least "half empty" again.

While still lying in bed, God reminded me right then of something that had happened the night before. I was at a very low point when driving home from work. My mind was swirling with tasks that seemed impossible to accomplish. It was late and dark. One of the things on my mind was to get the yard mowed. I just couldn't see how I could have time to do it when there was a good chance of rain. How could I spend the time to mow for hours with everything else on my to-do list? But as I drove up to the house, out of the corner of my eye I saw that the yard was mowed. Someone had done it. *Great,* I thought that night, *one thing off the list.* I kind of forgot about the lawn once I plunged into doing other pressing things that evening.

I woke up feeling particularly empty and drained, but God made me remember that at church several days before we had met a sharp young guy named Josh who was there for the first time. He needed some work for a few days before he headed to his summer job at a church camp. He had come and mowed the lawn for me! God prepared way ahead of time to encourage me. He had planned where I would sit in church to meet Josh, and had him come to mow just when I was at my lowest with all the stress. God whispered to me, "See, here's a sip to get you going. Remember that I love you enough to plan all this for you and to surprise you. Just watch, I will fill your cup." As I gathered strength from that sip of God's kindness, I wondered how God would satisfy the thirst I had and fill the emptiness in my heart.

Later that morning in my quiet time, I read from John chapter 2 in which Jesus turned the water into wine at the wedding in Cana. One of the thoughts I wrote in my journal was that the water pots were empty. There was nothing left to drink at all—no wine or water. The bride's father was humiliated and the guests were thirsty. However, Jesus didn't miraculously fill the pots with water. It took some act of obedience on the part of the servants for Him to do the miracle. They had to initiate something. They had to go and get the water. Similarly I needed to go to the graduation, go to all the parties, and enjoy the celebration with Peter's friends. I needed to do some hard work to get the water He wanted to give me. Then it was up to God to fill up my heart.

The interesting thing in the Bible story is that Jesus didn't just leave the pots filled with water and do the bare minimum of satisfying everyone's need for a drink. He turned it all to wine. He didn't settle for just keeping the wedding guests from getting too thirsty. He blessed them totally with the best wine they had ever had to drink. Wine symbolizes joy in the Bible. So in addition to giving us water to quench our thirst, Jesus wants to bless us with joy. I realized that Jesus wanted to do more than just get us through the graduation day. He wanted to continue turning our mourning to joy. He was up to something good with all that was going to happen.

As graduation day dawned I was feeling better. My cup was getting filled up with God's blessing and His Word. I wasn't feeling weak and dehydrated anymore. There was some strength there to draw on to face the day. I never dreamed how much He would continue to bless and rehydrate me!

The principal had planned for us to have assigned seats with the other parents of graduating seniors. When we entered the gym I became tearful when I saw the room set up for the event. Thoughts filled my mind that my tall, handsome son wouldn't be leading the class in and later speaking to the student body. (We could assume he would have been number one or two in his academic class rank, which would give him the task of speaking to his class. No one could prove us wrong.) Amazingly I was assigned to sit by a mother of one of the girls in the class. She is a clinical counselor. She was very compassionate and skilled as she listened to me talk about what I was experiencing in that moment while dealing with the loss of our son. It was a huge blessing to have her there, supporting me at that emotionally charged time. She was detached just enough to keep me calm and steady, and was careful not to reinforce anything that could increase my potential for crying and a meltdown.

As I sat talking to her, at first I couldn't identify something that was in my line of vision to the platform. There were three rows of empty seats ready for the seniors when they marched in. But in the front row, at the end closest to us, there was a graduation gown and shawl placed on the chair with the mortar board cap propped at the side. The band was practicing close by, and I assumed one of the senior band members left it there and was going to grab the gown, put it on, and rush back to get in line for the entrance to "Pomp and Circumstance."

When the seniors started marching in, the gown was still there. No one had grabbed it. Then it hit me. The seniors had marked with the gown the place Peter would have been in the lineup of the whole class. He would have marched in first because his last name started with an "A." They were coming into the room in alphabetical order. He would have been sitting in that first chair. His classmates were remembering him in a very obvious, tangible way. They wanted to make him part of their day as they were missing him badly. I broke down inside. It was too much. Their grief and mine mingled together silently.

Then it was time to receive the gift the class had prepared for us. Somehow Duane and I got up to the stage in front of everyone, and accepted a beautiful plaque they made for us and a diploma cover with signatures from the whole class inside. It was a touching moment. Before the ceremony I had noticed a memorial plaque of Peter hanging in the hallway, and had made a mental note that I needed to take a picture of it to treasure it. But the gift the class made was an exact copy of that plaque for us to keep! We were overwhelmed by their thoughtfulness.

God had more blessings in store for us. The three girls who spoke to the class—the class president, the salutatorian, and the valedictorian—had all been good friends of Peter's. They all mentioned in their speeches the things they had learned from his life and death, and the positive impact he had made on their lives. They, as a class, took his death very seriously and were better prepared to make much of their opportunities that lay ahead of them as a result. They remembered him. There weren't too many dry eyes at that ceremony. God encouraged me again that day that Peter's life and death were not wasted. He was once again using the pain everyone was feeling to bring ultimate good.

As we went from one graduation party to another later that evening, God blessed us over and over as we learned of the plans each of Peter's friends had for their future. So many of them were planning to serve and help people in the careers they had selected. There was a depth and seriousness and empathy that his classmates seemed to have developed due to the loss of their friend. Seeing God change the lives of Peter's friends has always brought smiles and some comfort. Once again God was turning our mourning to joy.

In all the events of graduation God taught me that the cup of my life isn't "half full" and Duane's isn't "half empty." In my own strength and ability and outlook on things it will always be totally empty. I will run dehydrated through life on my own. But He fills our emptiness with sips of little blessings to show He cares, and then fills us with truth from His Word to get us hydrated. But God doesn't leave it at that. He does unexpected things through loving, wonderful people to totally shower us with His love and give us joy. I don't ever have to face life on empty. If I look up to Him, God fills me—totally.

Right after graduation Duane and I took a group of twelve of Peter's friends on a mission trip to Haiti. I was looking to this trip to be one that would totally fill me with lots of joy to last for many months to come. It was to be the last time I would be able to spend much time with any of them. Some of these students had grown up with him in church. Some were his best friends at school. They had run with him in cross-country. Two of them spoke at the graduation, mentioning the impact Peter's death had on the class. They knew him better than anyone else. Being with them was the next best thing to being with Peter. It was a good time of being together, making them disciples in missions and considering together what God had in mind for them to do to serve Him with their lives.

The highlight for all of us in Haiti was taking a trip up a mountain to visit a new little church. Because Peter loved goats, the team decided to give a flock of ten goats to the people in the community where this little church was located. Some of the village people were not Christians, others were. Giving to anyone was in keeping with the philosophy of the local mission organization. The recipients of the goats were to give the first baby goat (kid) back to the mission. Then that kid would be given to someone else, to continue the process. We had the challenge of taking the flock of goats up the mountain, each one with a collar and rope leash. Most of the students had never been in contact with a goat. We had never climbed a mountain covered with slick mud and rocks. It was a hilarious time, pulling unwilling beasts, shoving them, and slipping and sliding in the mud on the path. Peter would have had a blast if he had been with us!

When we got to the top of the mountain, to the little community, we visited many homes and prayed with the people there for any needs they had. Then they all gathered at the place where the foundation for their church building had been laid. We sang worship songs as the bleating goats joined in, with the loud sound reverberating between the mountains. What an amazing time to praise Jesus together with the Haitian believers and Peter's friends! It was a healing time for me that set the stage so I could in my mind let Peter's friends leave to move forward and follow Jesus in life. Jesus filled me with that trip with those kids. I was able to say good-bye and start the process of letting them go to serve Him. It felt as if our nest was totally empty, but we were starting to see how God was filling it with new things. This was our last trip to Haiti, but it is a great and precious memory.

11

MOVING FORWARD

This morning, when reading my Bible, I found a verse I had high-lighted in the past. It summarizes the prayer of grieving people's hearts as they face the next phase of life and move forward into what God has for them to do without the person they loved with them.

> **"Satisfy us in the morning with your steadfast love,**
> **That we may rejoice and be glad all our days.**
> **Make us glad for as many days as you have afflicted us,**
> **and for as many years as we have seen evil."**

PSALM 90:14–15, ESV

I wrote in the margin that this verse means "Give us gladness in pro-portion to our former misery. Replace the hard years of suffering with good times." It is a prayer for God to fill our lives up to the brim in the gaping vacuum left by our loss.

The next verses say:

> **"Let your work be shown to your servants and your glorious**
> **power to their children.**

**Let the favor of the Lord our God be upon us, and
establish the work of our hands upon us,
Yes, establish the work of our hands."**

PSALM 90:16–17, ESV

After working through the strong emotions of grief, when the waves of pain lose their intensity and frequency, grieving people have a need to find new, positive outlets for their energy. One's spiritual growth no longer focuses on finding solace and comfort. Instead, the focus is on God giving a new identity and helping us to prioritize what is important in life. The old way of viewing oneself as only being the mother (or relative) of the deceased has to be replaced with a new vision of where to move forward. God's sovereignty is seen in new dimensions, and He puts new puzzle pieces in place to keep us focused on the Kingdom of God. But there is a crying need, when feeling weak and frail, for God to be the one on whom we rely when starting any new ventures. He needs to be the one who establishes our work.

Empty Nest

In the spring of 2015, our task of moving forward in our grief was expedited by our two middle kids. Matt was planning to continue ministry with the Navigators or go to graduate school in civil engineering. Julia was deciding whether to go to graduate school in vocal performance or to begin a career working in some capacity. The nest in our home was soon going to be totally empty, but God had some glorious surprises and lessons to teach us about His sovereignty and purposes through their experiences. As my kids left home Jesus and His Word became more and more precious to me.

Once my attention was off the things that consume the minds and energies of parents of high school kids, my other kids' needs stood out. Participating in their launching as adults was part of my "moving forward" process. Through their development and experiences, God continued to teach me about His love and sovereignty. My love for God deepened, and my dependence on Him to care for my kids increased. I grew in being able to see God's ability to use them for His glory. As Duane and I were in the process of setting them free to serve Jesus, our own interests in serving Him in other capacities intertwined with their stories. Our three kids all faced unique struggles dealing with their grief. They were all young adults, and were pushed towards figuring out how to move forward much faster than what felt comfortable to all of us. They all had to figure out vocations and God's will for their lives. Concurrently Duane and I had to lay aside the identity of being the parents of a deceased son, find a new identity, establish a new normal to our lives with a prematurely empty nest, and move forward to what God was calling us to do.

What God did in the lives of our other three kids after Peter died, and as a result of his death, demonstrates His power to transform us and shape us to be useful in His Kingdom. Our kids all responded differently to the tragedy. The amazing thing about God's sovereignty is that He can take the same event and use it differently in different people's lives. That, to me, proves what a big God He is.

The support, or lack of support, they had as they faced their grief made a big impact on what they experienced. They all faced the challenge to find new identities besides being the sibling of Peter. They all needed to find where God wanted them to go in the process of moving forward. Duane and I have been able to watch God direct them. We've had to learn to choose to have faith that God is working together with them to accomplish His purposes. God gives us daily peace, as we are able to rest in the fact that He is a huge God and is perfectly able to take care of them.

Julia

Julia had very close, supportive friends who stood by her initially. However, not many young college students have experienced the loss of a family member, and very few identify with someone who has so much deep pain in her heart. Furthermore there is a tendency for people to have no idea what to say to a person who is grieving, so they avoid the hurting person. So as the time went by the people in Julia's Christian campus ministry group seemed to be unable to relate to her as she became increasingly reclusive and depressed in her grief. We learned through her experience that we as followers of Christ must reach out to people who are hurting and isolating themselves. We need to be the place they can go to in order to voice their needs and pain. We have to be proactive when such terrible things occur. We have to give them the opportunity to talk and just listen and care. That simple thing, which doesn't require any problem solving or much insight, may make the difference between them finding joy at the end of the grief journey or turning their back on God.

When Julia came home for a visit one weekend, she joined Duane and me for lunch with a Korean law school student and an East Indian graduate student from USD who were going to our church. She was searching for what she should do after graduation with her degree in music (vocal performance) if she didn't get accepted into graduate school. Somehow Julia's interest in Korea and the Orient as well as her very good skills in learning languages came into the conversation. The Korean guy took that topic and, for about forty-five minutes, told her in many different ways how wonderful it would be if she'd go to Korea to teach English. He was so excited about his idea that it seemed he just wouldn't stop for a breath. During that plea for her to go back to her country to teach, she was thinking that it wouldn't be such a good idea to go to Korea: everyone would assume she could speak Korean and understand the culture, and not realize she's American. She envisioned many awkward situations living there. But she remembered a friend who was teaching English in Japan. A different Asian country was intriguing. Julia contacted her friend and got linked to companies that hire teachers. It was a long process, but she was hired by a Japanese company to go there to teach English for eighteen months.

Meanwhile God was getting Duane and me ready to move forward to other things He had planned. But what He was showing us to do was possible only because of the aftermath of a puzzle piece He placed in my life in 2009. At that time Matt was in his senior year of high school. He had been on the cross-country and track teams for Centerville. It was a very small boys' team of only three guys and an alternate younger runner. Centerville was the home of one of the best runners in the state. Matt liked to run, but he joined it so the team would be large enough to compete with other schools. Matt, and everyone else, wanted Adam, the talented, fast runner, to be able to compete. I got to know Adam's dad Tim when we watched meets together. Tim had liver cancer. He frequently told me how his condition was worsening and all the difficulties he faced with his treatments. Tim was a rough guy with a foul mouth. He was full of criticism of Matt's running, and lots of ideas how he could improve. (Matt did qualify for the state meets in his own right, so he was a pretty good runner himself.) It was clear that Tim really didn't let God into many obvious places of his life and heart. I knew that as he faced the end of life he really needed to hear about Jesus, but I was afraid to speak up. I rationalized that I just didn't know how to bring up the topic or what to say. So I put it off week after week, meet after meet. The voice of the Holy Spirit prompting me got softer and softer.

Tim didn't come to the last track meet of Adam's senior year. I heard that he was just too sick to be able to come. That wasn't a good sign at all. He always did his best to support Adam. I didn't see him at the graduation ceremony, either. Then things just got busy with the summer, and thoughts of Tim were out of my mind. The night of the fourth of July, about six weeks after school was out, I was washing dishes at the sink. Matt burst in the back door and into the kitchen, and cried out to me, "Mom, Tim died!"

I suddenly was filled with total shame and horror. Tim had died without hearing about Jesus. I was at fault. I hadn't obeyed God's promptings in my heart to share the gospel. It was too late. I had never felt so guilty and responsible for a person's spiritual condition in my life. I had failed Tim eternally and disobeyed God.

To dull my guilt I decided to organize the effort on behalf of the cross-country team to send flowers to the family. Tim's funeral was to be in a funeral home in Sioux Falls. I decided the easiest thing would be to just bring the flowers to the funeral. Julia wanted to come with me. I recall telling her on the way, in the car, that it wouldn't be like any funerals she had ever been to before. It wouldn't be a time of celebrating that a follower of Jesus had gone to heaven and was rejoicing there with angels after finishing the work that God had given him to do. I didn't know how sad and awful it would be but prepared her for the worst.

We sat near the back of the funeral parlor. The room was full of people from Centerville and Tim's family. I don't recall a minister leading the event. Tim's brother got up to share the obituary and tell memories about his brother. He told all kinds of crazy stories about growing up together. He told about how rough his brother had been and some of the abuse he had put his family through. He painted Tim to be a worse person than I had realized. It was rather miserable to hear all that.

Then the brother said that about a month before he died, Tim asked his brother to tell him about God. He wanted to know all about how to be sure he was going to heaven. I gasped loudly. Julia was rather shocked at me. I started to cry and sob (as softly as I could) as I heard the brother tell how he shared the gospel with Tim until he understood and believed. Tim accepted Jesus as his Savior. Tim's life changed in an obvious way in the last weeks of life. He told each of his kids how much he had hurt them, and asked for forgiveness. He expressed to each of his kids and wife that he was sorry for how he had led his life and hurt so many people. Tim wanted to learn as much about Jesus as possible from his brother before he got too confused from the cancer taking over to understand anything. He was as loving as he could be from that time on until the end of his life.

I was spellbound and so surprised at what God had done to rescue Tim. I was rejoicing so much it was hard to contain myself. Then his wife put the "frosting on the cake" in her remarks. She noted that in the last hour before he died, he opened his eyes for the first time in several days and said, "WOW!" She knew he was seeing heaven and was on his way there for sure. I don't think I had ever been so overwhelmed with praise to God in all my life.

That experience was a turning point in my life. I realized that God had rescued Tim despite my disobedience. I had missed out on the joy of talking to him myself. But God wasn't going to let Tim go to hell because of my negligence. He loved him too much. He reorganized puzzle pieces in people's lives so they would share with Tim and lead him to salvation. On the other hand I realized that if I ever felt God prompting me to tell someone about Jesus and the gospel, I needed to obey no matter the cost. That experience refocused my spiritual sight on the needs of people for Jesus and His gift of salvation. It made me more interested in local mission efforts as well as the huge needs of the world for their Savior. It made me willing to have my kids as involved as possible in evangelism and missions.

Years after this experience with Tim, I was sitting with my daughter Julia in the waiting area of the airport just before she was to take off for the first flight of her trip to Japan. She had talked frequently about the crowds on the buses she had been on in Ecuador, studying Spanish, the previous summer and how bad they were. I couldn't fathom that Ecuador's buses could be as bad as travel in Asia. I thought she needed to know something about crowds and the differences she could face once in Asia. (It wasn't the nicest thing a mother could do just before her daughter left for her adventure, of working and witnessing there for an entire year.) I pulled up a YouTube video of a crowded train of people in Bangladesh going home for one of their major religious holiday celebrations. You have to see the video to appreciate what we viewed. (*Google*: "Overcrowded Trains in Bangladesh.") In the video a train meant for 1,000 people was carrying six to ten times that many. People were jammed inside like squished sardines (most of the children and women were inside.) The men were clinging on the outside, to a window frame or other handhold, or standing or sitting on top of the train. You could hardly see the train for the masses of people hanging on the outside. I had taken rides on similar trains in the first class when I lived in Bangladesh thirty-five years before. First class is relatively spacious and comfortable. I was aware that the other classes in the train were terribly crowded, and had experienced the crowded conditions to some extent, having spent a miserable night in second class when I jumped into the wrong train car by mistake.

What affected me when I looked at the video with Julia was how long the train was. It lumbered by for minutes and minutes, with no end in sight to the humanity jammed together. They were all going home to celebrate at the end of the fast of Ramadan. They were hoping to find favor with Allah by doing some good in their lives to outweigh the bad so they could be in paradise at the time of their deaths. They were trying to make sure they observed the customs perfectly so their families wouldn't be disgraced and they wouldn't be shunned. They were willing to undergo terrific discomfort to avoid shame and achieve good works in the sight of their god Allah. They were totally lost, unaware of God's free gift of grace, honor, forgiveness, and reconciliation through Jesus' death for them.

Julia didn't seem to be too affected by the sight of the people on the train in Bangladesh, so she pulled up a video of a crowded train in Japan. That made matters worse. The Japanese people were crowded and jammed inside the commuter train so tightly that the train doors wouldn't shut. (*Google*: "Crowded train in Japan.") There were four officers who kept pushing and pushing the people physically to squeeze them in tighter so they could shut the doors. Finally they got the doors shut and the train took off.

It was a horrible sight on several levels. Selfishly I thought of my daughter enduring horrible train rides like that during her next year in Japan. (Fortunately she was able to walk to work each day, so such rides were infrequent, and the area where she lived wasn't as dense in population!) Secondly, I thought of the discomfort of the people there and how very challenging simple things in life are for billions of people. But finally my thoughts landed and parked on the immense number of people there are in Asia and the rest of the world who most likely are headed on an uncomfortable ride of their spiritual life, trying to appease a god to win favor and paradise. Their efforts are futile. They are totally lost without Jesus. The ride is terrible and the destination is hell.

The videos showed the harvest that Jesus spoke of up close. To use farmers' terminology, the "stand in the field" is terrific; there is potential for a bumper crop. The "harvest" is huge—billions of precious people who are there, in the field, ready to hear about Jesus, but unable to hear the good news as there are not enough workers to share the message of salvation and bring in the harvest.

I was overcome by the effort that it took to get our two kids sent to be workers in the harvest in difficult places, and the pain of losing our youngest son whose legacy has been, through his death, to bring people in the local community to a knowledge of their need for a Savior. It's a real job to get workers to go to the harvest. It's painful for their parents. The everyday emptiness of not having them close by is tangible.

The night before Julia left, she and Duane spent time with his family. The family mentioned Julia's cousins and their successes in their careers. Most were working as professionals in cities relatively close by. A cousin, who like Matt had been the valedictorian of his high school class, was happily working in a small town factory. He was working his way up in the company. He spent his time in his little house alone, or with local friends. He was and is a nice guy, and his parents were happy he was living close by. They were content with what he was doing. He was safe and seemingly secure in his lifestyle. The contrast of what my kids have done, to be willing to do hard things for God, to work in the "harvest," was obvious. The relatives may be happy and feel secure about their kids, but they may not experience the joy in seeing the harvest from what God does through them.

God assured me from Matthew 19:29–30 that He would reward us as parents one hundred times over for making it possible for our kids to go into the harvest to work. It's worth it. We'll see them and many others in heaven someday and Jesus' smile up close. God understands the sacrifice of letting our kids go to serve Him. He felt the pain of sending Jesus off to a very hard, difficult world to be the Savior.

I left Julia at the airport that morning, trusting her into God's care and the lessons He'd have to teach her so she can be used for His glory to work in the harvest. My job was done. True, it was hard to see her go. But the alternative of her settling for an easy life in the states seemed abhorrent after seeing the videos of the crowded train.

Those videos faced me with the fact that there are so many people in terribly difficult places who need Jesus. The harvest time has come for them. I realized that I couldn't hang on to my kids, keep them here in safety, in the USA, knowing that billions will be in hell if they don't go to share the gospel. Hell will be a terrible, crowded place with all those who needed to hear the truth. It will be a millions times more tortuous than the crowded trains in Bangladesh and Japan. God spoke to me, reminding me of the Great Commission. Not only did I need to let my kids tell people about heaven and God's plan to take us there but He also wanted me to actively participate in that work. The crowded train ride in hell will last an eternity. How could I look on and let people go on the terrible, crowded ride straight into an eternity without God's presence?

Julia loved Japan. It was the best thing God could have done to keep shaping her into His image and building the career and life skills she needed. Julia became a part of a local Japanese church, bonded to the missionaries there, and got a vision for reaching the millions of people in Asia who need Jesus. She was one of the best teachers the company has had in that location. She honed skills in teaching all age groups, but was surprised at how much she liked teaching very little children. She returned after fulfilling her contract, not knowing where God was going to lead her next. But with new teaching skills and an amazing natural ability to manage kids, God led her to a Montessori school in Sioux Falls and a ministry with Sunday school at our church. It's fun to see what puzzle pieces God is laying down in her life!

Matthew

After living with us in the spring semester after graduation, Matt set out to be on staff with the Navigators at SDSU. He led Bible studies, organized special events and trips, and taught guys to be disciples one on one. God had a special puzzle piece in store for him through that experience.

At a staff conference, Matt attended an international Navigator information session over lunch with a friend. He really didn't have any one else with whom he could eat lunch, so he just accompanied his friend. But at that session God focused his interest on missions. Matt had gone on three trips to Haiti with us and had seen what an engineer could do in a cross-cultural situation and how he could combine that with missions. He had been to Bolivia five times with his engineering club to work on a water project there. He knew he wanted to serve God cross-culturally in the future. So at that meeting Matt learned about a campus ministry in Beirut, Lebanon, that needed more people to be part of the ministry there. It would be about the same type of campus ministry that he was involved with at SDSU, but located overseas. He was intrigued by it, as he could pursue his goal of getting a graduate degree in engineering at the same time. He felt God calling him to Lebanon.

Matt came home from that conference, wondering how to talk to us about it. He realized that Duane and I had strong interests in missions, and his grandparents (my parents) had planned to be missionaries in China before my mom got sick. We had been on multiple mission trips by then, so he realized we would most likely appreciate his vision and calling to fulfill the Great Commission. On the other hand, going so far away from home to a difficult country might not be too appealing to his parents. He took a risk and told me about the opportunity. I don't recall my exact words, but I immediately told him it was awesome and that he should go. I was overjoyed that he could find some way to do his three most favorite things in life at once: campus ministry, missions, and furthering his engineering training. How awesome God was to give him this chance!

To make things better, he told me he would be going to the American University of Beirut (AUB). The name of the school rang some bell in my head. I knew there were some family ties to that particular place. Upon further investigation I found that my great-uncle as well as a cousin of my dad's had been presidents of the university. My aunt was the daughter of the founder of the university. Matt had some family ties to the place. My mom was overjoyed that Matt was going there to carry on the family connection. We all marveled that God had used so many things to redirect Matt's life after his little brother died. If Peter hadn't died, Matt most likely would have settled into a career in the states. He wouldn't have worked for the Navigators for a year in the states and then in Lebanon. But instead he became involved in missions and embarked on an adventure that has played a role in the Kingdom of God advancing.

I remember the morning we took Matt to the airport to go to Beirut for graduate school. He was so excited, full of dreams, courage, and hope. He was so happy to be preparing for the job God had for him to do. But I felt like I was sending him off to kindergarten again. It was terrifying and full of unknown challenges. There was potential for lots of new friends and exotic experiences. But there was also the risk of people who could persecute him for his faith. In kindergarten kids would just ridicule him for being different than they were. In this new phase of life persecution could mean death or imprisonment. I felt pretty powerless.

That same semester Julia was in the process of selecting a graduate school for continuing her vocal performance training (although she didn't continue to pursue that career and ended up in Japan instead). I knew I'd feel the same way again with her, although I didn't expect her to be leaving the country. So I thought about the difference between sending Matt and Julia off to kindergarten versus off to graduate school. I had taught both of them to obey the rules, to get along to some extent with their siblings and friends, and to be polite. They had learned those lessons and were very nice people. They had learned to manage their money, cook, take care of their clothes, and were good employees at the jobs they had. But had I really prepared them for this new phase of life?

I recalled that my most pressing question after Peter died was, "Did he love Jesus, and did other people know it?" I pondered over Jesus' command to "Love the Lord your God with all your heart, mind, soul and strength and love your neighbor as yourself." It was clear to me that morning, as Matt left, that if I love God totally with every part of myself, I will have a relationship with Him that will get me through anything that happens in life. I will never have to do anything alone. I will be able to trust Him to support and help me. If I love God fully, I will love other people, too, and my life will matter; it won't be wasted.

I wondered that morning whether I had taught Matt and Julia to love Jesus. Or did I just teach them to follow rules? I wondered whether I had taught them to know God, to trust in Him, to rely on Him. Had they learned that Jesus is there for them in everything they will face by watching my life? My heart was wrenched as I saw my two kids leave home. I wondered if my faith in Him had been strengthened enough through all my past experiences to face this new stage of life of learning to trust God to take care of them. I had no control over them anymore. They were God's.

But God knew just how to take care of them, strengthen my faith, and bless all of us in the process. Matt's story of God's direction in his life got even better. Matt had to attend an Arabic class once he got there, as well as take courses at AUB. He tried several options for language study but finally settled on a school tucked into a back street of the city. There were other expatriates in the class from several different countries. Seated across the room from him each day was a lovely young lady. Matt found her intriguing; she was from the USA, with a Southern accent. So he started passing notes to her, got her to sit by him, and invited her out for coffee. It turns out that Erica was in Beirut learning Arabic so she could work in refugee camps. Erica loves Jesus with all her heart, and has devoted herself to serving Him. Erica became good friends with the girls on the Navigator team and grew to know Matt more. Matt soon told us about her on a Skype visit one Sunday morning: "Mom, there's one more thing I have to tell you. There's this girl…"

"That girl," Erica, became his fiancée after they returned to the states. They got married in an elegant ceremony in Atlanta on February 24, 2018. God couldn't have given Matt a better wife to support him, share his passion for missions, and reach the world with the gospel. When I think of all God had to do in His sovereignty to get Erica and Matt to the same place at the same time, it's rather mind-boggling to me. I realize it's no big deal to God. He had it planned all along, getting everything set so that their lives would be joined together. It's exciting to see what God has in store for them as they seek to be part of establishing the Kingdom of God.

Both Matt and Julia were away from home, in Lebanon and Japan, respectively, on Christmas 2016. It was pretty lonely for Duane and me. I recall being pretty sad that I wouldn't have any kids home for Christmas at all. That Christmas Eve, as I was feeling very sorry for myself, these thoughts came to mind, as if from God the Father Himself: *Mary, I know exactly what it feels like to have my child gone from Me on Christmas.* As I meditated on that reality, realizing that Jesus was sent to earth, away from the direct presence of the Father, to bring hope to us, I realized that He was willing to go to great pain to bring the gospel to us. It cost God the intimate fellowship He had with Jesus at His right hand in heaven. He gave His son to live far away on earth for us for thirty-three years. His purpose is that all men would come to "the knowledge of the truth" so that "no one would perish" and have everlasting life with Him in heaven. My two kids Matt and Julia were sent to fulfill the Great Commission. They were on God's mission. They were doing the will of the Father, fulfilling His great purpose. Was I willing to embrace God's purposes and give up my own comfort for His cause? Could I love His purposes more than my own idea that families should be together on Christmas? Was spreading the gospel more important to me than having a tight-knit family and a live Hallmark picture of the holidays in my living room? I had set my kids free and told my kids as they left the states, "Go, serve Jesus—see you in heaven." (That's a little crass, but how can I hang on to them when the need is so great?) Did I mean this when I was lonely and missed them on a holiday? My heart cried out and asked God to renew my desire to serve Him and see people all over the world come to know Him, no matter the cost to me personally.

Ganesha

Since the time our "nest" emptied when Matt left for Beirut and Julia left for Japan, Duane and I have been excited to get to know international students who attend the university in the city where I work. We were pretty eager to return to our love of people from other countries. God has helped us to see how we can move forward and find new ways to serve Him through these relationships. Although we cannot go overseas right now to follow the Great Commission, there are many students from all over the world living close to us. They are the harvest that is ripe in which God calls us to work. While in Haiti on many mission trips, God impressed on me that our new purpose in life is found in psalms:

> **"Declare His glory among the nations, His marvelous works among all the peoples!"**
>
> PSALM 96:3, ESV

Figuring out specifically how declare God's glory to fulfill the Great Commission has been the driving task of these last few years. It has enabled us to move forward into fun, new, positive ways of serving God. It's exciting to see how the Holy Spirit works in people's lives to draw them to God!

A few months after Peter died I had a patient for whom I did nutritional counseling regarding gestational diabetes. Her name was foreign. I cannot remember if I figured out she was from Nepal from reading her chart or when I met her at the front office. She was nervous and didn't know how she'd describe her diet and food habits to an American dietitian. I quickly told her I had been in Bangladesh for three years, and had traveled to Nepal twice during that time. I knew what "*dal-bat*" meant (lentil stew and rice). I had eaten Bengali food for three years and many times since then; I knew what she was talking about and how to plan meals that would work for her. We had a good time getting to know each other and teaching her to count carbohydrate grams to keep her blood sugars under control. The baby was born about ten weeks later; a healthy little girl. I was able to visit her before she left for home.

In the meantime I got to know one of the dietary employees at the place where I work. She somehow mentioned that she was living with a guy from Bangladesh. It turned out that they were very good friends with the Nepali lady. We made plans to have a potluck at my house to eat great food. I met the Bengali guy when I visited the new mom and baby. He was there meeting the new baby and chatting with the parents. When I greeted him in Bengali, initially he didn't respond; he wasn't used to hearing his language spoken by anyone but his other Bengali friends. He was so surprised that someone spoke his language and was delighted that I had lived in his country. Plans for a meal together firmed up.

I eventually gave them some goat meat to cook for the event, to save them some costs involved in feeding a group of people. We all finally got together on a Saturday night. What a fun time, sharing memories, dredging up Bengali words and phrases, and looking at pictures from our time there! Those experiences had taken place about fifteen years before the Bangladeshi guest was born. He was amazed to see what his country was like before many modern changes took place.

It was like old times, having fun again with international people. I hadn't smiled and had such a good time in the two or three years since Peter had died. I felt like they were such good friends. They were so nice, such good, generous, hospitable, and helpful people. They pitched in and did the dishes in a flash so we could enjoy more pictures.

Their baby was tired and it was time to go, but we hadn't had time to look at the goats and other animals on the farm. To keep from getting many bug bites outside at dusk, I suggested that they drive the car up close to the barn. We chased the donkey and three goats out of hiding in the barn so they could see them, and chatted about the chickens we raise and their fresh eggs and good chicken meat. Plans were made to butcher chickens for them. They invited us to a party they were having for the baby's weaning ceremony. She would be fed solid food for the first time, and everyone would have a good time wearing their finest saris and clothes. I was excited to go! Then they walked toward the car to drive home.

I saw the back end of the car and their license plate: "GANESHA."

"What does that mean?" I asked. The Nepali lady answered that it is the name for one of her gods, "Ganish" (the elephant god). Other Hindus in South Dakota had already taken the technical, usual name for the god for their custom-made plates, so she changed the spelling a bit. We chatted a bit more and then they left.

It hit me then that although my new friends were so sweet and we had such fun together, they were all so terribly "lost." As I was running on my treadmill the next morning, it just overwhelmed me. They would not be in heaven at all with me, and would suffer forever in hell because of not knowing Jesus. They could look at me some day, my beautiful friends, with their big brown eyes, as they received their judgment and sentence, and ask, "Mary, why didn't you tell us how to be in heaven with God forever?"

I cried and cried for them. The gap was so huge. If you're so certain about the value of your god that you put his name on your license plate, how would they ever be interested at all in Jesus? Did they feel a need for a Savior? What could be done to show them their need for Jesus? They were so terribly nice; very good people. But lost for eternity. How could they be reached?

About this time I had another friend from a country in the Indian subcontinent who had a four-month-old baby. She wanted a recipe for a dish I had made, so one day I went to her apartment to take it to her. She made me some tea to drink while we talked. She was concerned that it was so hard to lose weight. She had tried to exercise at the wellness center on the USD campus, but found it very hot to work out wearing her hijab (head scarf). There were men in the exercise group and it was awkward. She asked if I could start a group for her. She was willing to invite all her friends to come. I felt like I was risking a lot, but asked if she'd be okay with working out at our church. All of them could exercise in privacy without any men around, so they could be free to wear regular clothing and could shed their scarves. Sure enough it was okay with her.

So then God stepped in and started putting things together in an amazing way. Over the Christmas and New Year's break a few weeks later,

Duane and I took off to Lebanon to visit Matt and meet Erica. Erica was part of an exercise group there, led by a Christian lady. They let me come to join them for a session. I was so amazed to hear the leader confidently say after the work out, "Ladies, we've exercised our bodies, now it's time to exercise our spirits." Then she led them in a devotional to focus their attention on God and what He wanted to do in their lives in the upcoming year. God gave me a vision then of how the exercise group my friend wanted me to start could be used for His glory.

Concurrently, back in South Dakota, a friend at church was working on getting her certification in leading yoga classes. She already had certification in aerobics. She needed a group to practice her teaching skills, and was at a loss how to get people to come. She contacted the pastor about whether she could use the church for her group. There was no problem in using a room in the church on weeknights. He told her about my friend who wanted to work out and didn't have a place. So God put it all together!

Soon after the group was organized and meeting, Pastor Steve challenged me to make sure this wasn't just another exercise group available for anyone in town to attend. It had to have some spiritual component to it to be able to meet at church. That was okay. God had given me a vision that it could be done, when He let me see a similar group in action in Lebanon with people from the same religious background. So we started. At the end of most yoga sessions there is time for meditation. We turned that time into a time to meditate on a Bible verse. One of the American women selected Bible promises each week and had the church secretary print the verse on a card with a beautiful scene in the background. They could take God's Word home each week as a reminder. I had the job of explaining the verse to the ladies after our exercise time. Then we'd pray for each other.

I'll never forget the verse for the week:

**"The thief comes only to steal and kill and destroy.
I came that you may have life and have it abundantly."**

John 10:10, ESV

I explained the verse to the ladies, explaining that Satan wants to ruin and destroy our lives, but Jesus comes to bless us and love us and be with us when we trust Him in faith. Jesus came to give us a good life of being in a close relationship with God. Then I asked for prayer requests. A young international student, who I'll call "Joyce," asked me to pray for her sister-in-law, who I'll refer to as "Irene." Irene was twelve years old. She was very disabled from a medication reaction she had when a baby. She must have had a seizure and had lost her ability to talk and walk and coordinate any part of her body. Her mother had to provide continual care for her daughter throughout each day, so she was unable to teach in the university. The family faced a great deal of shame due to the situation. It was heartbreaking for them all, and Irene was getting more difficult as she was realizing all she was missing in life. Irene was an adolescent, so transporting her anywhere was virtually impossible in a country that is not well-equipped to accommodate the needs of handicapped people. It was certainly a situation where it appeared that the "thief" was robbing them of any quality of life. Joyce asked me to pray for Irene.

I gulped and thought, *God you better show up now. I've just told them this promise. They won't understand all the nuances of the Christian life and how we grow to understand and wait when you answer no.* I took a leap of faith, not knowing any other way to handle the situation, and prayed that God would heal her and enable her to begin talking. Joyce missed working out with the group for about four weeks after that prayer time. When she returned I asked how Irene was doing. I about "lost it" when Joyce said that Irene was speaking in sentences that were about four words long instead of grunts. She could make herself understood on the phone! We praised God together and gave Jesus the credit for healing her.

Three months later I was helping a friend move; this friend is from the same country as Joyce's and Irene's. There were several others there helping to carry the heavy things. They were speaking in their language. I could understand some of it, but not all, so I asked them to clarify in English what they were discussing. One of them had gone back to the city where Irene lives and had visited her family. A new clinic with physical therapy had been started in the city, run by a nongovernmental organization. Irene was getting physical therapy for the first time in her life. She was getting stronger. I asked when the clinic opened, and put two and two together. God had opened the clinic at the same time we started to pray for her. God is sovereign!

It gets better. As time went on Irene's brother came over several times to visit us with his wife Joyce. He told us much more about Irene's progress. She now is talking fluently. She can feed herself now and is learning to walk. She needs help to get up the stairs to her home, but she's made amazing progress. How awesome God is to heal this little girl! How amazing it is to demonstrate to her brother His loving-kindness and power. As we continue to pray for the family, we know that they need to be drawn to Jesus and understand their need for a personal relationship with Him, freed from their shame and disgrace.

In the last few weeks God did another amazing miracle to show His love to these foreign students. A new woman from a Muslim-majority country came to USD in Vermillion to work on her PhD. She is very devout in her faith. Julia and I took this woman with two others for a ladies' afternoon out to visit the Butterfly House (mini zoo) in Sioux Falls one Saturday afternoon. We had a fun time together, chatting and becoming friends. The PhD student (I'll call her Rachael) posted many things on Facebook about her experiences in getting adjusted to the USA. The last post I saw, however, was a question regarding all the headaches she had been having. A few days later, a friend of hers texted me to say that Rachael was terribly sick. She had been flown to the big hospital in Sioux Falls due to having a serious brain bleed or hemorrhage. Her headache was not a migraine at all, but something life-threatening. I feared the worst. I knew other patients with the same condition who had been left without the ability to speak, or were paralyzed on one side. Any impairment at all would make it impossible for Rachael to stay in the USA as a student. And if she went back to her country, she wouldn't have access to good medical care. Her quality of life, if she survived, would be poor at best.

I notified Pastor Steve to contact the prayer chain at church immediately. The next morning, in my quiet time, I read the story of the woman who touched the hem of Jesus' robe. She had an impossible condition. Her situation, like Rachael's, was hopeless. Jesus said to that woman, "Take heart, daughter, your faith has healed you," and instantly the woman was made well. God gave me faith right then that He was going to totally heal Rachael. We were desperate for God to do a miracle. There was no hope for her otherwise. Due to her visa status she had to be able to continue to study to stay in the USA—she had to get totally well to work on her degree. If she went back to her country she wouldn't be able to survive without the critical medical care she needed. It seemed to me that the others from her country were a little oblivious to the seriousness of her condition. So when I took her friends to visit Rachael at the critical care unit, I made sure the nurses gave them sufficient explanations of how dangerous the condition was so they would understand her prognosis. At first Rachael was too groggy from the pain medication from her continued headaches to really understand that I was praying for her. But each time I went to visit I asked if I could pray. Muslims understand that Jesus (Isa) was the healer in Bible times. They are comfortable with Jesus in that role. So I used that understanding to tell Rachael and her friends how awesome it is that Jesus can heal today. I told those who were visiting her that Jesus was known to heal the little daughter of Jairus from a distance. He has the power today to heal, even though He isn't on earth in physical form anymore.

Within three days of the brain bleed occurring, Rachael was out of the coma. She could talk in her language and English. She could understand everything people said to her. She could move her feet, legs, fingers, and arms. She started to roll over in bed. She could see to some extent.

Gradually her memory returned and she could learn new information and retain new facts, such as the date and month. It shouldn't have been a surprise that God totally healed her and restored her in every way, but seeing it happen before your eyes is astounding. When the nurses told her friends and me that many young women die from similar brain hemorrhages, it was clear that Jesus was the one who did the miracle. She made rapid progress in physical therapy, and now that she's back home again in her apartment. She has totally recovered. Within three months of getting ill she is able to restart her graduate program. God is at work, showing Himself to be a powerful, loving God who cares deeply about those who are ripe to be harvested.

A lesson we've learned from these experiences is that believing in the sovereignty and power of God leads to action. If God is sovereign we can take steps of faith and risk, trusting in Him to work out His plan. Sovereignty doesn't mean that God does everything and we sit by and passively watch. No, He uses us in accomplishing His purposes. He uses people, you and me, to accomplish His will. He knows that we are blessed when we are part of His story. So if we're willing to be used by God, He uses us. It is exciting to be able to participate in His strategy to reach the world with the gospel! To sit and not be involved is to miss out on a grand adventure of working with Him as He puts the puzzle together.

Being used by God involves trusting Him, which develops over time as you see God work in your own life. Faith grows as the trust increases. Then love increases for this amazing God who cares so much for you. A passion for others to know this awesome God follows. Then God gives courage and boldness to get involved and reach out to other people. He's done this in my life. Without the difficult experiences and good times, I never would have thought Jesus is worth the risk involved in telling others about Him. But He is worth it all!

WAITING ON GOD

Jonathan

As I write this, right now at this very minute, God is setting down the next puzzle piece of our lives. It's kind of amazing to see this process as I've been writing. It's as if I can see God's sovereignty in action in a very raw, painful situation. I'm challenged once again to blindly trust God. He's been there before for me; I know in my heart and mind that He is in control this time. I know that the secret to keep my eyes on Jesus in this trial is to look for His lovingkindness. I haven't had time to process these events; it is a day-by-day adventure with God. On the way to an evaluation with a psychiatrist with Jonathan today, he was listening to Christian radio and heard one encouraging song after another. Suddenly he snapped off the radio and said, "We need to pray right now." He then prayed out loud, "God, you are in control of what's going to happen this afternoon. It's all in your hands, whether I go to the psych hospital to live or the penitentiary (for the rest of my life). I trust you for whatever You do and whatever happens this afternoon." Wow! Tears came to my eyes as I realized that my son, despite all his troubles, was able to trust Jesus to be in charge of His life, no matter the possible outcome. How did all this come about? How did Jon come to understand at a personal level the sovereignty of God?

Right after Peter died, Jonathan (Jon) was the most vocal person in the family regarding his feelings of grief. He missed not really knowing his little brother because he had lived in several different group homes and institutions during and after high school. However, within a few months of Peter's death he started having problems processing his feelings. He resorted to smoking and running away from the facilities where he lived.

One night I got a call while I was exercising with ladies at church. It was Jon. I heard cars in the background instead of the usual voices in his group home. He wouldn't tell me where he was, so I asked what he could see on the streets around him. From what he described I realized he was in downtown Sioux Falls, in a rather bad neighborhood. He had run away from his group home and gone on foot at least two or three miles. The police found him, but that began a series of serious problems with him not staying with staff and purposefully running into traffic to get hurt. He was transferred to a locked unit. Still, he managed to run away repeatedly when he'd go out to smoke. I recall one day going to visit him, and finding out that he had just escaped. The police were leaving to search on the streets and took me with them in the patrol car to help identify him. Three police officers finally found him at a group home he had lived at previously.

Jon began assaulting staff to get his way when they tried to put controls on his smoking. By the time he was transferred to the South Dakota Developmental Center (SDDC) he was smoking every fifteen minutes and wanting more cigarettes. Jon continued to have severe problems with handling his aggression, which resulted in hurting staff. There were three other clients at SDDC at the time who were also quite violent. The problems there were on the news. The last assault resulted in Jon punching a staff in the mouth. He was sent to prison, but while there a severe infection developed in the knuckle of the middle finger of his dominant left hand. That required surgery and a month-long stay at the hospital, with a guard with him the whole time.

Because Jon had three simple assaults on his record, they amounted to a felony. He was taken into custody and transferred to the penitentiary to serve a two-year term. At first the legal system there was quite concerned that he was going to be treated unfairly and hurt by other inmates due to being developmentally delayed. As soon as the evaluation period was over Jon was transferred to the prison in Springfield, SD, on a unit with other prisoners with special needs.

It was there that God got ahold of Jon's life. He had a roommate who witnessed to him. That guy prayed with Jon to accept Jesus. Jon started reading his Bible and growing in his faith. Incarcerated in the same prison as Jon was a friend of the family who had become a very strong Christian while in prison. He met with Jon many times and taught him to trust Jesus. When Jon's parole date came he was transferred back to SDDC in Redfield, where he had lived before. Within a few weeks of getting there he decided he didn't want to stay. He brought a butter knife back to his room from the cafeteria one day to be able to have on hand as a weapon. By doing that he violated his parole, and ended up in the penitentiary again to serve out the rest of his sentence.

He was placed with the general population. We don't know all the details, but one day he got angry at something he overheard and resorted to what had always worked for him in the past to stop the insulting interaction: he hit a prison guard, causing a concussion, and it took several guards to subdue him. One other person was hurt in the scuffle, and because of that he was transferred to the maximum security unit. Jon was afraid of the other prisoners, and chose to relinquish his rights so he wouldn't be around the others much. He preferred to be in a cell by himself for much of the time. He was in shackles and handcuffs whenever he was moved around the unit.

I don't think I'll forget the day we went to visit him at the penitentiary the first time. Through the glass I saw my little boy, all grown up. He was in a tan, shapeless top and pants, with his hands cuffed and chained to both the chain around his waist and the table at which he sat. His feet were shackled as well. He was totally subdued. He wasn't the wild little boy I had to restrain so many times anymore. He couldn't spit in my face this time. He couldn't bite me. He was paying the consequences for all he had done and the choices he had made to hit and lash out to get his way when his heart was full of pain, anger, and rage.

I had had a very hard heart toward Jon for several years. When he had come home for a visit a month after Peter died, he snuck out of the house in the middle of the night and walked five miles to Centerville to go to the bar there. He walked home and we didn't find out about it until he bragged about it to staff later on. I was terrified of having him ever come home again. I was full of fear at how he could hurt us. How could we ever protect him and others if he'd disappear in the middle of the night? What if he'd get into a vehicle and drive off (without a driver's license)? I didn't want him to ever set foot in my house again when I realized how violent he could be. Considering how terrible he was to control as a kid, it would be worse now that he was full grown. So how could we be expected to ever have him with us at home? I didn't trust him at all. But God melted my hard heart that night when I saw him in chains.

Jon's day of finishing his sentence drew closer. No group homes would take a person with a felony. No programs wanted to care for someone with such a violent history. We prayed and prayed for some place to send Jon, and the only thing that happened is that God changed my heart. Duane has always been more sympathetic and understanding toward Jon. I've been the one with the fear and hard heart, even though Duane had to manage Jon when he was at his worst as a teenager and really violent. God had been challenging me for months to rest in Him and watch Him work. He was asking me to just follow Him each day in regard to what was going to happen with Jon. All Duane and I knew is that it seemed God wanted us to take Jon home and try to get him established in working somewhere in the area. The mental image God gave me during that time was that I was to rest next to Jesus in the bottom of the boat while Jesus was sleeping during the storm. I could be utterly calm, because He wasn't concerned at all. He had the storm completely under His control.

We hadn't heard any more about his legal situation regarding the assault of the guard, and supposed that it was all dropped when he completed his sentence in the maximum security area. Shortly before Jon finished his two-year sentence we were contacted by a lawyer (public defender) in Sioux Falls regarding the charges the state of South Dakota had against him. We found out that Jon was charged with aggravated assault of a corrections officer. Because he was in prison for assault the judge determined that he was a habitual offender.

I'll never forget the day when Duane heard from the lawyer that the maximum sentence for the crime of assaulting a corrections officer was fifty years. I was shocked and horrified. Everything came crashing down around me. Where was God in this situation now? Could I trust Him this time, or was this just too much? Was He really in control of Jon's life and ours? God's sovereignty seemed like a cruel joke. Were we really going to have to go through a court trial and all the humiliation of that process? How would we ever survive all that stress? My heart broke for Jon. He was facing nearly his entire life ahead of him being locked up. That didn't seem possible—how could a person receive a sentence that long for hitting someone? I didn't want to minimize the seriousness of the problems he had caused the victim, but fifty years seemed excessive.

I think God realized that this was just a little over the top for us to handle on our own. We let the church secretary know that night that we were facing a crisis and needed Pastor Steve. He called Duane first thing the next morning. God was in this situation, caring for us through the loving help that our pastor gave us. He pointed our hearts and thoughts toward Jesus so we could find comfort and calm in the storm that we saw looming on the horizon.

The day came for Jon to be released from prison. The picture I had that morning from God as I meditated on being in the storm with Him in the boat was that it was time to get out of the boat now and follow Jesus on land. All I had to do is take one day at a time and just follow Him. Somehow He would give me supernatural peace, knowing that He was with us in this next phase of Jon's life.

Jon was to go to the county jail until the legal proceedings could take place for a jury trial. We didn't know much regarding the case at all. We had minimal or no contact with the lawyer because he was a public defender, not someone we hired. We were told that the trial was scheduled to take place within a month, on June 18, 2018. Both Duane and I realized that if found guilty he would outlive us in prison. This would be our only chance to spend any time with Jon as a free person for the rest of our lives.

Thinking that we'd only have him home about a month, Duane bailed him out on May 23, 2018. We felt pretty confident that we could trust God with Jon at home for a month. We anticipated him to stay with us as we awaited the legal proceedings. There was no news at all about his trial. Finally we got an appointment with his lawyer. When we met with him, which was only four days before the trial was scheduled to take place, he explained that Jon needed to have an evaluation done before he could be tried. The trial would be delayed. The legal system had to prove whether or not he was mentally and emotionally competent to be tried with a jury. If deemed incompetent, he would live at the Human Services Center (state psychiatric facility). If competent, he could have a jury trial with whatever outcome that would entail. The lawyer was having problems getting records from all the places where Jon had lived to give to the psychiatrist and psychologist to do their full evaluations for the competency evaluation. When all the documents were available and reviewed, Jon would face the evaluation and then things would proceed legally.

Waiting for the evaluation to occur has been another lesson in choosing to trust God and His control of the situation. It was many months of waiting, with several highs and many lows. Jon was baptized on Father's Day and confessed before the church that he wanted to follow Jesus. He had shown evidence of having a change of heart. He tried to be much more cooperative and offered to do household chores. He usually tried to control his temper and to be kind and considerate.

Within a week of his baptism he started having suicidal thoughts, and had to be hospitalized. He had several more suicide attempts, including two overdoses on his medications. On Sunday night, June 24, Jon woke us up, telling us that his friend Luke had told him to tell us that he just couldn't handle his suicidal thoughts anymore and needed some help. We ended up taking him to Avera Behavioral Health (psychiatric hospital) in Sioux Falls and got home by 3:00 a.m. I don't do well without sleep and it was a tough week. He came home by Wednesday night with a double dose of one of his antipsychotic drugs; he was very sleepy and lethargic from that time on, but subdued.

A week later, on Sunday night, July 1, he really freaked out and became very angry. We heard a sound of an engine revving. It turned out that Jon had gotten into our pickup and was driving away. He doesn't have a drivers' license. His intention was to wreck it and kill himself. There had been a great deal of rain that week, and the gravel road north of us was under about three feet of water. But he headed north and was driving through the water on the flooded road. He either intentionally tried to go into the ditch or slipped off and got stuck in about five feet of water. He couldn't get the pick up out of the ditch to keep driving the two miles out to the highway where he intended to cause an accident and take his life. He slunk home on foot. Duane gave him the number of the suicide hotline. The counselor ended up calling the Clay County sheriff to come and deal with the situation. Jon wanted to go back to Avera in Sioux Falls. Duane took him there again, and came home at 4:00 a.m. I didn't go with them; I couldn't face another week feeling horrible from getting so tired out from another long night in the admissions department of the hospital.

I picked him up from the psychiatric hospital later in the week. On the way home he asked about the pickup and if we had gotten it out of the water. I told him we could have had him legally charged for stealing the pickup. I told him how serious it would be if he had gotten in an accident and had hurt anyone without having a driver's license, including the terrible financial situation he'd put us in. (The usual result is getting sued for an average of $6 million for a death you cause when driving). He didn't want to hear about it and I reluctantly dropped the subject.

We went to Duane's family events on July 4 and Jon worked with Duane on the farm the next day. Those two days seemed rather uneventful. Matt called me as I was driving home from work on July 5. When I got home I handed the phone to Duane as I got out of the car so he could continue talking to Matt. I got some of the groceries into the house, started making supper…and TOTALLY forgot about locking the car and taking the keys and hiding them. (That turned out to be part of God's plan—Matt didn't know he was someone through whom God was working, when he distracted me with his happy story of getting a raise and favor at work!)

That evening Jon said he was tired from the new medication he was on and was going to watch a movie and go to bed. I went to the basement to work on laundry. When I came back upstairs he was talking to someone on the phone—the suicide hotline person. I couldn't hear much and went bed to read so I could overhear the conversation and be somewhat aware of what was going on. Soon Jon brought me the phone to talk to the counselor. She said his suicidal thoughts and plans were pretty strong and serious. He was planning to cut himself and take the car to cause a car accident. I told her that wasn't possible because we lock up the knives and keys, but she called the sheriff to come. This time we didn't feel safe transporting him anywhere. The hotline person felt he needed to go to the Human Services Center in Yankton for more extensive, long-term help. The sheriff took him away to stay at the jail in Vermillion until they could get him committed.

When we finally went back to bed at about 1:00 a.m., after the sheriff took him away, I suddenly remembered the key issue. I realized that I couldn't remember putting the keys in my purse and bringing it in the house. I bolted out to the car, and sure enough the car door was open and the keys were in the ignition. I just cried, realizing how close we had come to a disaster, and how strong God's protection was for us. Although Jon knew the keys were there (he spies out EVERYTHING and knows where EVERYTHING is in the house and outside), and it led to his terrible temptation to follow through with his plans, God kept him from harming himself. Later I realized how loving it was for Jon, knowing the keys were in the car, to take initiative to call the suicide hotline for help instead of carrying out his plan to wreck the car. He told someone recently that he couldn't follow through with his plans to really kill himself because we had already lost one son. Later I found a Boy Scout pocket knife of Peter's in the room where Jon sleeps, which he could have used to cut himself. So much for being the great mom who has stripped the house of everything possible that could be a danger to Jon. This experience was pretty humbling!

After realizing that God sovereignly protected us regarding the car keys, I recalled the verse that stood out to me in my quiet time the morning of July 5, not knowing how God would put it into action later in the day. In the story of Abigail and David, she said:

> **"If men rise up to pursue you and to seek your life,
> the life of my lord shall be bound in the bundle of
> the living in the care of the Lord your God."**
>
> 1 Samuel 25:29, ESV

What a beautiful picture of God's care! He "binds us in the bundle of the living," wrapping us up with other believers in the body of Christ to care about us. God protects us from harm. God is amazing at taking care of our failures and weaknesses and protecting us, and sovereignly keeping us from evil. We were so grateful for the prayers and concern of the pastor, his wife, and others at church. We really felt that we were on this journey with Jon because God wanted him to have a break before he would be locked up for many years. It's a hard adventure, but God is in control of it. We just have to follow Him daily and leave it to His power to work out. Paul told us in the book of Philippians:

> **"He Who began a good work in you will carry it on to
> completion until the day of Christ Jesus."**
>
> Philippians 1:6, NIV

Today as Jon and I drove to the appointment for the evaluation that would determine whether his future would be in a psychiatric hospital if mentally incompetent or in a prison if deemed competent, this song came on the radio, "You Are More" by Tenth Avenue. The lyrics to the chorus caused both of us to remember that Jon is a child of God. He's not just a sum of all the things he's done to mess up his life, including all the wrong choices, unfortunate circumstances of his birth, and his patterns of violence, lying, stealing, and addictions. He's not just a huge problem to us. He's being remade to be like Jesus. He's made in God's image, bears the stamp of His character. There is some fruit of the Spirit evident in his life at times, as he can be kind, considerate, and generous. Jesus has redeemed Him and calls him His own. Jon's life has a purpose and value.

As I continued driving, God had me recall a patient I had many years ago. That person was profoundly developmentally delayed. He had stopped eating so he needed artificial feedings. In South Dakota the law is that if there are no advanced directives to state otherwise, a person has to be tube-fed when they reach that nutritional condition. This patient had no relatives or guardian. He was a ward of the state. To obey the law we placed the tube. The doctor was very angry that the procedure had to be done on a person who he thought had absolutely no worth to society. He had no value—why not just let him die? But as the patient recovered from the procedure and we got his feedings stabilized, I observed many of the staff from his group home come to visit and share their love with him. They were tender and kind. They gave up time of their own when they were off work to visit him. It was beautiful to see these qualities displayed in the young staff who were fond of him. They valued him. He brought out the best character traits in people who knew him. I learned from that experience that even the most helpless, pathetic person with no obvious value to society is precious because of what they do in our hearts to change us and keep us loving and kind. They have value because of who we become in relating to them. Therefore Jonathan has value despite all the trouble and problems we face. He has kept me from having a hard heart, and kept me realizing how dependent on God I need to be to face each day. Jon keeps me following Jesus.

These verses from psalms have been helpful to me in understanding God's nature in regard to Jon's status:

**"If his sons forsake my law, and do not follow my statues, if
they violate my decrees and fail to keep my commands, I will
punish their sin with the rod, and their iniquity with flog-
ging. But I will not take my love from them, or will I
ever betray my faithfulness. I will not violate my
covenant or alter what my lips have uttered."**

PSALM 89:30–34, ESV

God is not going to take His love away from Jonathan or us due to
his actions. He is in control and will not be unfaithful to His promises to
never leave, nor forsake us.

The weeks and months of waiting for the legal proceedings to develop
drag on and on. On one hand I know that the timing of the determination regarding Jon's competency is in God's timing and plan. He's working
things out for His purposes, not only in Jon's life but also in our hearts.
I realize that the waiting time is causing me to just give up more control
and rest in God. Every day is a challenge with Jon. He is very unpredictable. Now he's addicted to smoking, which drives his compulsions to get
money and cigarettes in any way he can devise. He is prone to stealing
from anyone, so having guests come to our house or going anywhere with
him is tense. We feel exasperated with him most of the time, and have to
rely on God moment by moment for patience and words to express kindness. I pray daily for love for my son. Just when I've been at the end of my
rope, not knowing how to cope, God has sent some relief: Jon expresses
suicidal thoughts or makes another attempt and ends up in one of the
psychiatric facilities for a few days, giving us some respite. God is sovereign even in the hard times, when His timing is not mine. He's taught
me before that He is putting a puzzle piece in place to form His Kingdom
during hard times. Now I'm learning patience to wait for God to act.

FEELING LOVED

Max

One lesson I've learned is that God's sovereignty doesn't just affect the big things in life. He is in control of small things that seem rather inconsequential in light of the complexity of ruling the universe and keeping everything in order. He delights in helping us with the things that trouble us, just to tell us He loves us. Somehow when God helped me find our dog, my love for Him grew deeper. When He demonstrated that He cared about such an insignificant thing as my dog getting lost and orchestrated amazing things to get Max back, I was just overwhelmed with praise for His loving-kindness.

One Friday afternoon, my international student friend from Bangladesh came over to play with our dogs. He was heading soon to Montreal to begin his PhD study. We had a very good talk about his past, and I shared the gospel with him. It was very sad to see him leave. I thought it would be the last time we would see him. He posted pictures of Max, our other dog and me, on Facebook after the visit. The next day I had a conversation with Pastor Steve about how wonderful it is as Christians to have such a personal, warm relationship with God, in which we are assured over and over that He cares about what is on our hearts and minds, including even the little problems that plague us. Our view of God is different from that of my friend, who doesn't know God to be active in his life personally. We prayed God would show to my friend that He cares about him personally.

My friend wanted to see the dogs one more time on Saturday evening before he left the area for Montreal the next day. Neither dog could be found when he arrived. Max and Duncan (our other dog) often hunt along the creek or out in the fields, so I wasn't too worried. It just was disappointing to all of us that they couldn't have one last time playing together. When I got home late Saturday night from a shopping trip, there was evidence from muddy paw prints that Max had been in the house, but only Duncan was at home. I was too tired to do anything about it. Duane was away with Julia, and I was alone for the weekend. When I got up Sunday morning I took a walk and called Max, but he never showed up. I anticipated a long hunt, driving all over the area, looking for the dog. Max usually stays home, but when he runs he can run six or more miles without tiring. He isn't too good about finding the way back home by himself. I prayed God would bring him back by some miracle. Usually Duane goes on the search for Max when he disappears. I was dreading having to do it by myself after church. By the time I would get home from the worship service he could be anywhere and impossible to find.

A few hours later in church I got a text from my friend Jill, asking if I had heard her voice mail message about a lost dog. As it turns out, someone driving on Highway 19 saw Max Saturday evening, about three miles from my home. They took him to their place to get him off the road and posted a picture of him on the lost pet site on Facebook. Jill had seen the picture my friend had posted of Max with me, and compared it to the lost pet picture. She texted me and got me connected to the person who had found Max. Concurrently another friend noticed a spot of dirt on the forehead of the dog in both of the pictures and associated them together. She texted me as well. Golden retrievers can look pretty similar, but the dirt spot was too obvious a similarity between the two posted pictures to overlook. She was pretty sure the lost dog picture was of Max. I never noticed the dirt on Max's face before that day.

I drove as fast as possible after church to the place where Max was being held and protected in a garage. However, I had neglected to fill the car with gas before I took off. The gas light came on, and I barely made it to the town to find the place where the dog was being kept. Max was safe there. I got my dog back and took him the eleven miles back to our home. I never would have looked in that area if I had had to search by myself. Max had never crossed the highway to go that direction before. He would have been lost forever.

Are all these things coincidences? Could I have figured out how to find Max on my own? It's not likely. I don't take many pictures of my pets to post, and I don't spend much time looking at stuff that's posted by people who aren't friends, and I had never seen the lost pet site. Was the dirt on Max's face just a trivial characteristic that enabled him to be identified? I never would have found the stranger who kept Max for me overnight so far away from home. I would have given up for sure. Yes, I was very happy to get Max back, but more than that I was joyful that God demonstrated His affection in such a tangible way. I was totally awed that God chose to have my dog run away to answer my prayer that my friend would learn more of God's tender care for us. My friend learned Max had been found and he therefore saw God's sovereignty at work regarding something he found precious, that is, Max. He could see God at work in our personal problems. We pray his heart is softened to the gospel just a little more due to this experience.

Often our society views these types of events as coincidences. There aren't coincidences with God. He loves us dearly and is in control. He has planned everything in our lives to draw us to Himself so we become more like Him. He wants us to be ready for heaven. A verse in 1 John says:

"...When He appears, we shall be like Him, for we shall see Him as He is."

Psalm 89:30–34, ESV

We might as well get started now to recognize God at work. The more we acknowledge His work and see evidence of Him, the more we become like Him, and the more ready we are to be with Him forever in His Kingdom in heaven.

He wants us to see His actions in the really big events of our lives, as well as the small things. It's a much better feeling to give God all the credit for putting the pieces together than to call things coincidences. There's an incredible joy that wells up inside you when you realize the all-powerful God cares so much for you that He arranges everyday things to bless you, help you, and comfort you. He is a powerful, sovereign God and works out incredibly minute details to show all of us His loving, powerful character.

Thankful

The year of the fourth anniversary of Peter's home-going to be with Jesus was a difficult, painful time. One day at a meeting at work, my eyes glanced at the calendar on the wall. I had never stopped to figure out what day of the week the fourth anniversary date of Peter's death would be. I took a deep breath and tried to stifle a meltdown in front of all my coworkers as I realized that November 23 that year would be on Thanksgiving Day. My mind reeled, oblivious to the discussion among the staff. How would I ever face the anniversary date on Thanksgiving?

The plan was that we would go to Atlanta for Thanksgiving to meet the parents of our soon-to-be daughter-in-law. We were planning to stay with them a few days. We couldn't turn Thanksgiving into a time of mourning for Peter. It wouldn't be fair to Matt, Erica, or her parents, when they had so much joy to share with us. A few days before we started to drive to Atlanta, it crossed my mind that it was very fitting that Peter's anniversary date would be a day to focus on thanking God. As it turned out God brought renewed healing to my heart as I praised Him, so I didn't feel sad and want to detach from the family. He gave me grace to watch the football game and enjoy it and participate in other things the family was doing. Late in the day we shared a little of Peter's story with Erica's parents, just as a way of acknowledging our feelings and the pain Matt was feeling from missing his little brother.

The major lesson I've learned in grief over losing our son is that the key to getting through the pain is to focus on what God is doing to bless you in the midst of it all, and then to thank Him. I've found that being thankful is the outward expression of acknowledging God's action on our behalf. We are challenged by the apostle Paul to:

> **"Give thanks in all circumstances…"**
>
> 1 Thessalonians 5:18, ESV

This means that in the midst of the trouble, thank God for anything possible that you can. The psalms indicate:

> **"Enter His gates with thanksgiving and His courts with praise!"**
>
> Psalm 100:4, ESV

As we thank God even in tough times, we enter His gates to go through the courts and come into God's presence. We feel His nearness. We don't feel abandoned, as is common to feel when facing grief and other problems in life. The secret to me seems to be in acknowledging evidence of God's love and care and thanking Him for it.

Birthday

Peter's twenty-first birthday would have been September 19, 2018. Duane and I were feeling especially sad, missing this milestone in his life.

I took my eyes off God's purposes and focused on myself. There were lots of feelings of self-pity that surfaced in the weeks before his birthday. It helped in some ways that I went to a wedding during that time, of a girl who had accepted Jesus after Peter died. Four of the people who were influenced in their spiritual walks by Peter's life attended as well. As I talked to them God started turning my focus back to Himself. I could see the immense spiritual growth in these people. They were so changed and transformed. They had continued to increase in their faith as they sought God by themselves and were in close fellowship with other believers who had been with them in the last five years.

But seeing those friends at the wedding also made me realize how much I was missing, not being able to participate in these stages of Peter's life. The morning of his birthday, a new friend posted something on Facebook, noting this verse:

"Precious in the sight of the LORD is the death of His saints."

Psalm 116:15, ESV

The death of Christians is precious to Jesus. She said, "How awesome it is to witness a Christian cross over from this life and step into the presence of God Almighty."

I needed so much to remember that Peter's death is precious to God. He just didn't use Peter for His glory. Peter wasn't just a tool for God to use. No, He treasures my son and counts him precious. His death was very special to God. How eager God was to have Peter join Him in heaven to share His glory with Him! God delighted in gathering Peter to Himself. And to comfort me, how good God was to remind me of that truth the morning of September 19. When I was hurting so badly God made sure to comfort me. God is so powerful and in control that He can even plan when others post things on Facebook that we need to see, and place them in the sequence of things you scroll through so you see it just when you need it. I choose not to see this as coincidental. God figured out how to get through to my sad, hurting heart that was wrapped up in grief. God's sovereignty is a comfort. It brings joy that He cares enough to show us His power in incredible ways to meet our personal needs. God's sovereignty enables peace to surround us, because He is so powerful to take care of us.

After I read my friend's post I turned to my Bible. It fell open at Isaiah 61. This is a favorite passage of mine. Those verses say in reference to Jesus:

> **"The Spirit of the Lord God is upon me**
> **Because the Lord has anointed me to**
> **bring good news to the poor,**
> **He has sent me to bind up the brokenhearted,**
> **to proclaim liberty to the captives,**
> **And the opening of the prison to those who are bound.**
> **To proclaim the year of the Lord's favor, and**
> **day of vengeance of our God;**
> **To comfort all who mourn; to grant to those**
> **who mourn in Zion –**
> **To give them a beautiful headdress instead of mourning,**
> **The garment of praise instead of a faint spirit;**
> **that they may be called oaks of righteousness,**
> **the planting of the Lord that He may**
> **be glorified."**

ISAIAH 61:1–3, ESV

As I read the passage it was as if God was telling me that Jesus' purpose in coming to earth was to bind up my broken heart. He was going to comfort me that day and exchange my fainting heart that was focused on myself and what we had lost, and give me praise to put on to wear instead. His purpose in comforting me was to enable me to glorify God. As I praised Him the heaviness and grief diminished. He was the one who could transform mourning into joy. One of His purposes for my suffering was to bring glory to Himself. That may seem rather self-centered of God, but He knows that we are happiest when we are fulfilling our purpose in life, that of loving Him, knowing Him, and glorifying Him. We cannot do that by ourselves. It takes Jesus initiating the comfort so we can respond in praise, and find joy.

Thumbs Up

In the fall of 2013, I told Peter I wanted a nice picture of him smiling while running. Usually runners have very pained looks on their faces during races. He agreed to try to smile for me at the next race. The next competition occurred in a place with lots of woods and foliage. Parents of cross-country runners learn to find ways to intercept their kids at various places during the race to cheer them on. So as I followed him in his race I found a pretty spot as a backdrop for my photo. Peter was ahead of the pack and feeling confident as he ran. He gave me a thumbs up and a huge smile, and ran on. I snapped my picture, grateful for my dear son.

Peter had his thumbs up that day, knowing he was victorious and running a good race. Writing this book has caused me to examine why I can have my thumbs up, following Jesus in the race of life He's set before me. You know now that my race hasn't been pretty, free of obstacles. The secret is this: I have learned to trust the puzzle maker. As I've grown to know Him in all the struggles and pain in life, He's been there, demonstrating His love in obvious ways. And the more I've learned to trust His love, the more secure I've been in Him. In response, my love for God grows stronger and deeper in painful times. He hasn't abandoned me.

At the same time He's demonstrated His personal love, He's given me a glimpse of how He has used these problems to bring glory to Himself. As I've told my story, you've seen God's providence in the little things of life, and in the big things. I may bristle at thinking God allows painful things in my life for His glory. What kind of God is that—a deity who personally benefits from my pain? In times of loss we struggle with God's character. It's hard to see that God is good all the time. God's sovereignty isn't clear when I am in the middle of a mess in my life. I gain that from hindsight. But in the middle of problems God's providence isn't offensive when I feel His personal care for me. His character becomes apparent. His purpose may become clear.

There is joy in knowing that as I yield to His plans He is able to use the events in my life to draw people into the Kingdom. His sovereignty is glorious! My pain isn't wasted when I see it from His perspective. How awesome to be part of His powerful plan to bring as many people into the Kingdom of God as possible! How humbled I am to think that I could possibly play a role in God's glorious puzzle. It's too awesome to imagine that He would count me worthy to be part of His glorious plan.

The alternative to seeing God's sovereignty in my life is to view it from a self-centered perspective. The minute I take my eyes off Jesus, all I see is the ugly cardboard side of the pieces of my life. Nothing makes sense. There can be no joy when I focus on myself. I wallow in self-pity. God becomes a cruel puppeteer. My prayers become requests for my comfort, so I can have a nice life. And when God doesn't answer those prayers my heart fills with doubt. My trust in God dwindles away. No, the key is found in what my sixteen-year-old learned as he searched his Bible:

"He must increase, I must decrease."

JOHN 3:30, ESV

Viewing God's sovereignty at work on a personal level throughout life is a means of letting Jesus increase in my life so I decrease. It's only when holding onto that attitude that joy can be found.

I welcome you to join me in being part of His glorious puzzle, a life in which God's sovereignty is demonstrated to you personally through His love and cosmically through being part of His plan for the ages. What we do in life won't be in vain if we see it as part of God's plan and the means by which we fulfill the Great Commission. The place to get started in seeing your life this way is to begin looking for ways to acknowledge God's action in your life on a daily basis. Start by thanking Him for all the evidences you see of His loving-kindness. Continue by setting your mind to view coincidences as evidence of His powerful work on your behalf. When the hard times come, pray immediately for God to show you that He is with you. Praise Him and tell other people what God is doing.

As I've written my account of God's action in my life to teach me to trust Him and then to grow in my love for Him, I've identified my life verse:

> **"Oh, magnify the LORD with me, and let us**
> **exalt His name together!"**
>
> PSALM 34:3 ESV

As we praise God, we know He is with us in all the hard times in life. Join me in doing that together. You'll be amazed at the awesome acts of God!

Peter finished the race of life. He kept the faith. He's received the crown of life that God awarded him for trusting Jesus as His Savior. He has his thumbs up eternally, rejoicing in heaven with Jesus, praising Him that his life wasn't lived in vain. He is yearning for all of us to receive the crown of life someday, as we await Jesus' coming and the final stages of the establishment of His Kingdom. How wonderful it is to be part of that awesome, glorious puzzle our sovereign God is creating!

Appendix

Puzzle Box

(Further thoughts regarding the Kingdom of
God and His purpose for us.)

T his verse in Colossians is intriguing in light of God's sovereignty and
how He acts in our lives:

**"He has delivered us from the domain of darkness
and transferred us to the kingdom of his beloved Son,
in whom we have redemption, the forgiveness of sins."**

Colossians 1:13–14, ESV

How amazing! God takes us out of the darkness and isolation of the
inside of the puzzle box, where Satan wants to keep us locked up, and
puts us into His puzzle that He's forming into the Kingdom of God. Satan
would like us to keep focused on how horrible the inside of the box is. In
there we are jostled around, where no one appreciates us or notices us.
We get banged up in there as the box is shaken. It's lonely and terrifying.
We're stuck, with the box sealed shut. We focus on Satan and the power he
has over us. We are bullied by him and spend a great deal of effort giving
him credit for our problems.

But God has opened the puzzle box. He has freed us from that miserable view of life. How? At salvation He takes all the puzzle pieces out

of the box and they are laid out before God. Then He gives us a purpose. Our purpose for living as Christians is to be part of His overall purpose. God transfers pieces of our lives, piece by piece, to put into His puzzle. He allows us to have a big part in enabling all people to come to the knowledge of His redemption and forgiveness. How wonderful to be a part of that process! How freeing it is to understand life from this perspective. It's glorious to be part of His sovereign puzzle!

So today it may be hard to be thankful in the middle of problems you're facing. My challenge is to look for ANY evidence of something good going your way. Attribute whatever good thing or coincidence you see as a demonstration of God's love. Choose to thank Him for it. Tell someone else what God has done for you. Step out in faith. Give Him the credit and glory. Feel the pain, but realize that by thanking God you will feel Him carrying you and supporting you in this rough part of life's race. It's His way of comforting you. The result will be a straight path through it, because you can follow Jesus. There will be joy and adventure along the way, discovering God's loving-kindness and comfort.

The High Cost of the Gift

(Facebook post written regarding the
outcome of tissue donation)

About eighteen months after Peter died we got a letter in the mail from a lady who had received one of Peter's corneas. I have no idea who she is or her full name. Through connections made by the South Dakota Eye and Tissue Bank, I had told her in a letter in the past that it would be wonderful to meet her if she wanted to do so. Theoretically those types of meetings can be very healing and helpful to donor families, as they see some good that can come from a tragic loss. I tore open the envelope, eager to read her response. This is what she wrote:

> *"Even though I have been blessed with the gift of sight, I cannot meet you. You see, I know for me to have my sight restored, someone had to lose their life and that saddens me. I'm afraid that if I would meet you, I would dwell on that sadness. For your family, you feel some peace knowing that your son in a way lives on in me. Yet for me, I cannot quite get my mind to think that way. So please forgive me for not having the strength to meet you. But still know that I will think of Peter often and keep him in my prayers."*

I cried. I had to respect her for her decision not to connect in person. I was honored by her very deep appreciation for the gift of sight she had, and the understanding that it had come at the very high cost of someone's life. She was taking Peter's life very seriously, so seriously that she couldn't face the giver of her sight. It was too unbearable for her to deal with. A life lost for good sight, the cost seemed too great.

My thoughts turned to Jesus and the fact that He willingly faced torture and death for me to be able to face God and live in His presence on earth and in eternity. Jesus gave me spiritual sight by His death. He made it possible for me to see God in person someday. I asked myself, "Am I taking Jesus' suffering and loss of life so seriously that I would be like this lady, feeling so humbled and unable to face Him?" Or have I heard it said so frequently and told others myself, "Jesus died on the cross for your/my sins," that it has lost its significance? Do I still feel the horror of His death in my place? Have I gotten calloused to the cost of my salvation? Do I feel sad that He had to suffer so much for me? Do I feel like I don't even have the strength to meet God—that I'm so humbled by Jesus' gift to me? Do I really value salvation and understand the implications of what my life would be without Jesus dying for me?

I must say I think I feel a little like what God must feel when people refuse to accept the gift of salvation fully and establish a relationship with Him. I felt a little let down that for now this lady doesn't want to form a friendship with us, based on the gift of Peter's eyes. To a much greater degree God must feel really let down when we don't accept the grace He offers and the free gift He offers of a relationship with Him. He expects nothing in return but our nearness, praise, glory, and worship. The whole purpose of salvation is to restore the relationship with God that our sin destroyed. He must feel like Jesus' death was wasted—its purpose cannot be accomplished when the gift He offers is refused.

"For by grace you have been saved, through faith, and that not of yourselves so that no one can boast. But the free gift of God is eternal life in Jesus Christ, our Lord."

EPHESIANS 2:8–9, NIV

This lady's response helped me to see things a little from God's perspective amidst my sadness. It caused me to value His gift of salvation more and love Him in return.

These verses from Habakkuk came to mind to refocus on what is true:

> **"Though the fig tree does not bud,**
> **and there are no grapes on the vines,**
> **though the olive crop fails and the fields produce no food,**
> **though there are no sheep in the pen and no cattle in the stalls**
> **yet I will rejoice in the LORD;**
> **I will be joyful in God my Savior.**
> **The Sovereign LORD is my strength;**
> **He makes my feet the feet of a deer;**
> **He enables me to go on the heights."**
>
> HABAKKUK 3:17–19, NIV

This truth is something people in grief can cling to: when you seem to have lost everything important to you and the future is bleak, focus on Jesus' gift of salvation. Keep your attention on God, your Savior.

I found it to change my attitude. Jesus' suffering for me was so amazing. He chose to die for me. God chose to put His Son to death and grieve for Him; it wasn't something that happened by accident. Jesus' death was planned to take place for me. The Father grieved that He had to make His Son suffer so much to accomplish salvation.

So when in mourning, as we focus on God's grace, demonstrated in Jesus' salvation, we can be joyful. Our awesome God shows Himself to be our strength. Our eyes can't stay focused on our small miserable world if we worship Him. As we chose to be joyful in our grief, He gives us the energy to face each day and live in the high places with Him.

Dancing

(Thoughts regarding God's goal for our grief)

Dancing isn't something I do. I'm uncoordinated and struggle with keeping the right rhythm to a tune, so the possibility of moving to music is a challenge to me. Furthermore dancing was expressly forbidden when I was growing up. My parents made it very clear that Christians did not dance to secular music AT ALL. I grew up being pretty inhibited. The ironic thing is that when I was about twelve years old we started going to a charismatic church in the heart of Chicago. At Faith Tabernacle we sang scripture songs that had been put to music during the worship. Frequently people would break out in dancing before the Lord. I spied my dad doing a jig at times!

One of the praise songs we sang that became engraved in my heart was as follows:

"Thou hast turned my mourning into dancing for me
Thou hast put off my sackcloth,
Thou has turned my mourning into dancing for me
And girded me with gladness.
To the end my glory may sing praise unto Thee
and not be silent,

Oh LORD my God, I will sing praise
unto Thee forever!"

PSALM 30:11–12, NASB

We sang that song over and over. I can't say I ever danced there, but it was amazing to see others who had been through really rough times in their lives letting loose. This song gives us a picture of what grief looks like when God has healed us. I read that psalm recently and noticed new things from its truths:

1. It is God's goal that we get to a place of joy in the grief process. I see so many people being content after they've stuffed their grief or medicated it to the extent that they can live life and be productive again. However, they remain sad inside, living in a shell of respectability, with a growing hardness toward God.

2. Grief is as horrible as the pitiful state of a beggar who wears rags or just burlap sackcloth, begging for any crumb to sustain them for the next few minutes. It starts as a state of being totally wretched, unable to function and dependent on God to meet our needs through love expressed by other people.

3. It is God who turns our mourning to joy; it is God who takes off the sackcloth of our grief and replaces it with gladness. There is no other way to heal than to allow God to do the work.

4. The purpose of the healing is that God gets the credit and glory. The phrase in the psalm "To the end my glory may sing praise unto Thee" is difficult to understand. I explain it this way: when we look like we are doing well in grief recovery, and people take notice of our progress, we must give God the glory and not take credit for being 'such a strong person,' Our responsibility is to give God all the credit for healing our hearts and being the strength people notice.

5. We are not to keep silent about the marvelous God we have

who comforts us. Praise and magnifying God will make the joy multiply to the extent we will thank Him forever. A healing heart is one that is joyful before God and praises Him for His loving-kindness and tender care of us while we grieve.

6. Give God the credit for any tiny kindness people show, or the encouragement of a bird or sunset or flower that causes us to turn our thoughts from the darkness of mourning to see God's blessings for that moment. He will clothe us with gladness instead of the hard shell of being stuck in grief or the stinky scratchiness of sackcloth.

Brokenness Is the Reason for the Season

(Facebook post written during the
Christmas Holiday Season 2014)

Several years ago I attended a GriefShare holiday event, organized to help grieving people face the emotional issues at Christmas and other holidays. A statement made in the video I watched at the "Surviving the Holidays" event pierced my numbed mind: "There is no need for Christmas if there is no pain and suffering and sin. Jesus came to end it all, to end brokenness. This is the sufferers' holiday. Christmas guarantees that God is there for me and others with losses."

Broken lives from any loss through death, violence, injustice, or negligence are the reason Jesus came to live among us. Jesus' binding up of our wounds will ultimately be accomplished when we meet Him in heaven someday. His death accomplished this for us when we have faith in His sacrifice for our sins. But He also binds up our wounds to heal our brokenness here on earth. How does He do this? One of the frustrations of the broken person at Christmas is hearing about joy and peace. It doesn't seem tangible to a hurting, broken person. How does the Christian find this state of mind? I found in facing my grief that God heals through two means: His presence and His people.

To a grieving, hurting person, God's presence can be remote, intangible. I've found that to feel His presence requires a conscious effort to look for any evidence of God's goodness or love in every situation. Proverbs 3:5–6 (NIV) say, "Trust in the LORD with all your heart. Do not lean on your own understanding. In all your ways acknowledge Him, and He will make your paths straight." Finding anything good in a bad, painful situation and attributing that as evidence of God's care and love are the ways to put this verse into practice. Don't chalk it up as a nice coincidence. Consider finding something you lost, or a beautiful South Dakota sunset, or the narrow escape from hitting a deer on a country road, or realizing things could have been worse as evidence of God's work on your behalf. As you praise and thank God for every very small thing that happens, those events start to piece together so you see a big picture of how He's caring for and loving you in the terrible conditions you face. God straightens the broken, shattered paths of our lives when we are able to see His hand holding us in the situation. He comforts us through His presence.

God's people are the other means by which He brings healing to broken hearts. If you're hurting, let people know honestly how you are feeling. It's important to talk about the loss to trusted people. Those who want to be supportive often shy away from hurting people because they "don't know what to say." Our culture pushes us to avoid the emotional pain. So what can you do? Just hug them, ask how they are and indicate you have time, and wait for them to start talking. Just listen. Tell them any memories you have of the person; they really want to hear as much about the person as possible so memories don't fade, which makes the person seem more remote and "gone." Grief drains away as people cry and talk about the person they've lost and what happened. Giving them a safe situation in which they can tell their story is very healing. God demonstrates that He's listening to us through the people who He brings to hear our grief story. A word of caution: don't be put off if a grieving, hurting person doesn't open up to you. Maybe they are on the verge of crying and can't face doing that in the social situation where you both are. That's OK, the hug, smile, and your welcoming attitude will feel good.

At Christmas, we think of Jesus coming to live on earth. He came as Emmanuel: God with us. God left the perfection of heaven to enter our pain in a world suffering the consequences of sin. He came into our brokenness to bring healing. Jesus Himself declared this to be His mission at the start of His ministry when he quoted from Isaiah 61.

> **"The Spirit of the Sovereign Lord is on me because He has anointed me to preach good news to the poor, and sent me to bind up the brokenhearted, to proclaim freedom for the captives and release from darkness for the prisoners...to comfort all who mourn and provide for those who grieve in Zion – to bestow on them a crown of beauty instead of ashes, the oil of gladness instead of mourning, and a garment of praise instead of a spirit of despair. They will be called oaks of righteousness, a planting of the LORD for the display of His splendor"**
>
> Isaiah 61:1–3 (NIV)

Jesus came as Emmanuel, "God with us." He came and experienced grief. He came to a world that was broken due to the consequences sin brings. He suffered emotional losses just like we do. He hurt for us when He saw death, sickness, injustice, cruelty, and negligence. He not only experienced what we experience as Emmanuel, but He took all that brokenness on Himself. He stated at the Last Supper, "This is my body which is broken for you." He allowed himself to be broken on the cross to bind up all our wounds. He took on Himself all our pain. He is the only one qualified to do anything to bring healing and fulfill His promise to bring back joy to our lives. He knows what it feels like to face grief, loss, and pain. He came to redeem us from our broken state.

Now that He's in heaven preparing a place for us to join Him, He continues to make His presence known in our brokenness through His people. We feel it in tangible ways through their expressions of love. Our brokenness is the whole reason for Christmas. If the world was not sinful and broken, then there would not have been any reason for Jesus to come. The massive celebration we engage in at this time of year never would have been needed. In the midst of our pain we can celebrate joyfully, because Jesus' birth promises healing for our wounds. Maybe in our grief we don't have the physical energy to celebrate as much as in the past, but the joy inside that the season brings is all that really matters. Christmas is a time to celebrate Emmanuel and feel the joy His presence brings. Reach out to Him: He's there to love you. Brokenness is the reason for the season.

LEMONADE

(Facebook post written regarding God's comfort in grief)

I've been thinking about lemonade a lot in the past few days. Perhaps it was because the yellow and green decorations were so beautiful at the South Dakota Eye and Tissue Bank tribute luncheon. The striking yellow napkins reminded me of the color of lemons. I looked around at the couple of hundred people in the banquet room last Saturday, and saw a room full of people who had been given "lemons" in their lives—not just small lemons, but large sour ones. The people there had either been faced with a terrible diagnosis and lots of health struggles and pain or they had lost a very important person in their lives who gave of themselves to bring healing to other people—the recipients. There were lots of grief evident in the room, a quiet suffering. And yet there was joy that the donation of tissues had brought about some good.

It reminded me of the saying, "When life gives you lemons, make lemonade," which sounds nice but trite. When the lemons of life are large, and are cut open by a sharp knife and squeezed until dry, I believe it's impossible to make lemonade by yourself. I came to the conclusion after watching all those wonderful, hurting people at the banquet:

When life gives you lemons, God enables you to make lemonade to share with others.

How does this happen? If we can't make the lemonade ourselves, how does God enable us to make it? Real lemonade is made of lemons, water, and sugar, along with some stirring or mixing action. God gives us the living water, Jesus, who promises to never leave or forsake us when we walk through the valley of the shadow of death and troubles. Our relationship with Him and His nearness are not dependent on whether we feel His presence in the midst of the cutting and squeezing pain of our lives. He's there, showing His love and care in many ways. The more we understand the nature and character of God, and the more we look for what He is doing to demonstrate His love at bad times, the easier it is to participate in the lemonade-making process.

The sweetness in the recipe is the Word of God. Psalm 19:10 says that God's Word is "sweeter than honey, even honey from the honeycomb." We find a lot of comfort and sweetness as we read God's Word when facing the lemons of life. He speaks to us through what we read. Without reading and knowing what He has to say, it's a pretty sour drink to swallow.

If we don't mix it all up to dissolve the sugar in the water and squeezed-out juice, we just have isolated ingredients in the container of our lives. What helps us to get it all dissolved and palatable? I was reminded of the verse in Hebrews 10:24: "Let us consider how to stir one another on to love and good deeds." We need to be with other people to be "stirred up" to get the healing God wants to achieve in our lives. We need to be challenged and encouraged and comforted by real people, not just devotionals and books about grief or whatever problems we face. This was so very evident at the Lion's Eye and Tissue Bank luncheon. Patti Auch, an employee of the organization and distant relative, was one of the people I noticed going from table to table, encouraging and thanking everyone for making the healing possible in the recipients' lives. She was "stirring" the people there to feel the comfort God had available for them by thanking them for their gifts that brought life. In the same way, if we hadn't paid attention to the people who made the request for tissue donations at Peter's death, we never would have felt the awesome comfort and joy that came from blessing Peter's recipients of his tissues. We needed to be stirred to do something positive in the midst of the worst "lemon" we've ever faced. It was real people who showed us God's love and comfort. We needed real people to speak God's Word to us, when our tears clouded our eyes. It took a strong support group to urge us to keep doing necessary things to bring healing.

The last part of the lemonade-making process requires sharing it with others. God doesn't just enable us to turn our lemons into lemonade so we drink it all ourselves. He allows those experiences to come into our lives so we share the lemonade with others who are thirsty to feel and taste the goodness of God in their pain. In 2 Corinthians 1:3–5, it reads, "Praise be to the God and Father of our Lord Jesus Christ, the Father of compassion and the God of all comfort, who comforts us in all our troubles, so that we can comfort those in any trouble with the comfort we ourselves have received from God."

After the Lion's luncheon we drove to SDSU for a choir concert. As I sat there listening to my daughter sing, I was thinking about lemons between being blessed by the various beautiful choral music works. The last number was based on the Prayer of St. Francis. I listened to the words, knowing that in the midst of all the pain we feel, if our attitude is to be an instrument of God's peace, then He can not only continue the healing process in our lives, but also bring comfort to others. I was challenged to open my eyes with compassion to see others with the same lemons I've had in my life: infertility, miscarriage, failed adoption attempts, a special needs child, a child who has gotten in trouble with the legal system, a father and sister who died from cancer, a mother dwindling away in a care center, the death of a son, and the separation from family by large distances. People with similar issues are the ones to whom I am to give the lemonade God has made in my life. Maybe I can't feel the hurt other people feel by the types of lemons they have had in their lives; God only offers me the chance to make lemonade of the problems I've faced.

As you read the Prayer of St. Francis, consider how you can use the lemons of your life to bring comfort and bless others.

"Lord, make me an instrument of Your peace. Where there is hatred, let me sow love; where there is injury, pardon; where there is doubt, faith; where there is despair, hope; where there is darkness, light; where there is sadness, joy.

O, Divine Master, grant that I may not so much seek to be consoled as to console; to be understood as to understand; to be loved as to love; For it is in giving that we receive; it is in pardoning that we are pardoned; it is in dying that we are born again to eternal life."

Teddy Bear

(Thoughts regarding God's purpose for us in our grief)

In the GriefShare groups I've led, toward the end of the thirteen sessions one of the lessons focuses on purposes of our grief using the message from this passage:

> **"Praise be to the God and Father of our Lord Jesus Christ,**
> **the Father of compassion and the God of all comfort,**
> **who comforts us in all our troubles, so that we**
> **can comfort those in any trouble**
> **with the comfort we ourselves have received from God.**
> **For just as the sufferings of Christ flow**
> **over into our lives,**
> **so also through Christ our comfort overflows."**
>
> 2 CORINTHIANS 1:3–5, NIV

To demonstrate this lesson I usually bring my old, beat-up teddy bear that Duane gave me the year we were married. I slept with it for many years, needing something to wrap my arms around at night. It's not a pretty sight, with matted fur and a torn ear from the kids playing with it too much. It's been through a lot. It can be hugged and cried on. It cuddles back. It comforts.

I also bring a beautiful white teddy bear that was given to me by a grief support organization. It is perfect. It has a cute, little perky blue shirt with some sweet statement of comfort embroidered on it. It's so pretty that it can't be touched or slept with or hugged for fear it would be messed up; its fur would get matted down, and it wouldn't look nice anymore. Its purpose was to bring comfort, but it's too perfect to relate to. It's a decoration.

God doesn't want us to be Christian decorations that look pretty to the world. He allows us to be beat up by life, then He comforts us and sends us out to love others who are experiencing similar problems. He wants us to be like my beat-up old teddy bear. We are much more lovable and able to comfort because of the hard things we've experienced. We can share what God's done for us, and give people faith in the God who showed up for us and demonstrated His loving-kindness. The grief experiences we have as well as other difficulties in life have a purpose when "through Christ our comfort overflows." This brings God glory, and we can praise Him.

Night Light

(Thoughts for parents who have kids serving
God in hard places away from home)

On Mother's Day recently, I was missing my role of being a mom to take care of my kids. One child was with Jesus, the next one was pretty far away with his new bride, one was at home with us, and the eldest was in prison. Trusting God for your adult kids is different. You have to allow Him to do His work in them. You have to allow Him to place the puzzle pieces of their lives in the right places to serve Him. You have to trust that God will tenderly care for them in your place. Mother's Day morning God lovingly assured me that He was going to take care of my kids for me, now that my role had changed so much. God spoke to me through His Word.

While reading straight through the Bible in the morning, I came to the passage about Samuel hearing God calling to him in 1 Samuel chapter 3. I thought to myself, *What new thing can I possibly learn from this familiar story?* Then I prayed and asked for the Holy Spirit to speak to me through the chapter.

I only got to verses 2 and 3 before God impressed me with something I had never thought of before. The verse reads, "At that time Eli, whose eyesight had begun to grow dim so that he could not see, was lying down in his own place. The lamp of the Lord had not yet gone out, and Samuel was lying down in the temple of the Lord, where the Ark of the Lord was."

Here was this precious little boy, whose mother had given him to God's service. He was learning to serve God in the tabernacle, doing many chores as Eli had taught him. But imagine this little boy having to go to sleep at night far from his parents, and in a room far from Eli. He was lonely, I'm sure, and missed his family terribly. He must have longed for other kids to play with and to see the little brothers and sisters God had given to Hannah after he was born. He cuddled up in the old little robe his mother brought him last year to stay warm and tried to sleep.

But God did something very special for this little boy who had been dedicated and given to God's service. Samuel laid down to sleep in the holy place inside the tabernacle. The holy place was the middle area of the tabernacle. On one side was the outer court, where the animals were slaughtered and offered and sacrificed. On the other side was the holy of holies, where the Ark of the Covenant was resting. That was the place where God's presence dwelt among His people. He had probably done his chores and swept the floor in the holy place earlier in the day, so it was clean. But he was alone.

Samuel could see the three pieces of furniture in the holy place: the table of showbread, the altar of incense, and the lampstand. Verse 3 says that "the lamp of the Lord had not yet gone out." The lampstand had to be filled with oil in the morning and evening to keep it burning. So envision this precious, little lonely boy, lying down to sleep, perhaps afraid of the sounds outside the curtains of the tabernacle. Yet God gave him a glorious nightlight to comfort him. The lamp hadn't yet used up the oil that night. He wasn't alone—the oil signifying that the Holy Spirit was still with him.

As he became drowsy he could smell the aroma of the frankincense that was burned earlier in the day on the altar. The frankincense, symbolizing our prayers to God, reminded him to talk to God before he slept. He calmed down as God comforted him. He remembered that God's very presence was on the other side of the thick, heavy curtain that divided the holy of holies from the holy place. God was with him and he could almost feel His touch. Samuel could sleep soundly because God was close to his little heart, showing him he didn't have to be afraid of the dark. The light of the Holy Spirit, God's comfort, was right there with him. God was taking care of him because his mother had given him to God's service.

God blessed me so much as I read this and envisioned little Samuel with God's night light. When we give our kids to God's service, often we can fear what will happen to them. We hurt for our kids, who have gone far away to serve God in hard places. They can be alone and afraid, learning to trust God on their own. But God doesn't leave them. He is right there with them.

God showed me that He gives our kids, whom we have dedicated to His service, a night light: the very Holy Spirit to comfort them when we cannot be with them. He makes it tangible. He doesn't let the light of God's presence go out. Then on top of that, God gives them an extra gift of aroma therapy through blessing them with joy as they pray and pour out their hearts to God. How awesome He is to love my kids when they are far away and I cannot express my love to them!

Love Has The Power to Transform Death

By Joy Anna Rosendale

(Article printed in many small newspapers,
written by Peter's aunt)

On Saturday morning, November 23, the phone rang in my Pittsburgh condo. It was my sister Mary, but immediately I could tell something was wrong. In a low, muffled voice she confirmed it: "Joy, last night Peter was in a head-on car collision, and he died early this morning." "What! Peter? That's so horrible! Oh, I'm so sorry, honey! I'll come as soon as I can!"

Then I stuffed my feelings and swung into action getting my business affairs in order to make the trip to Mary's Centerville farm via Sioux Falls. But that night at my church prayer meeting, I broke down in deep sobs. "Oh God, why did you let this happen? It's such a waste! Why Peter? God! What's the point of all this?"

He had been Mary and Duane's "surprise from heaven" sixteen years before when they thought they couldn't have any more children. He had brought much joy to our family, and had brought much inspiration and delight to the many school kids who loved him as their friend, mentor and role model. Every teenager's death brings pain, but Peter, being the outstanding young man he was, triggered unusually sharp shock and grief by his sudden tragedy. A brilliant cross country runner, Peter had recently won a medal for placing 17th in the State competition. His straight-A academic record combined with his generous words of encouragement, offered freely to the kids on his team and at school, had penetrated deeply, motivating them to make something noble of their lives. And his fun-loving, prankish nature, full of zest and the joy of living, had endeared him to a great array of friends.

"God, where are you? Why did this happen?" I sobbed. My pastor and his wife and other friends from church gathered around me, praying for me, offering hugs and words of comfort. And it helped. It renewed my determination to trust God's love in a very dark hour.

By the time I arrived in South Dakota Monday evening, an amazing miracle was in process. Mary's church was filled to the brim with Peter's classmates, their parents, and concerned family friends who had gathered to share memories of Peter and to support one another with poignant, loving thoughts that came from the depths of their hearts. Instead of the despairing gut-wrenching grief I could have expected, a powerful network of love was forming. I opened my own heart to it and let it carry me.

A couple hundred condolence cards arrived at Duane and Mary's home. Memories, tender encouragement, words of faith and hope... And the outpouring of love continued the next day at Peter's funeral. Rightly sensing that the church wouldn't be big enough, the family was given permission to hold the service in the school gym. Including the Monday evening gathering, over one thousand people attended Peter's services. Peter's twenty-two-year-old brother Matthew delivered a powerful speech about Peter's goals and his resolve, as expressed in his notebook, to "not waste his life." Peter's passion had been total commitment to Jesus

Christ as his Lord and Savior, and Matt exhorted us all to follow Peter's example, to carry on his legacy. Peter's death could result in new life if it helped us find a close and meaningful relationship with God through Jesus.

In the sacred moments while Matt was speaking, a new understanding broke open in me: how God felt about Peter's death. In earth's tragedies, God's overwhelming emotion is compassion. He feels what we feel. He grieves what we grieve. He draws very close to us, partaking of everything we are going through as vulnerable, pain-filled human beings. That's why Jesus came to earth—to carry our sorrows and heal them, and to die a death far worse than Peter's to forgive our sins and remove everything separating us from God.

God's compassion is filled with hope and determination. God's intention is to bring good out of sorrow, beauty out of what would otherwise be a disaster if God's love were not permeating it with heaven's peace. God's compassion is also filled with yearning, wanting to draw everyone into that place of comfort where we can find new life in His love.

It is love that makes the grand difference. God lives and thrives in the love we people express to one another: the comfort cards, the hugs, the prayers and gentle words, the cooked meals prepared for a bereaved family, all the thoughtful and kind things people do to try to alleviate each other's pain. I believe that suffering and sorrow and tragedy can be the doorway into a deeper and richer experience of love, and God's love transforms even death into something profoundly life-giving.

The Peter Auch Story: Ready to Run

By Andy Coy

It was the fall of 2011 and the Beresford boys' cross-country team had just placed fourth at the state meet for the first time in their school's history. In South Dakota, a team must finish in the top four to warrant an award-stand appearance. Needless to say the Watchdog boys were excited to be recognized on the big stage. For most of these boys this was their first taste of success in any avenue.

It was an exciting day for Beresford cross-country.

Perhaps none was more excited than Peter Auch, an eighth-grade rookie who had earned a spot on the team as an alternate. Peter had been running cross-country for only a year, but had already caught the attention of Head Coach Matt Coy.

Part of a coach's job is to identify leaders within the team, and it was clear to everyone in the program that Peter was "the one" to lead the next generation of Watchdog distance runners.

Peter's talent was obvious, but it was the intangibles that made Peter stand out, even as an eighth-grader. He was punctual, precise, and, most importantly, internally driven and focused.

Thus Peter was chosen as an alternate for the state meet. The trip was not only a reward for his hard work and race performances, but a chance for Peter to experience the pressure-packed state-meet atmosphere. Peter would need to know the ins and outs of the meet's structure, as he would help lead the Watchdog troops as early as next season.

From the initial Friday course jog to the prerace warm-up, Peter studied every detail.

Ready to Run

Rarely do alternates actually end up racing, but they are expected to pack a uniform in their bag in case one of the "starters" is sick or injured and can't race. An alternate would also need their uniform to wear on the medal-stand if their team finished in a coveted "podium" spot.

Coach Coy, whose team wasn't predicted to finish on the podium, didn't think to go over award-stand routines the night before.

Just before the awards presentation, Coy found all of his runners and made one last request.

"I told the boys they needed to wear their uniforms on the awards stand to look like a team," said Coy. "I looked at Peter and said he could wear his warm-up jacket since he likely had his uniform in his bag."

Peter's uniform wasn't in his bag.

"Little did I know, he was wearing his uniform all day. He ripped off his jacket and running pants and had his uniform on," said Coy.

"He had been ready to run all along."

Driven

As Coy would find over the next three years, Peter was unlike any athlete he had ever coached.

Underneath the kind, shy smile was a relentless athlete determined to make the most of every opportunity presented to him. In an era where apathy can be the norm, Peter was rare.

It didn't matter the workout, the race, or the task—Peter was always (figuratively speaking) ready to run.

"He never missed a practice, he knew every calorie he put into his body, he studied the correct running shoe for his body type, he studied training and tapering, and he was always picking my brain about what we were doing and what my overall plan was for him and the team. He was one of those rare competitors who you only get to coach once in a lifetime. He didn't want to be mediocre and didn't want his team to be mediocre, either. He was determined to be great."

This all-or-nothing attitude wasn't limited to just running—this was the way Peter approached life.

"He was determined to get from life what he needed," says his mom Mary Auch, a registered dietician at Sanford Health. "He couldn't just chill out and just enjoy free time and leisure. He used it for something he wanted to accomplish. He knew his weaknesses, and was honest to list overcoming them as a priority."

As the years passed Peter's relentless determination to be great began to reveal itself through running.

The Goal: "Top 25"

After a great summer of training before his sophomore year of cross-country, Peter began to produce a level of success far surpassing anything he'd accomplished in his young career. As the season progressed Peter established himself as one of the best runners in "Class A" cross-country.

By the time of the state meet in October, Peter was excited and confident in his preparation that he could finish on the award's stand with a top twenty-five finish—a goal that he had set before his training began the previous summer.

This "podium" finish was the spark that drove Peter out the door for hundreds upon hundreds of training miles, battling eastern South Dakota's oppressive summers.

The night before the race, the team went out to a restaurant for a traditional premeet meal, which is more or less an opportunity to unwind with teammates and family before the excitement and anxiety of race day.

While most of the team, consisting of thirteen- to seventeen-year-old kids, was typically giddy with nerves and excitement, Peter was a different story. Dialed-in and focused—and mildly annoyed at the energy of his teammates—Peter seemed ready to run, right then and there. Race day couldn't come any sooner.

"Watching the video of the team eating the night before the state meet, you can see that Peter was not goofing off like the others," said Mary as she recalls the video Coach Coy made of the events that weekend. "He was thoughtful as usual, thinking I'm sure of his strategy and how to make sure he would win."

Race Day

Although just a sophomore, Peter and his senior teammate Riley Schapp led the Watchdogs through the morning of the state meet like veteran leaders. In fact everything the day of the big race went as planned—a rarity in high school athletics.

The state cross-country championship is a unique event. The meet consists of over one hundred athletes, all competing in one race, all with similar goals, and all ready and determined to run their best race of the season.

"Winning," per se, means hundreds of different things to cross-country runners. At the state cross-country meet, the peak of success is often associated with cracking the top twenty-five—the goal Peter had set for himself several months prior.

With the firing of the starter's pistol, the runners were off. Peter and the rest of the Beresford squad started off near the back of the pack. With the slow start, one couldn't help but wonder, *Are they ready to run? Had nerves conquered the young group? Did they peak too soon?*

However, halfway through the five-kilometer race, Peter started to make his move from forty runners into the pack to the thirties, and closer to his goal. As the closing kilometer loomed, Peter's tactics were working, and his goal of a podium finish—the coveted top twenty-five—was within reach.

Peter continued to pick off his competitors, one by one. As he neared the final straightaway, it was clear that his goal of reaching the podium was becoming a reality.

The official results confirmed it—Peter had just placed seventeenth in Class A at the 2013 State Cross-Country Meet.

And as it turned out the conservative start to the race was all part of the plan—Peter and the Beresford boys were ready to run after all.

The 2013 state meet was the best race of Peter's life. All of the focus, determination, and commitment to all of the little things had paid off.

But even in the midst of his excitement Peter was still thinking of the people around him.

His teammate Riley Schapp had also come from the back of the pack with Peter, but the effort was too much. Schapp passed out and crashed into the woodchips just before the finish line, to miss out on his own top twenty-five finish. It was a heartbreaking end to a career for Schapp, a senior.

Peter knew Schapp had gone through the same "trial of miles" as he had the previous summer in hopes of a podium finish. He was well aware of their shared top twenty-five goal.

In respect for his teammate, Peter saved his celebration and ran a victory lap far away, in a circle around the team camp.

As Peter jogged by himself in a mini-celebration, Coy recalls him letting out a controlled scream of excitement.

The Next Step

His performance at the state cross-country meet was a sign of great things to come for Peter Auch. The once shy, quiet eighth-grade alternate had matured into a confident, talented distance runner.

He was progressing very quickly, and both Coach Coy and Peter knew the next step from the podium could be an all-state selection, and perhaps even higher accolades after that.

Even more exciting for Peter was the anticipation for the upcoming track and field season, a sport where he had already shown incredible potential as a freshman. A breakthrough track season seemed inevitable.

Peter knew the possibilities, but he also knew dreams were nothing without the foundation of hard work. Although only early November, he had already started training for the spring season, doing all of the little things that make champions.

He continued to stick to his incredibly strict diet (his mother is a registered dietician, after all), and he was juggling his academic and athletic commitments admirably. Peter was consistently receiving high marks in the classroom and was in a tight race for valedictorian of his class.

The younger guys looked up to him as a role model, and his easy-going, positive outlook on life made him a popular kid around the school.

In fact, as Coach Coy recalls, Peter seemed to be smiling everywhere he went.

"Maybe because he was up to something, or maybe because he was just enjoying life," he says. "Probably a little bit of both."

By all accounts Peter was just simply a really great kid. As a parent I'd want my kid to hang out with Peter Auch.

Given Peter's outstanding reputation, it's with no surprise why the events of Friday, November 22, were such a paralyzing blow to the Beresford community.

Black Friday

After finishing a workout at the school, Peter drove to his home in Centerville to get ready for a gathering with some friends at a local church.

It was a Friday night and his friends were already at church, waiting for his arrival. But after an extended period of time Peter's friends began to worry. Typically punctual and dependable, Peter had yet to arrive.

And then came the sirens.

On his way to church Peter was struck by a vehicle trying to pass another car on the highway, just a mile and a half from the turnoff to the church.

The next day, due to the injuries he received in the accident, Peter passed away in a Sioux Falls hospital.

It was all too sudden. It was all too confusing. It was all too very, very sad.

Peter was just sixteen years old.

The Purpose of Peter Auch

But in the days following this tragic event, Peter's family—and the Beresford community—were beginning to learn some incredible things about the kid behind that memorable smile.

It was clear that a bigger story was beginning to unfold—a story that would reveal a purpose far greater than distance running.

In fact, as it turned out, Peter's story wasn't about running at all.

If you were to visit Peter's *Twitter* account today, you would see that purpose written out very clearly in the description under his username.

Like a silent message of reassurance, it reads, quoting from John 3:30 (ESV), "He must increase, I must decrease."

Peter was not done with the people in his life. He was determined, even in his absence, to leave an impact.

The Notebook

Following the accident, Peter's family discovered a notebook in his room with a long list of goals addressing his spiritual, mental, physical, and social life. From Peter's writings one could see a teen who was reflective and analytical about his own life and the impact of his life to those around him.

Deeply religious, Peter wanted to bring people closer to the God he had come to love. He wanted his peers to see a higher calling beyond alcohol, drugs, and the many other superfluous objects of our everyday existence.

He not only strived to lead a fulfilling life for himself, but he wanted those around him to be happy and fulfilled, too.

Keep in mind, this kid was sixteen.

The selections from Peter's notebook that were read at his prayer ceremony had a profound impact on the entire Beresford community, and especially on Coach Coy and the Beresford cross-country team.

"After some of his goals were read at his prayer service we realized Peter was going to have a lasting impact on all of us. He had a number one goal of bringing people closer to Jesus, especially his classmates, and he also wanted to win a state cross-country championship. Those will stick with our cross-country family for years and years to come."

Peter lived his life deliberately and purposefully, and that was the permanent impression he left with everyone who knew him.

It's a lesson we can all take from the sixteen-year-old: live life with a distinct, well-defined purpose.

"Peter read a book with his dad this last year called *Don't Waste Your Life*. It is a saying that I remind myself about daily," says Coy. "He had a purpose in life and fulfilled it. He wore his emotions on his sleeve. He loved life."

His mother Mary wholeheartedly agrees.

"Peter would be so glad to know the effect his life had on his classmates, and that in the end he pointed them toward the God he loved. His real purpose for his life was fulfilled in his short sixteen years; he had accomplished the job God had made him to do."

What will be remembered as the most tragic day for Peter's family, teammates, and friends, was simply a new beginning for Peter, one which I can only imagine began by God asking, "Peter, are you ready to run?"

FUNERAL SPEECH

(Speech given at Peter's funeral by his friend, Riley Schaap)

Hi everyone, my name is Riley Schaap. I was a buddy of Petey's and a good friend of his on the cross country team as well. If you ever saw Peter racing against somebody just neck and neck during the race it was probably me. We were probably jostling people around, and pushin' each other to keep goin' on.

I just want to start out this service by tellin' a quick little story about Peter. This last month the Beresford XC team was headed to state XC. Naturally, as a team we seek to intimidate our rivals. The easiest way to do this Peter thought, along with the rest of us, was to bulk up in the weight room. Can't you just picture the Beresford XC team up there just slammin' on those 45 plates? People aren't gonna' be shakin' in their shoes unless that bar is bending. Unfortunately, big broad shouldered XC runners just don't exist, ya know, so we decided to do something different. After some consideration, it was decided that we would have to bring a big boom box and start crankin' out some dub step at the state meet, I mean that stuff will scare anybody. So, we got to the state meet, but soon realized that we did not have a big stereo to do as we wished. Instead we had to settle for some speakers that were roughly the size of the palm of my hand. So we walked around the state meet, up and down the course, crankin' this dubstep music, we were a force to be reckoned with, I mean,

I'm sure people could hear us for well... a good 20 feet. But, we were there to intimidate them, strike fear into their hearts. Apparently that music wasn't enough, because about halfway through walking the course, Peter suggested that we start bobbin our heads to the music, as if we didn't have enough swag already... So, I remember our Beresford team bobbin our head to that music, walking the course backwards so we could stare people down haha. I don't know if we really were intimidating them, I hope so, who knows?

Petey meant a lot to this school as well. You could always count on Peter to have a great smile, and to bring excitement to any activity, especially dodge ball! Every student knows that if they needed extra help on a worksheet, or just had a general question, they would find a truthful, honest answer from Petey, and support there as well. Peter never gave up. He was a gutsy go get 'em athlete, but perhaps even more than that, what stood out about Peter was the high priority that he held concerning his faith. Peter stressed his relationship with God in his personal life as was evidenced by the way that he acted, and held himself in his other aspects of life.

Throughout Peter's life, he taught me numerous lessons. He taught me how to give it my all, even in the tough times, when it hurts. He also taught me to be diligent in my work, whatever that may be.

Some of the greatest lessons I've learned from Peter however, have come in the last few days. I have had many emotions and many questions flying through my head recently. After talking with Mary, Peter's mom, and being alone with God and other followers of Christ, I have been profoundly challenged. I was on the phone with Mary on Saturday afternoon, and she asked me these questions about Peter:

- What was Peter like?
- If Peter saw someone alone and hurting, what would he do?
- Could you see Jesus in Peter's life?
- How did Peter confront certain sin struggles in his life?

After considering her questions in regard to Peter, I couldn't help but begin asking these questions of myself. I've begun asking new questions relating to my own spiritual walk. I'd like to slowly run through a couple of these questions again. However, this time I would like to ask each of you to insert your name into the question and allow them to challenge you.

These past days I have asked myself "What is Riley Schaap like?" What do I identify with, is it XC, track, academics, the performing arts, my faith. What is Riley Schaap like?

The second question I would like you all to ask yourselves is "If I saw someone alone and hurting, what would I do?" This question was very convicting to me. Often times I fail to look on others with love, to push past my own selfish desires and reach out. God calls us to do this, and we all know the blessings associated with helping another through pain, yet why is it so difficult to do? If I see someone alone and hurting, what do I do?

The third question, "Can you see Jesus in my life?" I have asked this question of myself before, but in these past days the question has taken on new meaning in my life. The importance of my response has grown dramatically. Am I allowing God to mold me and make me into the man He wants me to be, or am I continuously fighting His will for my life? If somebody passes me on the street or sees my actions, are they seeing traces of Christ in me?

The final question I asked myself is probably the most significant of all. After the events of this weekend, and having seen tragedy firsthand, this question constantly reverberates in my mind. "If I were to die tonight, would my life be filled with treasures that will last or empty pursuits of this life?" Will my life be filled with lasting treasures, relationships with people and souls reached for the Kingdom of God, or a bunch of worthless pursuits, goals focused on myself and short-lived desires?

After considering these questions I was not satisfied with my response. Peter's legacy has given me a renewed desire to serve my Creator. I know I cannot do this on my own, but through Christ I know even the most extraordinary things are possible.

"Praise be to the God and Father of our Lord Jesus Christ! In his great mercy he has given us new birth into a living hope through the resurrection of Jesus Christ from the dead, and into an inheritance that can never perish, spoil or fade. This inheritance is kept in heaven for you, who through faith are shielded by God's power until the coming of the salvation that is ready to be revealed in the last time."

1 Peter 1:3-5, NIV

"Do you not know?
Have you not heard?
The Lord is the everlasting God,
the Creator of the ends of the earth.
He will not grow tired or weary,
and his understanding no one can fathom.
He gives strength to the weary
and increases the power of the weak.
Even youths grow tired and weary,
and young men stumble and fall;
but those who hope in the Lord
will renew their strength.
They will soar on wings like eagles;
they will run and not grow weary,
they will walk and not be faint."

Isaiah 40:28-31, NIV

Press On

(Booklet written for Peter's classmates as a gift
for their graduation from high school)

The class of 2016 is amazing. God used you to change my life. You and other students in the high school were used by God to give me purpose when life lost any sense of direction. You have clarified to me what the meaning in life is—a meaning that lasts and endures. You have given comfort to my family when faced with a huge emptiness. You have been our joy when feeling despair. You've helped me to accept the loss of Peter and move forward in life.

Three of you were there when I got out of the car at the gate to the cemetery at the time of the internment. You asked me the real story about how Peter got the scar on his face and got me laughing so hard about the crazy stories he told you. As a result I was able to face what I thought would be the worst part of the whole day. Many times you've cheered me up with your texts and memories of your friend.

You helped Peter's brother Matt, who had a very difficult time with his grief because he had missed out on spending much time with his little brother. He was too engrossed in his last year of studying engineering at SDSU to be at home much. He didn't know the fun side of Peter much and how he acted around his friends. He needed you to share your memories to help him to know who Peter was as a real kid. You didn't realize it, but you were helping him when he assisted the track team in the spring of 2014. You helped him in his journey of grief to find joy and peace.

I didn't really know many of you until eighteen hours after Peter died, when we all met at Brooklyn church. I had no idea when I opened the door to the church that night how important you would become to Duane and me. That night it was too early to ask why Peter died. You were a sea of tears and sniffles and misery and broken hearts when I talked to you that night, too stunned to know what to say or do. I was in shock. But the mom in me kicked in when I saw your pain, and I was bonded to you guys.

When we met at Brooklyn that night I hadn't even started to ask why Peter had to die; maybe you did when you heard the news. But three days later my son Matt, at the funeral, answered the question we had barely begun to form in our minds: "Why?"

To quote him in the funeral speech he gave, he said, "I'm not asking, why did this happen? I know why. I hate it. I would have never done it this way. I wish God had chosen another way, would have never put us through this agony. But I know why. It was for you. For you who knew him, for you who would hear of him. It was so you would understand and love the gospel. It was so God could show you His love, and sovereignty, grace, and glory. So God could show you Himself in ways that were impossible otherwise."

Most people struggle forever with the "why" question after a death and never get a good answer. They eventually replace the why question with, "What do I do about my loss now?" I never had to ask why since God made it very clear to all of us that the loss of our son and your friend and classmate was because of this: it was for His glory to be spread. Peter's life and death caused you to confront your Savior, to see His glory up close—to see evidence of God's worth and value displayed in His actions. You had to determine whether you could follow this glorious God who took Peter home. Peter challenged us to determine what in this life is worth living for and what is worth dying for. You had the privilege of learning this lesson early in life. Many graduates flounder and waste a lot of time learning these lessons. You are better prepared for life as a result of this loss.

You have changed as a class. Many of you in the last two and a half years have deepened your relationship with God and grown to know Him personally. I realize some have drifted away. But you are aware and may have come to know that you do not want to waste your life on doing trivial, unimportant things to serve your own interests. You have taken Peter's death very seriously and now face a fork in the road of your life. You can continue on in what you've learned and use your life to glorify God. If you do, you'll lose your life by common American standards. Or you can follow the path that promises success and a comfortable American dream life.

Press On

Matt read to Peter as he was dying at Avera hospital, from Philippians 3:13–15 (NIV): "I press on toward the goal to win the prize for which God has called me heavenward in Christ Jesus." He's attained that prize of eternal life. Peter pressed on in life and achieved his goal of being with Jesus forever that night. He's in heaven now, enjoying being with his Savior close up every day. The verse is directed toward us now. We have to apply it with the choices we make. How do we "press on" with our lives?

You've seen and worn the shirt you designed in his memory over and over in the last two years: "Don't Waste Your Life" on the front, and "I press on to the goal of the upward call of God in Christ Jesus" printed on the back side. You've brought me joy whenever I see you wear it. What does it mean now that you will put it away or wear it as pajamas, and exchange it for wearing college attire in public? What does "pressing on" mean now? What does "pressing on" look like in everyday life, and what skills and beliefs do you need to "press on" lifelong?

When I consider how to "press on," I think of the little bit of running or jogging I do. Most of the time it isn't totally pleasurable. It's work, but I have an end result in mind. I press on to finish the next mile or go faster or add a few more minutes to reach the goal I set for the day. "Pressing on" isn't easy. It doesn't come naturally; it's easier to sit on the couch to read a book or watch TV.

"Pressing on" involves making hard choices to reach the goal and prize of eternal life in heaven. You may be called to go to a hard place to live and work to spread the glory of God, looking forward to that prize God has for you someday. You may be like Peter's brother Matt, who has willingly gone to the Middle East for graduate school to make friends and show them Jesus' love, fully knowing it could cost him his life should the political situation there deteriorate.

You may be like Peter's aunt Beth, who is a missionary in Pakistan. She lives inside the gates and walls to the Christian college campus where her husband is the president of that institution, much like the Muslim women in the community. It's too dangerous for her to leave and shop by herself and have the same freedoms we thoughtlessly enjoy here in the US. She and her husband go outside the gate with an armed guard wearing body armor. Beth has watched ISIS videos of beheadings, to be prepared for that possibility of martyrdom for her Savior if she were to be kidnapped outside the gate to the compound. She knows families of the Christians in the city who have died in bombings of local churches—the threat is real. The recent bombing in Lahore on Easter this year took place two miles from where they live, and the college is on the list of terrorists' targets.

But Beth loves the students there and supports the efforts of the college to help them grow in their Christian life. She's pressing on, despite lots of discomfort from feeling confined and from the possibility of pain and death and being martyred. It's worth it to her to make sure Pakistanis know how much Jesus loves them. She realizes that without the Christian presence in that college, the Muslim students there may never hear of the gospel and see Christians up close to be drawn to the Savior. It's sobering and motivating to do what is needed so they will have the opportunity to be with her and her Savior in heaven. It's worth it to her to suffer for others in hopes of their salvation, because the alternative is too horrible to think much about. As her husband Jim wrote recently: "...But just as this is a cause to live for, so it also is one that is worth dying for... There is nothing better in life than living for a cause that is worth giving your life for."

In "pressing on," we are willing to be part of God's plan. It involves following Jesus wherever He leads us. It may be hard for us; it could be easy. We don't know. For Peter it meant dying at age sixteen. Was Jesus worth it? Is He worth it for us to give our lives in service? I heard a relative say of Matt's few years of service with the Navigators campus Christian ministry at SDSU: "People shouldn't be expected to give so much of their lives." *What!?* I screamed inside. Didn't Jesus leave the glory of heaven to come to this world to live with us and give His life for us? He died an excruciating death so we wouldn't be separated from God forever in eternity. Is it too much to devote all our lives to serving our Savior in thanks for the costliest gift of eternal life He has given us? Isn't that what will last in the end?

In Matthew 16:25 (NIV), Jesus said, "For whoever wants to save his life will lose it, and whoever loses his life for me will find it." Be prepared for the pressing on toward the goal God has for you to be costly. There is a saying, "God doesn't use anyone greatly until they have been hurt deeply." We do not attain greatness in God's Kingdom without great pain. Initially He accepts us as His children on the basis of Jesus' sacrifice. Salvation is a free gift; we can't do anything to work for it. But after making that initial decision of faith, following Jesus is costly. God does reserve a special reward for those who suffer for Him. It will be worth it someday if we press on through great difficulty.

You also need to be prepared for the "pressing on" to cause long-range changes in your lives and the lives of others. If my father, who was an alcoholic in college, wasting his brain and life, hadn't accepted the help a friend offered him, he would have totally wasted and ruined his life. Where he was headed was totally hopeless. Instead he accepted the gift of eternal life and his life was transformed. He became a renowned and beloved professor of theology and affected many students' lives. He "pressed on" to follow Jesus through a lot of very difficult struggles in his life. He was a father who trained his children to love Jesus through his example and teaching. If he had continued to get drunk and flunked out of college, he never would have met my mom, and I would never have been born. You never would have known Peter. You never would have had this experience that has shaped us all. It's like ripples that form when a rock is thrown into a calm lake. There is an initial splash, but then the ripples keep forming an ever-widening effect that can be seen. My dad's life has rippled far and wide in the last ninety years because he pressed on to do what God made him to do. It's affected you.

We've seen many ripples from the day Peter died, as your lives have been changed. I am constantly amazed at the people who mention that they still remember Peter, and mention that they think about whether what they are doing is worth it or not—whether they are wasting their lives or making it count for Jesus.

There is a memorable ripple caused by Peter's friendship with Breanna Swee. When feeling lonely after Peter died, she formed a friendship with Anton. Breanna made it her goal to help Anton understand Jesus and what Christianity was all about before he went back to Germany. Several of you took the step in the fall of 2014, when it wasn't popular to befriend a quiet German kid, to spend time to get to know him. You showed him Jesus' love. You made it easy for him to see what a difference God makes in a person's life, such that Anton accepted Jesus as Savior, and now is home growing in his faith. The ripples extend now to Germany. Your life will create ripples for many years to come. It's awesome to think about.

"Pressing on" is costly, tough, and long-lasting. It's worth it. I'd like to challenge you with some beliefs and behaviors that will make it easier to "press on" as you face this as graduates. Although you are all on a high now as you face graduation, and everything looks rosy, you will face problems at some time in the future. Life will be difficult for all of us at times. Jesus said to his disciples, "In the world you will have trouble, but I have overcome the world." When we believe that Jesus is able to overcome the troubles for us, we can face life confident in God's power. However,

I've observed that life is a lot tougher for some people due to some fundamental things that they believe that are not the truth. They have trouble in life just due to the things they believe. But when we cherish some basic truths about God and who we are in relationship with Him, life makes sense and is fulfilling. What I've learned and believed have enabled me to jump over the hurdles caused by the loss of Peter. These beliefs have kept me on the track, able to "press on."

Begin the Right Race

The first belief that is crucial is to understand how to be in the right race spiritually. "Pressing on" is needed to run the marathon of life; it's not for the fun runs. How do we register for the marathon race to heaven? We all have to understand that we cannot get to heaven by anything we do. Nothing we do will earn God's favor except the sacrifice of His Son Jesus. If we confess our sins, accept God's rule in our lives, and accept and believe that He was punished in our place, we can be confident that we are forgiven, made perfect in God's sight because of Jesus' righteousness, and we will be in heaven forever and ever. It's that simple. This is how we get into the right race and get started running. Placing your faith in Jesus is how to start the marathon God wants all of us to run.

Love Motivates Us to Run the Race

Jeremiah 9:23–24 (NIV) gives us the second belief or behavior that is necessary to press on lifelong. "Let not the wise man boast of his wisdom, or the strong man of his strength or the rich man of his riches; but let him who boasts boast about this: that he understands and knows me, that I am the LORD who exercises kindness, justice and righteousness on earth." What we will be able to carry with us lifelong and forevermore are two truths: that we know God personally and understand what He shows us about Himself.

The whole reason God made us is to have a close relationship with us, to show us His love. If we neglect a love relationship with God in an effort just to do good things for Him, we are just like "noisy, clanging cymbals" according to 1 Corinthians 13. Jesus summarized all the Ten Commandments like this: "Love the Lord your God with all your heart, mind, soul and strength, and your neighbor as yourself." Loving God is our top priority.

Knowing and loving God are the motivations for everything we do in life, in the race we're on. It keeps us going when it's hard. Love Him for the amazing thing He did in sending His Son to suffer in your place and die just so you could spend eternity with Him. It's amazing and humbling to consider. Of all the world's religions and gods, He's the only one who loves His people so much.

We get to know God through reading the Bible diligently and letting Him speak to us. We grow to love the God we learn about in the Bible. And we feel His love and care for us in hard times. Get to know God as your strength in hard times. He is there with you, loving you in whatever life brings. He is all we have to boast about, as Jeremiah 9:23–24 say. When all are done someday, people will be at peace at your funeral if it's clear to all that you knew God and loved Him like Peter did. The sting of the loss will be lessened because of your relationship with God. It is God's love and loving Him back that give us the encouragement to press on.

God Has Planned the Race

To make it to the end in the marathon, the third thing to understand is to make sure you believe that God is in complete control of your life. He has your race planned in every turn and valley and hill you'll face. The race is not easy, as I've said. Sometimes the directions on the path often don't make sense. The hurdles in the race loom high and huge. Turns in the path often seem to have no purpose. But God has every intricate detail and minute planned on the race of your life. He has a purpose for it all. All of it. There is a huge security in knowing that what happens in life is not by random chance.

There is a huge master plan that God made prior to creation. Each of our lives is part of that huge overall plan. I like to view that plan as a universe-sized puzzle. We only experience a few tiny pieces of the total puzzle. God puts down one piece at a time for us as individuals as we are faced with decisions or as notable events take place. The puzzle pieces of my life fit in with yours. What I do influences your life and how your puzzle pieces fit next to mine. Who my parents are, where I go to school and college, who I marry, health challenges, my kids, my job, and so on are all puzzle pieces. Even the conversations we have with others are significant puzzle pieces.

We just see little puzzle pieces as we live our lives. Usually it doesn't make sense how it all fit together. The problem is that most of the time we don't see the picture on the box top of the huge puzzle God is putting together. What is the picture? It goes back to creation. God made us to be His friends, in a close-friend relationship with Him. Eve and Adam destroyed that relationship with God when they sinned, and we've been affected ever since. So since then God has been at work, putting together a universe-sized plan or puzzle to restore the relationship of all of us to Himself. It's called the Kingdom of God—letting Him take control of our lives so He is in charge.

Picture a castle of where God lives as King in heaven, with each of us there loving Him, enjoying being with Him, wearing the crown prizes we've earned and enjoying basking in His love for us. God is doing whatever He pleases and whatever is necessary to bring all of us to the place where we accept that He has to be in control so we can join Him in His kingdom. He wants all of us to accept His gift of salvation through Jesus. His master plan is to cause people to be saved and be with Him for eternity.

As Christians our lives are all about joining God in accomplishing His plans. Our job is to do whatever God has for us to accomplish His greater purpose. He wants us to be engaged in causing as many people as possible to enter the Kingdom and spend forever with Him. He wants us to have the attitude: "Lord, I am willing to do anything necessary for furthering Your Kingdom." So whatever we do as Christians in life, it is part of God putting His huge puzzle of the Kingdom of God together.

Sometimes it hurts us personally when puzzle pieces are put together for God's overall picture. It can be really uncomfortable and painful. When you look at it, Peter's death was one of those puzzle pieces He placed in all of our lives. He worked in all our hearts to draw us closer to His kingdom when Peter died. It was part of His huge plan.

If we don't see life this way, as part of God's huge puzzle, not much makes sense. It's pretty meaningless to struggle to get a degree, make money, and just focus on enjoying the time. Life brings pain and hardship. These experiences of pain and hardship make life appear to be cruel and out of control when our lives are focused on seeking pleasure. We despair at all the pain and suffering. Current events seem tragic and terrible. Tragedies seem to be the result of a cruel being who is harsh and punitive and allows horrible things to take place. With that worldview it doesn't make any sense why a smart, nice, athletic kid like Peter should be killed. He could have done so much with his life and been so successful. We have the right to become bitter and full of self-pity if it's due to a random event. And we give up on God if we think that life is all about getting to the end with as much stuff and as healthy and happy as possible without any ugly scars.

Peter's death does make sense, though, when you understand that God had a much bigger plan in all of this. He loved all of us so much that He worked out a trillion details to have Peter born when I was infertile, transfer to Beresford from Centerville, get to know all of you, go to Boy Scouts to learn how to make plans and goals, buy a notebook with me at Walmart just as school started, take the time to write down all he planned to do in the next year that revealed to us his heart, read the books he did, change his thoughts and plans, increase his desire to follow Jesus, pick out his life verse (which was John 3:30), see the book on Matthew's bookshelf (*Don't Waste Your Life*), decide that he wasn't going to waste his, and have the accident happen at the precise time, place, and way it occurred. If he had left the house on the way to church one second later, or waited longer at the intersection when turning onto Highway 46, the accident wouldn't have happened. God was planning each detail. Why? To point all of us toward Himself, to bring us into His Kingdom. He has been in total control of it all. I can love a God who has a purpose in this. I can serve a God who makes good come of our loss. Life makes sense and I am secure that it will all work out in the end for a glorious purpose. I can rest and have joy when feeling sad. I don't have to wallow in bitterness and despair. God is doing His job, drawing people into His Kingdom, and chose my son and your friend to be part of that.

We Don't Run Alone

The fourth, huge lesson I learned in the last two and a half years is that we don't face the race alone. Jesus is running beside me, just as Riley Schapp and Peter ran together, often side by side, urging each other to excel and keep going (fast!). We don't have to "press on" through all the tough stuff by ourselves. When you find that life isn't as fun and rosy as is promised to eager graduates, remember that Jesus is in the race with you. He at times runs a little ahead, showing you the way, so you can keep your eyes on Him rather than the tough parts. He is the one who enables you to "press on." He will be with you to the end, and then you will gain that prize we all desire: to be in heaven forever. If you "fix your eyes on Him," you will be able to go through the pains of life joyfully.

When I attended the grand march for your prom I was tempted to take my eyes off Jesus, sit there and cry, and feel really sorry that Peter wasn't there to enjoy it and that I couldn't enjoy the experience like all the other parents there. I wouldn't have tons of pictures to post on Facebook of my son in his tux, looking terrific. My mind wanted to dwell on who he would have taken to the prom and what cute, goofy things he would have done despite looking handsome and awesome as an adult son. I wanted to wallow in self-pity that I was robbed of that experience. All I could envision was Peter dying on the bed in the ICU at Avera, a very different picture than what everyone else was seeing. But instead Jesus reminded me He was there with me. He made my thoughts turn to realize Peter was enjoying all the glory of heaven, with beautiful angels at a stunning party, having the time of his life. The dresses of all the angels far surpassed all beautiful gowns the girls were wearing at the prom (no offense!). The decorations in heaven were far more stupendous! Jesus turned my eyes back to Himself, so I could fix my eyes on Him and rejoice instead. Peter wasn't missing anything at all. He just wished you could be with him at his party!

That's happened over and over in the last two and a half years. When I'm really sad, Jesus reminds me of the reason why He ransomed Peter, and His right and plan to do with Peter's life whatever would bring Him glory. He reminds me of all of you and how He's used Peter to change your lives. Then joy fills me as I think of Jesus increasing in your lives and your growth in Him. Fixing my eyes on Him enables me to face it all. Learn to do that in whatever pain comes to you.

Keep Hydrated

How can I forget to mention the importance of hydration? Perhaps it's because we all find it easy to forget to keep drinking enough to be hydrated for the upcoming race—both physically and spiritually. I woke up today thinking of whether my cup was "half empty" or "half full." Yesterday, after having a day of working thirteen hours to get ready to be off for two weeks to go to Haiti, I felt completely drained, parched, and dry. My emotional cup was empty, realizing our house and my heart will be empty this weekend of Peter and all his siblings—alone. There won't be any graduation party here.

I usually try to see life as "half full." Duane sees it as "half empty." Neither of us are right. Life drains us to be totally empty, dry, and parched. There's nothing "half full" about your son dying and an empty house with only memories. The race you'll run will leave you totally dehydrated at times.

But there's water to drink. In John 4:13–14 (NIV), Jesus said, "Everyone who drinks this water will be thirsty again, but whoever drinks the water I give him will never thirst. Indeed the water I give him will become in him a spring of living water springing up to eternal life." Jesus comes and brings us a drink of Himself when we're dehydrated. He floods us with the water of His Word when we're ready for it and can accept it.

So how does He give us this water? One way is to recognize that the good things that happen each day are due to God blessing us, not luck or coincidence. As we respond in thanks and praise and worship for those small good things, God gives us a drink of the water of life. For example, this morning I remembered that when I drove up to the house in the dark last night, I noticed that the lawn was mowed. It was one of those bothersome things on my mental to-do list that was nagging at me. How in the world was I going to get the lawn mown between all the rain and last-minute shopping and parties and packing? But God had prepared a blessing long in advance of last night's drive home. Last Sunday I sat down in church by a sharp-looking guy who was there for the first time. He had just finished his first year at USD. Duane talked to him at length after the service, and told him he had some work for him to do if he was interested, before he headed off to work at a camp. The guy showed up this week and mowed all the big areas for Duane. The smaller parts I do around the house still had to be done. But God knew my need and had him come back yesterday and bless me and finish it all—when I was spent and emotionally dehydrated.

Here's another example of God demonstrating His love and giving us a drink when we're dry. Matt was finishing up his first semester of grad school. The projects were tough and difficult. Matt was committed to doing everything excellently to bring glory to God. He was running on complete "empty" in the last few days, not seeing how he was going to finish it all on time and give a decent presentation of his work to the class. So what did God do to hydrate him? His professor's daughter got sick, so the time for giving the presentation was pushed ahead a day, giving Matt twenty-four more hours to polish it up and make it a quality job. God is good. It wasn't coincidence. He answered the prayers of many for Matt this week and He gave my son a drink of His water to sustain him. (I'm sure He's taking care of the little girl, too!)

But how do we get hydrated for the marathons? That's where all the things you hear over and over in church come in. God gets us and keeps us hydrated when we faithfully do all the basic disciplines: personal quiet time in prayer and Bible reading; fellowship with others, sharing what God is doing in your life and in study together; memorizing and letting your mind dwell on the verses you learn so your attitudes and hearts change; and finally in sharing your faith with others.

Remember Peter's Gatorade bottle (that he squirted you with)? Use that image in your mind and follow his example to keep spiritually hydrated. An important aspect of staying hydrated is this: the water has to get used up to be able to get more. Runners sweat it out, drink, and get rehydrated. As Christians in the race we have to give the water Jesus hydrates us with to others. Then we are empty again, and He can fill up our dry emptiness once more to sense His nearness and blessing. Keep sharing the water with others, and you'll be given more and more. You will be a "spring of water welling up to eternal life." You will be hydrated to "press on."

The Purpose of the Race

The last crucial belief necessary for "pressing on" that I challenge you to accept is to understand the purpose of the marathon—your purpose in life. The most important purpose for which God made us is to glorify Himself. That sounds really selfish of God. It's not. The awesome creator of the universe has the right to do whatever He wants. If He saved us through the death of His own Son, then He has the right to do what He wants with our lives to bring glory to Himself. He really does deserve all the glory and credit for being supreme. If we really understand how magnificent God is, we can do nothing else but glorify Him.

So what does it mean to glorify God? To live so we attract people to Him and make Him famous, not ourselves. This was the essence of Peter's desire when he chose the verse from John 3:30 to characterize his life: "He must increase, I must decrease." He wanted people to think of his Savior, not himself. He was in second place, Jesus was first.

Pressing On in Everyday Life

So "pressing on" requires these five beliefs and behaviors: knowing that we will spend eternity in heaven with Jesus, understanding that we need to know and love God personally, believing that He is in control to draw people into His kingdom, fixing our eyes on Him, staying spiritually hydrated, and finding that our purpose for our lives is to glorify Him.

Practically what does that mean we are to do with our lives? If we really understand that God is in total control, forming His kingdom so as many people as possible join Him in eternity to have fellowship with Him, and that our purpose is to glorify Him, what does that mean we are to do? What should we do with our lives to fulfill our purpose?

Jesus made this pretty clear in the Great Commission: "Go into all the world and preach the gospel…" Jesus' intention is that the message of salvation be spread all over the world. It's not just for us to stay at home and enjoy God's blessings and be successful and comfortable; the message is for everyone, even people in very difficult and dangerous places. It's up to us to spend our lives doing the most significant thing ever, letting the world see and know about how much God loves us and offers us the chance to be with Him forever. It is an adventure. It's costly. It's demanding. It will take you to exciting places. It's worth it. The end result is awesome. I read the book *Three Cups of Tea* several years ago. It included a story about a woman who spent her life starting schools for girls in Afghanistan. It was a dangerous job. Her motto was, "I want to die, being used up in helping women be educated." I have changed that somewhat to form my motto: "I want to die, being used up spreading the gospel."

How many of you have watched adults give all their energies to earning enough money to have a bigger boat, a bigger house, a nicer lawn and garden, a nicer car, more toys, and hobbies? Those things just demand more and more of us and our time to keep repaired, cleaned, and mowed. In the end it all decays. You've probably seen very successful people who really aren't too happy when it's all done. It's pretty empty and meaningless. In contrast I haven't seen a single person who "lost their life" in obeying

Jesus' command to go into all the world to spread the "good news" who regrets it. It cost them comfort, but they knew they would win the terrific prize that awaits them in heaven, and bring lots of awesome people with them. There is time for comfort in eternity and pleasure beyond imagination there. Now is the time to go.

In John 15:16 (NIV), Jesus said, "You did not choose me, but I chose you and appointed you that you should go and bear fruit and that your fruit should abide…" God has chosen and appointed you, just like He did the disciples, to go to spread the gospel. Going is not optional. It's our appointment, our role and job in life. Jesus did not say to his disciples, "Stay at home, get a good job, earn a lot, and be comfortable with your family and friends close by." No, He gave them a very important mission. Those eleven disciples plus Paul were able to say good-bye to each other and travel far into the known world and established Christianity. Just those twelve guys were able to transform the world by glorifying Jesus wherever they went. What can we do if we fulfill the same command Jesus gave them?

You may not have to go outside South Dakota to obey God. "Go into ALL the world" does include your immediate surroundings as well as far-away places. So in whatever career you choose, make your foundational purpose to be to glorify God in how you do your work, making God famous and attractive in the process. You can be a physician who is the best in the field who lives to get more stuff, or you can be a physician who is the best in the field who lives to care about your patients in such a way that they want to know God personally like you do. You can repair cars just to get the job done so you can get home to do your hobbies, or you can do your job, caring about the people who need the repairs and finding ways to encourage them; in the process you are a magnet for Jesus and are glorifying Him. The quality of your work may be the same, but the manner in which you do it is what makes the difference in life. So whatever we do, we can find some ways to glorify God in the process. This can be at home, or far away. It will be exciting to see God at work through you!

My challenge to you is, don't waste your life, serving your own self-interests and being absorbed in trying to be successful. You should strive to get the most education possible and do the best in your future academic preparation. But success for personal gain is not the goal. Success so you can do the best possible job in serving Jesus is the reason for excellence. As my son Matt said, "To settle for anything less than excellence in what you do is to rob God of glory."

A wasted life is one that is not devoted to following Jesus and bringing Him glory. A wasted life is one in which you are first place and are not pressing on to know God. Go and follow Him here or far away for an exciting, amazing adventure in life. I promise you that you'll see Him change and transform people as you interact with them. You will spend eternity with the people whose lives you touch. Those people, in turn, will touch others' lives, to turn them to the truth. Let the ripples form as you press on to win the prize He offers you.

John Piper said, "If you live gladly to make others glad in God, your life will be hard, your risks will be high, and your joy will be full… Some… will die in the service of Christ. That will not be a tragedy. Treasuring life above Christ is a tragedy." That is wasting your life.

Right now, as graduating seniors, how do you start to "press on"? What can you do starting today and tomorrow? Make special effort to serve Jesus today in anything He prompts you to do, to love other people and follow Him. Don't put it off. God will give you small assignments to do every day as you "press on." Do them immediately. Realize it's Him guiding you in the little things. As you obey and do what He tells you today, knowing His will for the big decisions will become easier and easier. You will grow to trust Him, and it will be exciting to follow Jesus. You will be prepared for the marathon of life if you do well with the 5k races and the daily practices. Remember Philippians 2:13 (NIV): "For it is God who is at work in you, enabling you both to will and act for His good pleasure." Obey what you do have direction to do, and He will lay down the puzzle pieces of your life to form His kingdom. If you "press on daily," your life will not be wasted.

God bless you, class of 2016, as you "press on." Jesus is worth it.

"...Forgetting what is behind, and straining toward what is ahead, I press on toward the goal to win the prize for which God has called me heavenward in Christ Jesus."

PHILIPPIANS 3:13–14, NIV

Peter's Strawberry Flax Muffins

Mix together:

4 eggs

1 cup buttermilk (or 1 tablespoon vinegar or lemon juice plus milk to equal 1 cup)

1 cup canola oil

2 teaspoons vanilla extract

In a separate bowl, combine:

2 cups whole wheat flour

1½ cups all-purpose enriched flour

2 cups ground flax meal

2 cups sugar

1 tablespoon baking powder

1 teaspoon salt

Add egg/oil/buttermilk mixture to dry ingredients and stir by hand until evenly mixed.

Add to batter:
2 cups walnuts, chopped
4 cups strawberries, chopped

Portion muffin batter into muffin tins, filling ¾ full.

Bake at 350 degrees until done, about 20–25 minutes.

CPSIA information can be obtained
at www.ICGtesting.com
Printed in the USA
LVHW111058270919
632476LV00001B/1/P